D1104411

ESSENTIALS OF FORENSIC ANTHROPOLOGY

Frontispiece. Thomas Dwight, M.D., LL.D. (hon). From Warren, *Anat Rec*, 5:491, 1911. Courtesy of *Anat Rec*.

ESSENTIALS OF
FORENSIC
ANTHROPOLOGY

Especially as Developed in the United States

By

T. D. STEWART, M.D.
Anthropologist Emeritus
National Museum of Natural History
Smithsonian Institution

With a Foreword by

ELLIS R. KERLEY, Ph.D.
President
American Board of Forensic Anthropology

CHARLES C THOMAS · PUBLISHER
Springfield · Illinois · U.S.A.

Published and Distributed Throughout the World by

CHARLES C THOMAS • PUBLISHER

BANNERSTONE HOUSE

301-327 East Lawrence Avenue, Springfield, Illinois, U.S.A.

© *1979, by* CHARLES C THOMAS • PUBLISHER

ISBN 0-398-03811-2

Library of Congress Catalog Card Number: 78-7441

With THOMAS BOOKS *careful attention is given to all details of manufacturing and design. It is the Publisher's desire to present books that are satisfactory as to their physical qualities and artistic possibilities and appropriate for their particular use.* THOMAS BOOKS *will be true to those laws of quality that assure a good name and good will.*

Printed in the United States of America

N-1

Library of Congress Cataloging in Publication Data

Stewart, Thomas Dale, 1901–
    Essentials of forensic anthropology.

    Bibliography: p. 275
    Includes indexes.
    1. Forensic osteology.   2. Human skeleton.
I. Title. [DNLM: 1. Anthropology, Physical.
2. Forensic medicine.   W800 S852e]
RA1059.S73   364.12'5   78-7441
ISBN 0-398-03811-2

To the memory of

Georges Fully (1926-1973)

Calvin Wells (1908-1978)

FOREWORD

IT IS A RARE pleasure to find something that fills a void as completely and satisfyingly as this volume fills the long standing need for a comprehensive and up-to-date discussion of forensic anthropology, particularly one written by someone who has been a leader in that field for over three decades. The material in this book is drawn from all facets of forensic anthropology, but, equally important, it is drawn from Dr. Stewart's own vast experience and participation in shaping the course that this exacting discipline has taken and is pursuing.

With the establishment of a Physical Anthropology Section of the American Academy of Forensic Sciences, forensic anthropology achieved status as a recognized specialty, and, with the increasing number of courses in forensic anthropology being offered at universities, the need for a current text has become urgent. This book is more than just an excellent textbook, it is a well-documented history of forensic anthropology, a mirror for forensic anthropologists, and for anyone interested in the medical, legal or anthropological aspects of skeletal identification it is a fascinating and informative book.

Dr. Stewart received his Doctorate in Medicine at Johns Hopkins and pursued his professional career in physical anthropology at the Smithsonian, where he became the Director of the National Museum of Natural History. In addition to working extensively with the thousands of human skeletons in the research collections there, he has been engaged in forensic anthropological consultations for the FBI, the Armed Forces and various medical examiners over the last thirty-five years and has conducted research for the Army Graves Registration Service in Japan during the Repatriation Program of the Korean War. He is highly respected among his colleagues for his extensive knowledge of all aspects of the human skeleton and for his thorough and imaginative research. Author and editor of several books and numerous research reports, Dr. Stewart has been honored repeatedly by his colleagues. He is past President of the American Association of Physical Anthropologists, Viking Fund Medalist and Honorary Member of the American Academy of Forensic Sciences, as well as a member of the National Academy of Sciences.

This book is a major and definitive contribution to the growing literature of forensic anthropology. It explains in detail just what a forensic anthropologist contributes to the investigation of death and how he or she goes about reconstructing the biological nature of an individual from the skeleton. Any forensic scientist might profit from the wisdom contained in the chapter dealing with evidence and testimony. Any lawyer or medical examiner could learn a lot about identification by reading this book. For the forensic anthropologist this book summarizes the entire field and its methodology in great depth and is a most valuable and readable volume.

It is a pleasure to recommend a book written by an old friend —especially when it is an excellent book, well written by one who is most eminently qualified to make an important contribution to the subject. This is such a book.

ELLIS R. KERLEY, Ph.D.

INTRODUCTION

Forensic anthropology is that branch of physical anthropology which, for forensic purposes, deals with the identification of more or less skeletonized remains known to be, or suspected of being, human. Beyond the elimination of nonhuman elements, the identification process undertakes to provide opinions regarding sex, age, race, stature, and such other characteristics of each individual involved as may lead to his or her recognition.

This definition takes into account certain practices in the forensic field growing out of the fact that identity depends primarily on the soft parts and only secondarily on the skeletal parts. Coroners and/or medical examiners (today usually forensic pathologists), whose duty it is in the first instance to investigate unexplained civilian deaths,* are trained primarily to deal with fleshed remains. When confronted with remains, the flesh covering of which no longer yields identification clues, these investigators realize that the only possibility of getting the desired information is through study of the skeleton. At this point they often call upon forensic anthropologists for help on account of the latter's greater osteological expertise.

In some instances, of course, the remains that coroners and/or medical examiners refer to forensic anthropologists may have been completely skeletonized when discovered. Also, remains that were partly flesh covered when found sometimes are skeletonized before being sent to the forensic anthropologists. Anyway, the point is that, although the bones themselves are the main concern of forensic anthropologists, and all remnants of flesh attached to them obscure the osteological details, forensic anthropologists do deal with remains that are *more or less* skeletonized.

Of all the human dead that require forensic investigation, those whose soft parts have deteriorated to the extent that they

---

*The Armed Forces operate separately and they, too, employ forensic pathologists.

can be considered more or less skeletonized are a small minority. For this reason forensic anthropology has never been, and most likely is not soon to be, an overworked profession. Indeed, so far as most forensic anthropologists are concerned, the word "branch" in the above definition can be replaced by "sideline," for it is still rare for a physical anthropologist to have fulltime employment in the forensic field. In this respect forensic anthropologists and forensic odontologists are much alike; both apply in forensic cases the knowledge gained from, and used in, their regular occupations.

Generally speaking, the regular occupation of most physical anthropologists involves one or another activity directed towards gaining greater biological perspective on mankind. And since the study of physical man through time is possible only by means of surviving skeletal remains, the physical anthropologists who pursue this line of study necessarily acquire extensive knowledge of skeletal anatomy. Furthermore, the anthropological study of a skeleton from the past is very like the forensic study of a skeleton from the present, for the object of study in each case is an unknown who must be identified as to sex, age, height, etc. Regardless of purpose, physical anthropologists sharpen their interpretative skills by practicing on collections of documented skeletons derived from dissecting rooms.

Forensic odontologists, to whom in a preceding paragraph I likened forensic anthropologists, are concerned in their regular occupation mainly with the maintenance of normal-appearing and normal-functioning dentitions in living people. Thus, in contrast to the anthropologists, the dentists look to the present much more than to the past and to the living much more than to the dead. However, my reason for mentioning this other profession is to make the point that those anthropologists and dentists who enter the forensic field are rivals to the extent that they both are concerned with the dentition. That this is so is due to the fact that in life the teeth are the only viewable and therefore easily reachable part of the skeleton, a distinction that they lose after death when the body becomes skeletonized.

Fortunately, there is a tacit understanding in this matter of jurisdiction that satisfies both groups: The anthropologists have to take into account the natural state of the teeth, especially when this aids them in making their traditional determinations, but they recognize the necessity of deferring to the odontologists when most forms of unnatural alteration or restoration are present. The exceptions are the ethnic mutilations and decorations which anthropologists are more accustomed to dealing with (see Ortner, 1966; Stewart and Groome, 1968).

In actual practice, then, identification of human remains for forensic purposes necessarily is dominated by forensic pathologists, but is shared as circumstances dictate, with other forensic specialists. The dependence of forensic anthropologists upon coroners and/or medical examiners for a role in forensic identification is reflected in books on legal or forensic medicine. In most of these books, skeletal identification rates only one chapter (cf. Boyd and Trevor, 1953; Kerley, 1973; Krogman, 1949; Stewart, 1954a 1968, 1973). In one exception (Krogman, 1962) the subject is treated in book length, but is still labeled as forensic medicine.

One of my reasons for writing the present book was to emphasize through the title the recent breakaway of forensic anthropology from medicine to be considered in more detail in the first chapter. Another reason was to extend the coverage of the above-mentioned general publications to include other aspects of the field besides skeletal identification *per se*. In none of those publications does this coverage take into account the legal responsibilities of forensic anthropologists or trace the development of the identification procedures they employ. The importance of historical orientation in this instance rests on the verification it has to offer of anthropology's long peripheral relationship to medicine.

In keeping with the emphasis on history throughout this book I have selected the likeness of Thomas Dwight (1843-1911) to grace the frontispiece. So far as I can discover, Dwight was the first American to make major contributions to the field. He also participated in forensic cases, the number and nature of which appear to be unknown (Warren, 1911, p. 533). For these reasons, and especially on account of the nature of his contributions, he fully deserves, in my opinion, to be designated the *father of forensic anthropology in the United States.*

Dwight was concerned primarily with a factor that underlies every determination in forensic anthropology, namely, *human variability.* The existence of this variability places limits on one's ability, when dealing with skeletons, to state in precise terms such things as sex, age, race, and stature. The resulting lack of precision in these matters precludes consideration of forensic anthropology as an exact science. In tribute to Dwight, this idea will be emphasized again and again throughout this book.

                                                              T.D.S.

ACKNOWLEDGMENTS

Primarily this book is the outgrowth of my forensic activities. They started soon after my appointment in 1942 as Curator of Physical Anthropology in the National Museum of Natural History when agents of the FBI's headquarters laboratory across the street from the Museum began asking me to identify bones collected under forensic circumstances. Toward the end of the war then in progress, the FBI agents were joined by officials from the Army's Memorial Division, also headquartered nearby. The latter sought my counsel on identification problems connected with the repatriation of the war dead. Also, in succeeding years several state medical examiners and/or coroners sent in skeletal remains now and then for identification. Although these forensic activities rarely took up much of my time and remained a side line to my regular curatorial duties, they provided me with useful insights into what physical anthropology has to offer in the forensic field.

I would like to name the individuals in these organizations who made it possible for me to have eye-opening forensic experiences, but the list would be too long. Moreover, after all this time it would probably fail to include everyone, and the omissions, although unintentional, might be misconstrued.

Necessarily I have had to supplement my personal experience by drawing upon the work of other physical anthropologists who also have turned to forensic anthropology. The amount of literature cited—and I have not tried to be exhaustive—indicates how woefully incomplete this book would have been otherwise. Most pleasing to me is the fact that everyone I called upon for help responded promptly and generously. I have been only too happy, therefore, to indicate the source in each case of borrowing.

Lastly, it should be noted that this book is a product of my retirement years. As such it could not have been carried to completion this soon except for the Smithsonian Institution's liberal policy toward its retirees. To S. Dillon Ripley, Secretary of the Institution, I am indebted for being allowed to retain my office, my parking space, and many of the other privileges available to me in my active years. In this connection I am indebted also to my anthropological colleagues, and especially to J. Lawrence Angel, my successor, for respecting my need to maintain freedom from involvement in museum affairs during the writing period.

T.D.S.

CONTENTS

SECTION III
SPECIFIC SKELETAL TRAITS

ESSENTIALS OF FORENSIC
ANTHROPOLOGY

Section I

PRELIMINARY CONSIDERATIONS

As its title indicates, Section I deals with several rather diverse subjects that serve to prepare the reader for the detailed identification procedures to follow in Sections II and III. Since each identification procedure will be documented, especially as to the American input, an outline of the record of American involvement in the forensic field is needed at the very beginning, both to give perspective and to show that most identification procedures are old, and that only the improvements are new.

Forensic identification implies an obligation on the part of its practitioners to the legal system intrusted with the investigation of unexplained deaths. This obligation is fulfilled when a forensic anthropologist files a report of his examination of submitted remains and follows this up, if required, by testifying in court. This is why an explanation of the role of expert witness is important for understanding the proper handling of skeletal remains recovered in forensic situations.

The preliminary handling of the bones affords a forensic anthropologist an opportunity to distinguish between animal and human, to decide whether or not the human bones have been altered by exposure to fire, and to size up all signs having a bearing on the cause of, and duration of the time since, death. With these matters settled, a forensic anthropologist is ready to turn to the general and specific identification traits, the subjects of Sections II and III, respectively.

Chapter 1

HISTORICAL SETTING

BY BESTOWING upon Thomas Dwight the title of *Father of American Forensic Anthropology* (see Introduction), I have in effect consigned the whole history of this branch of physical anthropology in the United States to the 100-year period beginning in 1878 (the date of Dwight's prize-winning, medicolegal essay; the first sign of his entry into the field). A search of the anthropological literature onward from Dwight's time to the beginning of World War II (when American forensic anthropology entered its modern period) has revealed three other individuals variably engaged in what would now be considered as forensic anthropology. Only the highlights of the activities of these four pioneers and their successors will be given here because the fuller picture is covered in two readily-accessible publications (Stewart, 1977b, in press).

AMERICAN PIONEERS

Dwight, a Bostonian, spent nearly forty years as an investigator and teacher of anatomy. Although in his time physical anthropology was not an organized science in the United States, by 1919 Hrdlička could include him among those contributing significantly to the early history of American physical anthropology. It is clear now that these contributions were on the forensic side of the field.

During the last twenty-eight years of Dwight's career he held the Parkman Professorship of Anatomy at Harvard, having succeeded Oliver Wendell Holmes to that position (Warren, 1911). Many readers will recall that Dr. Parkman, for whom the Professorship was named, had donated to Harvard the land upon which the medical school building stood, and that it was in this building in 1849 that Dr. Parkman met his death at the hands of Professor Webster. In the ensuing memorable trial (Bemis,

1850), one of the witnesses for the prosecution was Professor Holmes.

Dwight was only seven years old at the time of the trial. However, I sense more than a coincidence in the fact that Professor Holmes' successor first came to wide attention twenty-eight years after the trial through winning a prize for an essay on a medico-legal subject (Dwight, 1878). Very likely Dwight had heard the story of that trial recounted many times. Be this as it may, his essay shows remarkable insights into forensic matters at a time when other American anatomists were not looking at human skeletons with applied purposes in mind.

The essay was only the beginning of Dwight's work in forensic anthropology. Over the quarter of a century following the appearance of the essay he investigated a number of intriguing questions to which he had been able to give only tentative answers at first. Among those raised in the essay, or in his Shattuck Lecture (Dwight, 1894b), and elaborated on separately were: How best can stature be estimated from skeletal remains without resorting to the proportionality of the long bones? How indicative of sex, height and age is the sternum? What is the range and significance of variations in the human skeleton? Do the skull sutures close regularly enough to provide a reliable estimate of age? How indicative of sex are the size differences in the articular areas of the long bones? His answers to these questions appear at appropriate places in the chapters to follow.

George A. Dorsey (1869-1931), the next figure in this historical sequence, showed a notable awareness of Dwight's contributions. Probably while still an anthropology student at Harvard, he picked up from Dwight's Shattuck Lecture (1894b) an observation about the size of the articular surfaces of the long bones being good indicators of sex. This led him shortly afterwards (Dorsey, 1897) to test the observation on Indian skeletons in the Field Columbian Museum in Chicago where he had become Curator (Cole, 1931). As a result, he appears to have been the first to learn that the head of the humerus is a better indicator of sex than the head of the femur. Later (1905) Dwight confirmed this.

Dwight's influence on Dorsey appears also in references cited in the latter's lecture on *The skeleton in medico-legal anatomy* (1899) given before the Medico-Legal Society of Chicago after the Luetgert murder trial was concluded (Wigmore, 1898). Severe criticism of Dorsey's testimony at the Luetgert trial by opposing anatomists (see discussion section in Dorsey, 1899) may have induced him to drop his forensic interest at that point.* Dorsey quit anthropology during World War I; this is why Figure 1 shows him in naval uniform.

H. H. Wilder (1864-1928), one of Dorsey's contemporaries, rates a place in the history of American forensic anthropology for a different reason. He was primarily a European-trained zoologist who came by an interest in physical anthropology late in his career while teaching at Smith College (Pratt, 1928). The aspects of physical anthropology that interested him most—dermatoglyphics and facial reconstructions on skulls—are, of course, very much a part of forensic identification. Not surprisingly, therefore, one of his books is on personal identification (1918, with Bert Wentworth as coauthor). The fact that this book contains no reference to the work of Dwight indicates, perhaps better than anything else, the extent to which by World War I forensic anthropology in America had failed to fulfill its earlier promise. Wilder's appearance is shown in Figure 2.

Wilder's career was overlapped by that of Paul Stevenson (1890-1971), a medically-trained American anatomist who spent twenty years in China prior to World War II. Because he was abroad for such a long time and published only two contributions to forensic anthropology (Stevenson, 1924, 1929), one of them in England, his position in the field must be regarded as fairly peripheral. Indeed, he may not have given much, if any, thought to the forensic applications of his findings. Figure 3 shows Stevenson late in his career.

The names of the two most important American physical anthropologists during the early decades of the twentieth century —Aleš Hrdlička (1869-1943) and Earnest A. Hooton (1887-1954)

---

*I corrected this impression in a paper read at the 30th Annual Meeting of the American Academy of Forensic Sciences (St. Louis, MO, February 23, 1978). This paper will appear in the *Journal of Forensic Sciences.*

Figure 1. George Amos Dorsey, Ph.D., LL.D. (hon.).

Figure 2. Harris Hawthorne Wilder, Ph.D.

—do not come readily to mind in connection with forensic anthropology. Although certainly both were asked by investigative agencies to make skeletal identifications, Hooton alone seems to have expressed an opinion on the subject in print. The opinion was not very flattering: ". . . modern physical anthropology has contributed comparatively little to the improvement of methods of individual identification . . ." (1943, p. 1613) .

Figure 3. Paul Huston Stevenson, M.D., D.P.H.

MODERN PERIOD

The revival of forensic anthropology in the United States dates from 1939, the year when W. M. Krogman published his *Guide to the identification of human skeletal material* in the *FBI Law Enforcement Bulletin*. I feel justified in using this event to signal the beginning of a new period, not only because of the scarcity of significant anthropological developments in the forensic field during the preceding four decades, but because here for the first time to my knowledge was an identification article by an anthropologist appearing in a periodical devoted to forensic matters.

In 1939 Krogman had the advantage over his colleagues of having participated in the advanced research on growth and development being carried on at the Western Reserve University Medical School by, and under the direction of, T. Wingate Todd (1885-1938), one of the most energetic and imaginative anatomists of the time. The results of Todd's highly-respected work were so evident in Krogman's *Guide* that they gave it an aura of authority and infallibility new to the field. Partly for this reason and partly because the *Guide* had no competition, it came into wide use. I well recall my own reliance on it when I began identifying skeletal remains for the FBI in 1942 after I had become Curator of the Division of Physical Anthropology, National Museum of Natural History.

World War II

The maximum utilization of the *Guide* was in connection with the U.S. Army's program of identifying the skeletonized dead from World War II for repatriation and reburial. Because of the course of American involvement in the war, the program had two geographical divisions, European and Pacific. In the former, European personnel did the actual identification work under an arrangement worked out through consultation with H. L. Shapiro, Curator of Physical Anthropology at the American Museum of Natural History, New York (see Simonin, 1948; Snow, 1948a; Vandervael, 1952, 1953).

Only when the program shifted to the Pacific were American

anthropologists called upon to help in the identification work. More and more at this stage the selection of anthropologists was aided by Francis E. Randall (1914-1949) of the Anthropology Unit, Research and Development Branch, Office of the Quartermaster General. Charles E. Snow (1910-1967) of the University of Kentucky was the first physical anthropologist to serve in the Central Identification Laboratory in Hawaii when it was established in 1947.

By 1948 enough interest in this and other aspects of applied physical anthropology had developed to enable Randall to organize a symposium on the subject for the annual meeting of the American Association of Physical Anthropologists in Washington. As the program finally evolved, Randall was able to enlist only four speakers to cover the field of medicolegal applications: W. M. Krogman, H. L. Shapiro, Charles E. Snow, and T. D. Stewart. The papers of the last two were the only ones published in the Association's organ that year (Krogman's remarks were embodied in his 1949 publication).

At the time this symposium was held (April 3, 1948), the Army was seeking a replacement for Snow at the laboratory in Hawaii because of the expiration of his leave of absence from the University of Kentucky. The leading candidate for the position was Mildred Trotter, Professor of Gross Anatomy at Washington University, St. Louis, and a charter member of the American Association of Physical Anthropologists. Knowing this, I took the opportunity at the Washington meeting to urge her to take the position, citing statements that Snow and I had made in our symposium papers as part of my argument. The point of these statements was that stature estimation from the long bones still was based on a series of fifty male and fifty female French cadavers, many of them senile, measured by Rollet in 1888-89. The position in Hawaii, I argued, offered the opportunity to combine identification with research and provide a more reliable means for stature estimation based on a youthful American sample.

Later I realized that I should have advised Dr. Trotter also to make her acceptance conditional upon being granted permission in advance to do the research, because after she arrived in Hawaii she was told that she was there to identify the war dead and not to do research. Eventually, however, she was enabled to do the research, which at that stage consisted simply of securing accurate length measurements of the long limb bones of known individuals. The outcome of this research work (Trotter and Gleser, 1952) is discussed in Chapter 9.

Korean War

The next opportunity for American physical anthropologists to engage in human identification on a large scale came only five years later with the signing of the armistice on July 27, 1953, ending the Korean War. In anticipation of this event, officials of the Memorial Division, Office of the Quartermaster General, asked for my ideas about further research on the war dead. The fact that the concept of using the war dead for research directed toward improving identification techniques no longer met with resistance within the military, and that on the contrary it was now being advanced by the military, is a measure of the administrative break-through achieved by Dr. Trotter in Hawaii.

I am not sure now whether my conversation with the officials of the Memorial Division took place before or after I wrote an invited editorial on *Research in human identification* for the August 28, 1953, issue of *Science*. In any case, the following paragraph from the editorial expresses what I had in mind:

> Additional research is needed, especially to improve the estimation of age after skeletal maturation. Present information on this subject [as provided in Krogman's *Guide*] comes from the population dregs of large cities which reach the dissecting rooms. Those unfortunate individuals have not always given their ages correctly; nor have they led healthy lives. Well-identified skeletons of healthy Americans from the middle period of life are seldom obtainable. This fact emphasizes the unique opportunity afforded by the military reburial program.

Following the establishment of the identification laboratory in Kokura, Japan, the Memorial Division arranged with the Smithsonian Institution for my services for the period from mid-September, 1954, to mid-February, 1955, to carry out the research

I had proposed. During that time, assisted by a small assigned staff, I recorded in detail the age changes in 450 skeletons (only 375 were satisfactorily identified). The results of this work, which will be dealt with in Chapter 8, constitute a report, prepared under my direction by Thomas W. McKern (1920-1974), in the *Technical Series of the Environmental Protection Branch, Quartermaster Research and Development Command* (McKern and Stewart, 1957).

During my stay in Japan the identification team there included two American physical anthropologists: Ellis R. Kerley, now of the University of Maryland, and Charles P. Warren, now of the University of Illinois at Chicago Circle. Two other physical anthropologists, Russell W. Newman of the Quartermaster Research and Engineering Center, Natick, Massachusetts, and Paul Baker, now of Pennsylvania State University, were engaged in another research project. They were seeking a means of estimating the weight of the body in life from dry-bone weight. Following the pattern being used in this chapter, consideration of the results of this work (Baker and Newman, 1957) will appear in Chapter 10.

Two further developments stemmed from the work in Japan: (1) A summer seminar in 1955 on *The role of physical anthropology in the field of human identification;* and (2) a re-examination of the Trotter and Gleser formulae for the estimation of stature from the long bones. The seminar was the eighth since the late 1940s funded by the Wenner-Gren Foundation for Anthropological Research of New York. None of the preceding seminars had dealt with forensic applications, but the growing involvement of American physical anthropologists in this field seemed to me to warrant one.

The Wenner-Gren being receptive to this argument, I arranged for the seminar to be held in Washington, September 6 to 9. The main program consisted of half-day panel discussions on the following five topics (with the chairpersons) : (1) Qualifications for identification specialists (W. M. Krogman), (2) identification of small remnants of the human body (William S. Laughlin), (3) sex and age (J. Lawrence Angel and T. D. Stewart), (4) stature, body build, and facial features (Mildred Trotter), and (5) educational and administrative aspects (T. D. McCown—1908-1969).

One of the concluding statements of the published report on this seminar (Stewart and Trotter, 1955, p. 884) is noteworthy:

> Like most scientists, [physical anthropologists] have been accustomed to working from the known toward general principles. If they have assumed too often that these general principles can be applied readily to the identification of an unknown individual, whatever disillusionment the discussion produced should be salutary. Also, it is likely that from now on certain researchs in physical anthropology will be carried out with a view to direct application in identification.

The World War II-derived Trotter and Gleser formulae for stature estimation were published just in time (1952) for use in identifying the American dead of the Korean War. Having a personal interest in these formulae, as explained above, I took the trouble while in Japan to compare the estimates that they yielded with the recorded statures in life for all of the 375 known individuals whose skeletons I examined. As plotted out, the estimated statures seemed to me to deviate unduly from the actual statures at the extremes of the range. This observation provided Dr. Trotter with an excuse to apply to the Quartermaster General for a contract to re-evaluate the reliability of the formulae from the standpoint of the different population sample represented by the Americans killed in the Korean War. The outcome (Trotter and Gleser, 1958) was that so far as whites and blacks are concerned, the 1952 formulae need no adjustment (cf. Trotter, 1970) and as a bonus tentative formulae were derived for Mongoloids and Mexicans, while the formulae for blacks were judged to be appropriate for Puerto Ricans.

Vietnam Conflict

American involvement in the Vietnam conflict, which began in the early 1960s, accelerated in earnest with the landing of the first troops in 1965, and for the next 8 years was accompanied by heavy American casualties, did not lead to any new research in identification. This was due to the nature of the fighting and to various technological advances that permitted the rapid recovery of the dead and hence for the most part prevented loss of identity. Nevertheless, from the beginning of the invasion Support Services (the new name for Memorial Division) of the Army maintained identification facilities, known as the Mortuary Central Identification Laboratory, at Saigon (Neep, 1970).

By 1968, however, Support Services became concerned about the uncertain future of the conflict and decided that some sort of meeting of identification specialists was in order. I became aware of this when a delegation from Support Services came to my office to talk over the matter. The arrangement worked out was that, if the Smithsonian Institution, my employer, could be persuaded to serve as host for the meeting, I would organize it and the Army would provide the funds.

A subsequent letter of request to the Secretary of the Smithsonian from the Chief of Support Services (Stewart, Ed., 1970, p. iv) sets forth the Service's need as follows:

> While we believe that accepted scientific techniques and procedures are being applied in our identification laboratory in Vietnam, we wish to have the benefit of current, expert, unbiased, and disinterested guidance from specialists in all phases of identification . . . The results of the [meeting] would, at a minimum, permit reassurances that all possible steps are being taken in the identification process—in short, this would represent a backup vote for the Department of Army from the scientific community. We see, however, a broader purpose and, looking to the future, believe such a meeting would tend to increase the dwindling interest in the field [since the end of the Korean War], permit the development of recommendations for research, and hopefully yield a breakthrough immediately applicable to our war dead program.

In the end, taking my cue from the other meetings of this sort mentioned above, I called the one arranged for Support Services a *seminar* and scheduled it for December 9 to 11, 1968. Although the seminar was not widely advertised, sixteen physical anthropologists were among the 106 registrants. Furthermore, papers by physical anthropologists take up nearly half of the published report (Stewart, Ed., 1970). Among these physical anthropologists are three whose names have not yet been mentioned: Eugene Giles, now of the University of Illinois, Urbana-Champaign; W. W. Howells, Harvard University; and D. Gentry Steele, now of the University of Alberta. Details of their contributions appear elsewhere in this book.

It is worth emphasizing at this point in the modern period of American forensic anthropology (1970) that the remarkable developments since 1939 outlined in the foregoing were stimulated and made possible mainly by the U. S. Army through its repatriation and reburial programs abroad. Although the immediate needs of these programs often were limited and specialized, the field at large has greatly benefitted.

Formal Organization

One more development—potentially the most significant of all —remains to be mentioned in bringing this account up-to-date, namely, the founding of a separate Section of Physical Anthropology in the American Academy of Forensic Sciences. This came about through the efforts of Ellis R. Kerley, who was named above as one of the anthropologists working in the Memorial Division's identification laboratory in Japan in 1954-55. Kerley joined the Academy's Section of Pathology-Biology in 1968 and immediately began inducing other physical anthropologists to apply for membership. Thus by 1972 there were more than enough physical anthropologists in the Academy to meet the requirement for founding a new section (14; minimum needed, 10). I was pleased to be granted Honorary Membership in 1974. Having attended annual meetings since that date, I can vouch for the fact that the Section's sessions provide a valuable forum for the presentation of new ideas on identification. Also, the *Journal of Forensic Sciences,* the official organ of the Academy, provides a logical outlet for papers the members may wish to publish.

Prior to the formal organization of the Section of Physical Anthropology in the Academy the expressions "forensic anthropology" and "forensic anthropologist" were seldom heard. This is no longer the case. Hopefully, the impressive historical background of this branch of physical anthropology provided in this book will extend the popularization of these expressions still further.

Chapter 2

ROLE OF THE EXPERT WITNESS

A NY POST-DOCTORAL physical anthropologist with extensive experience in human osteology qualifies as an expert in the
field of forensic anthropology.* This being the case, if such a
physical anthropologist responds to the requests of investigative
agencies to identify human skeletal remains recovered under
forensic circumstances, sooner or later he or she will be served a
subpoena to appear in court as an expert witness in connection
with one of the remains examined.

The word subpoena (L. *sub,* under + *poena,* pain, penalty)
has been used in law since the fifteenth century to designate "a
writ issued from a court of justice commanding the presence of a
witness under penalty for failure" *(Oxford Universal Dictionary).*
The fact that a court puts a witness under subpoena is a measure
of the seriousness of the obligation to which all potential witnesses
commit themselves when they examine evidence in forensic cases.
It is for this reason that I have given this subject such a prominent
place in this book.

An experienced law-enforcement agent may remember to
warn a forensic anthropologist of the obligation being assumed in
accepting a forensic case, but he is not obliged to do so. I do not
recall ever having received such a warning in any of the cases I
handled. Maybe this was because so often the material I dealt
with had a poor prospect of ever reaching court. Anyway, having
come the hard way by the experience of testifying in court
through serving as an expert witness in several forensic cases, I
appreciate the need to prepare others facing this prospect. Some
of these experiences will be used here to illustrate the points I
feel should be made.

---

*A program of certification is underway in the American Academy of Forensic
Sciences. In the future, therefore, it may be necessary, or desirable, for a physical
anthropologist entering this field to become a Diplomate of the Academy.

Since a forensic anthropologist will serve most often as an expert witness for the prosecution rather than for the defense, I shall refer to the principal lawyer in court with whom he or she deals as the prosecutor.

ADVANCE ARRANGEMENTS

Usually in advance of having the subpoena issued the prosecutor inquires about the witness' availability and takes this into account in setting the date for the trial. Where travel is involved, advance arrangements of this sort are helpful in conserving everyone's time and in keeping court costs to a minimum. The prosecutor also will arrange in advance with the witness for the payment of expenses and a fee (as a government employee, I was allowed only expenses).

Prosecutors often take the precaution of having their witnesses present well in advance of the times they expect to need them. One reason for this is the variability of the time required to select a jury. I recall circumstances of this sort in connection with a trial in a rural part of Arkansas where I went, in company with an FBI agent, to testify in a murder trial. We arrived in Little Rock in the morning of the day set for the trial and spent most of that day driving by car to the county seat where the trial was being held. During the afternoon I raised the question about our need to arrive sooner, to which the agent—an old hand at attending trials—replied, "They won't have picked the jury yet. It is a small town and everyone there has an opinion about the case." Sure enough, the last juror was not picked until around 10 o'clock that night.

In another case tried in Dover, Delaware, I was one of a number of expert witnesses who, over a period of nearly a week, were transported morning and night by police car between the courthouse in Dover and a hotel in Wilmington, over 40 miles distant. Finally, at the beginning of the second week, after being excused over the weekend, I was called to testify.

The Dover case was one of two in my experience involving in some manner two victims. In each case upon reaching court I was cautioned in the matter of giving testimony against referring in any way to the victim who was not the subject of the trial. Since the reason for a trial is to establish guilt for a crime, usually in multiple murders the suspected criminal is tried for the murder of the one assumed victim for whom the best case can be made out. Reference to another victim could result in a mistrial. Advance knowledge of this practice aids a witness in organizing his or her testimony properly.

A forensic anthropologist who undertakes to serve as an expert witness seldom, if ever, will have the victim's skeletal remains at hand during the trial and be able to demonstrate features thereof to the jury as a supplement to verbal testimony. However, should the bones show some feature crucial to the victim's identification, the witness can arrange to bring to the trial photographic enlargements of the feature in question in the hope that they will be introduced as evidence and shown to the jury.

Another way to demonstrate skeletal features is by means of color slides made in advance for projection on a screen. This necessitates getting the judge's permission and, if granted, a further delay while the screen and projector are set up. All of these extra activities tend to distract the jury from the matter at hand. The prosecutor will decide, of course, whether the showing of the slides is worth the trouble.

While waiting to be called to the witness stand a forensic anthropologist may be approached by the lawyer for the defense and asked about the skeletal findings in the case. This is entirely proper. The defense has the right to know what was found in the examination of the skeletal remains and to discuss it with the witness. Nevertheless, it is not a bad idea for the forensic anthropologist to sound out the prosecutor on this score at the first meeting with him upon reaching court.

EXCLUSION FROM THE COURTROOM

As a rule, all witnesses are excluded from the courtroom except, of course, while giving testimony. The location of the waiting room for the witnesses varies, depending on the layout of the courthouse. I have whiled away time in little rooms not far from the witness stand, and on one occasion, there being no witness room, loafed around the corridor outside the main entrance to the courtroom.   Although short on seating arrangements, the corridor was the more interesting place to be, because it gave me a chance to talk to some of the local people. Also, in that location, occasionally I could get a clue from people leaving the courtroom as to how the trial was going.

At most trials requiring expert testimony about skeletal remains a forensic anthropologist can expect to be called to the stand fairly early in the proceedings. This is because the human skeletal remains involved usually signify a homicide. As such they are important in establishing th*e corpus delicti* (L., the body of the crime) .   The *corpus delicti,* in other words, "constitutes the substantial and fundamental fact of the death of the person alleged to have been murdered, and as a result of criminal agency" *(Webster's New International Dictionary).*

A trial in Manassas, Virginia, the first in which I ever testified, illustrates this legal principle especially well.   Although a man had disappeared fifteen years prior to the trial, and there was evidence that a certain man had murdered him, the latter could not be tried without proof of the missing man's unnatural death. My identification of a skeleton from a nearby abandoned well as that of the missing man established the *corpus delicti.* The conviction of the suspected murderer ensued.

The *corpus delicti* can be any part of a skeleton that appears to the expert to be human and to conform to the description of the suspected victim. In each of two cases in which I testified (the ones in Arkansas and Delaware) the body of an adult had been incinerated and all I had to go on was a handful of calcined bone fragments. Yet I could still say that these fragments were human and adult.

ADMINISTRATION OF THE OATH

Traditionally, each witness is sworn in immediately upon being called to the stand. As now generally known, the witness is asked to stand, to raise the right hand, and to reply in the affirmative to the oath. However, in the Virginia trial just mentioned all of the witnesses were lined up at the rear of the courtroom and sworn in *en masse.* We were then sent to the witness room to await our turns in taking the stand.

The sequel to this experience offers an interesting contrast. It was after the Virginia trial that I participated in the trial in Arkansas referred to above in connection with the time consumed in jury selection. In the Virginia trial enough time elapsed between the swearing-in ceremony and my appearance on the witness stand for me to lose sight of the connection between the two events. Consequently, when I was called to the stand in the Arkansas court soon after the start of the trial there and immediately asked a question, I had time for only a fleeting sense of something being wrong. It was not until after I had completed my testimony and left the courthouse that I realized I had not been sworn in. Upon bringing this omission to my companion's attention, he realized that it could cause a mistrial and rushed me back to the courtroom. The solution worked out by the judge was to get the prosecutor and defense lawyer to agree to accept my testimony "after the fact" instead of having me go through it again.

QUALIFYING THE WITNESS

After being called to the stand and sworn in, the forensic anthropologist is asked by the prosecutor to state his or her full name and professional connection. The prosecutor then proceeds to prove to the trial judge, through a procedure known as *qualifying the witness,* that as a matter of law the witness is competent to give conclusions or opinions relating to the skeletal remains.

The prosecutor may do this simply by saying "State your qualifications," but more likely he will elicit the information through a series of agreed-upon questions. The latter method is the preferred one, partly because it emphasizes the different aspects of the qualifications (education, training, experience), and partly because, not being in the form of a continuous narration, it sounds to the jury less as if the witness were boasting. But regardless of the manner in which the expertise of the witness is developed, coordination between witness and prosecutor is important to ensure that the recital of the facts produces the desired effect upon judge and jury. This is an occasion when a witness must discard all modesty.

At some point early in the qualification procedure the lawyer for the defense may interrupt the proceedings to stipulate to the acceptance of the forensic anthropologist's professional qualifications. If this occurs, it is then up to the prosecutor to decide whether or not to continue to develop the witness' qualifications. In only one of my court cases did this happen, but Philipps notes (1977, p. 457) that

> Lawyers who in the past were willing to stipulate to the qualifications of the forensic witness . . . are now . . . conducting vigorous examination of the witness . . . on his professional qualifications. Lawyers are trained to 'not give an inch' where this will guarantee a client his constitutional right to a complete legal defense. Even for those lawyers who lack substantial skills and knowledge, if they can succeed in 'rattling the expert' they have taken a step in the direction of providing an optimal defense for their client.

ESTABLISHING THE CHAIN OF POSSESSION

Before the prosecutor asks the forensic anthropologist to describe what was found in the examination of the skeletal remains, he asks when and from whom the forensic anthropologist received the remains and what was done with them following the examination. This is to establish the witness' part of the *chain of possession of the remains* and to connect this evidence with that of other witnesses, thereby providing confirmation that the court is dealing with the remains of the assumed victim.

Establishment of the chain of possession of skeletal remains is particularly important when they have passed through many hands, as was the case in a trial in Louisiana at which I testified: The victim there had been murdered in one parish; the remains buried in a shallow grave in an adjoining parish; the burial opened by animals, and the exposed remains discovered by children and removed by a sheriff to a local farm building; the collected remains turned over to authorities in the first parish and sent by the medical examiner to me in Washington for examination; finally the studied remains were returned by me to the same medical examiner. When I attended the trial I learned that the medical examiner in the meantime had re-excavated the grave site and recovered a molar tooth lacking one root through fracture. This new find enabled me on the stand to confirm the chain of possession simply by pointing out that the separated root was still in the proper alveolus of the skull I had examined in Washington.

Some of the recommendations given in the next chapter, particularly those relating to record keeping, if followed, will go far toward helping forensic anthropologists in establishing their part in the chain of possession of the skeletal remains.

GIVING TESTIMONY

When the time comes for the prosecutor to begin eliciting the forensic anthropologist's findings, the lawyer for the defense may demand to know whether the witness intends to prove that the remains are those of the supposed victim. In such an event the witness should follow the directive of Thomas Dwight, the father of American forensic anthropology, given (1878, p. 7) in the following words:

> Let the expert never forget, both in giving his evidence and in making his investigations, that the result does not concern him. He should not permit himself to be employed either to prove that the remains are those of a certain person, or that they are not. He should be as impartial as the judge.
>
> Let him also remember that absolute certainty can very rarely be reached in the solution of questions of this nature; exceptions and various causes of error are so numerous that strong probability, amounting sometimes to moral certainty, is the most he can generally hope for.
>
> . . . it is for the jury, not the expert, to decide on the identity of the skeleton; it is for the expert to show whether the identity is possible or probable. The opinion he will give will depend not only on his professional acquirements, but on his honesty and common sense.

As in the matter of qualification, the prosecutor simply may ask the forensic anthropologist to tell what was found in the examination of the skeletal remains, or he may chose the more usual course of bringing out this evidence piecemeal by asking a series of agreed-upon questions. The success of the latter course depends, of course, on the prosecutor's familiarity with the skeletal findings and his knowledge of what questions to ask about methods used, reliability of estimates, etc.

Philipps (1977, p. 460) urges the expert witness to be candid with the prosecutor, especially in regard to scientific procedures that may be mentioned in the testimony and that may be attacked subsequently by the lawyer for the defense. He points out in this connection that

> . . . once the cross-examination is ended the prosecution has an opportunity on redirect examination to rehabilitate [the witness'] trial credibility if by chance it has been impeached. Unless there is a full understanding by the prosecutor of not only what [the witness] did, but also why [the witness] followed a particular procedure, he will be unable to ask the necessary rehabilitation questions that will enable [the witness] to give the answers which will restore [the witness'] credibility.

On the other hand, while giving testimony a forensic anthropologist should make every effort to maintain composure and to give the impression of being confident. Statements and answers to questions should be formulated carefully, using easily-understood phraseology and speaking in a clear voice, loud enough to be audible to all the jurors. Whenever the witness can address the jury directly in a natural-seeming way, he or she should do so. Since under the circumstances reference to anatomical parts is unavoidable, lay terms should be substituted for technical terms: Cheek bone for zygomatic arch, collar bone for clavicle, shoulder blade for scapula, thigh bone for femur, shin bone for tibia, etc. A good idea, even when using the lay term for a bone, is to touch simultaneously with the hand the indicated part of the body.

From time to time while testifying a forensic anthropologist will need to admit that an exact estimate of some trait cannot be given; that, for example, age based on molar-root ossification cannot be stated reliably within a certain range of probable error. This is an inherent limitation in human populations and should be frankly admitted even though, as we shall see, it gives the defense lawyer ammunition to use in his cross-examination.

Another thing in testimony that can play into the defense lawyer's hands is an answer to a question that is not directly responsive or includes volunteered information that is only partially relevant. I committed the latter error in the Arkansas case re-

ferred to above. When asked by the prosecutor for my estimate of
how long it had been since the bones had been burned, I said that
it was impossible to say since once bones have reached the calcined
state they remain that way indefinitely. But I did not leave good
enough alone; I added that the burned bones in this case looked
just like those of prehistoric Indians I had seen. Quite innocently
and unintentionally I had planted the idea, which the defense
lawyer enlarged upon in his cross-examination, that burned
Indian bones from earlier times could have been mistaken for
the bones of a recent victim.

CROSS EXAMINATION

From some of the wording I have used above in connection
with the lawyer for the defense, readers without trial experience
may have gained the impression that this officer of the court is the
expert-witness' enemy. This is true only in the sense that he is
sworn to do the best possible job for his client. Whenever I was
cross-examined the defense lawyer always treated me respectfully
and always seemed to be fair in his necessary efforts to weaken the
effect of my testimony. Yet I must say that as a group the defense
lawyers that I faced gave little evidence of knowing much about
forensic anthropology, although that, of course, was some time
back and more often than not in out-of-the-way places.

In this connection I am reminded of a defense lawyer who
cross-examined me in a trial held in a small university city.
Arriving there the day before the start of the trial, I seized the opportunity to call upon a professor of anthropology with whom I
had corresponded. In greeting me the professor admitted that
he was not surprised by my presence in town because the lawyer
for the defense in the trial I was attending had sought him out and
asked him for some questions to put to me on cross-examination.
Since by now the professor was embarrassed over the matter, we
struck a bargain: I taught his evening class and he gave me the
list of questions. As it turned out, the defense lawyer had trouble
formulating the unfamiliar questions from memory, and I took
pleasure in rephrasing some of them in order to make my answers
relevant, thereby exposing his incompetence in the field of

anthropology.

Incompetence of this sort is disappearing. Today, according to Philipps (1977, p. 457), a forensic anthropologist "may be shocked in confronting a defense lawyer not only versed in the skills of the courtroom, but also possessing substantial expertise in the scientific field about which the expert witness is testifying." He goes on to say that,

> More and more lawyers are becoming knowledgeable in the varied fields of forensic science. Many have been prosecutors who have 'switched sides' and take with them the knowledge that they have gained from professional association with forensic scientists. Others are attending seminars and symposiums or engaging in independent research with the assistance of a retained scientific expert.

This new proficiency on the part of the defense lawyers makes it necessary for a forensic anthropologist when serving as an expert witness to rely on more than subjective impressions in forming opinions. For example, in the case of a skeleton an attribution of sex based on inspection alone opens up possibilities in a trial for the defense lawyer to question the reliability of the attribution. On the other hand, a supporting objective attribution derived by means of a tested discriminant-function equation, enables a forensic anthropologist to pin down the matter of reliability and at the same time to give the appearance of being more "scientific." However, the forensic anthropologist should be sure that he or she can explain in lay terms what a discriminant function is.

Because the sexes form a pretty-sharp dichotomy, skeletal sex is less of a problem to a forensic anthropologist on the witness stand than the traits that grade between extremes, as for instance, from small to large and from young to old. Here an estimate must be stated as falling within a range, but where within the range no one can say. For this reason an estimate of skeletal age falling within a certain range of years does not distinguish that individual from all the other individuals within the same age range. So when a situation of this sort arises in connection with a victim in a trial, it allows the lawyer for the defense to raise in his cross-examination the possibility that the remains serving as the *corpus delicti* in the trial may not be those of the supposed victim but some other person in the age range.

A defense lawyer questioned me regarding this point in a trial I attended in Mississippi where the assumed victim was a white, teen-age girl. I testified that the tips of the roots of her lower second molars were incompletely ossified, and that from this observation, using the findings of Garn, *et al.* (1958), I judged her age to be between 11.8 to 14.0 years, but I refused to be pinned down as to where in this range. Thus, when the lawyer for the defense asked me whether the age of the remains could be twelve years or fourteen years, all I could say truthfully was, "Possibly." The age of the girl whose identity was accepted by the court was 12.5 years.

REDIRECT EXAMINATION

As an earlier quotation from Philipps (1977) stated, "the prosecutor has the opportunity on redirect examination to correct any impeachment of the witness' credibility that may have occurred during the cross-examination." In the Mississippi case just described the prosecutor countered the defense lawyer's question about the age of the supposed victim by asking me whether the skeletal remains could indicate an age of twelve and one half, and again I answered "Possibly."

I was subject to redirect examination also in the Arkansas case, and in particular about the possibility of the burned bones being Indian, a point made by the defense lawyer in his cross-examination regarding my volunteered information. The prosecutor wanted to know whether I had any reason to believe that the bones before the court were Indian. In my reply, as I recall now, I was able to make the point that the Indian bones referred to in my testimony had been found underground where they could not be confused with bones from a recent fire, and therefore, if the bones before the court were recovered on the surface, it seemed to me unlikely that they could be Indian.

DISMISSAL OF THE WITNESS

A witness must remain in the vicinity of the courthouse until granted permission by the judge to leave. Since it is up to the prosecutor to request the judge's permission for this, the witness should keep the prosecutor informed of his transportation possibilities. Sometimes a little forethought along this line will allow the witness to make an airplane connection that otherwise would be missed. In this way the witness spends no more time than necessary away from the office and keeps the expenses chargeable to the court to a minimum.

Chapter 3

HANDLING THE SKELETAL REMAINS

T HROUGHOUT the two decades beginning in the early 1940s, when I was actively examining skeletal remains recovered in forensic situations, the bones always arrived in my laboratory in paper bags or cardboard cartons. Those that now come to my successor, Dr. J. Lawrence Angel, in ever increasing numbers, still arrive in the same manner. The only times when there has been an opportunity for either of us to view any of the remains *in situ,* or to participate in their removal from the places where they were found, were when the medical examiners had determined already that the remains were early burials.

This situation is understandable in view of the fact that most of the remains we have seen have come through the Washington headquarters laboratory of the FBI from various parts of the United States. However, the same thing applies to the local Washington-Maryland-Virginia area. In a large metropolitan area it is seldom feasible for the authorities to call in a forensic anthropologist whenever skeletonized remains are found. The same is not necessarily so of smaller communities where there are fewer homicides and where the medical examiners are better able to establish rapport with the forensic anthropologists in the local universities or *vice versa.*

So far as surface finds are concerned, I doubt that a forensic anthropologist can learn more from seeing the remains *in situ* than a well-trained forensic pathologist can. But in dealing with buried remains a forensic anthropologist with experience in modern archeology has a distinct advantage. Arguments on this score have been advanced by Morse, Crusoe, and Smith (1976). Also, a training course for uncovering burials has been developed at Florida State University by Morse, Stoutamire, and Duncan (1976). It remains to be seen how much more of the action forensic anthropologists will see as a result of these propagandizing and training activities.

Forensic investigators tend to be remiss not only in applying archeological methods to the recovery of buried remains, but also in making sure that they have recovered all parts of skeletonized remains discovered above ground. In the latter type of case the investigators may fail to look for or recognize some of the less-conspicuous bones that may have become mixed with the underlying dirt, leaves, or other debris. Sometimes, too, scavenging animals may have carried some of the bones away from the main part of the skeleton.

Dr. Angel had an unusual case of bone scattering recently (Kernan, 1977). Investigators from a Washington suburb brought to him a skull without a jaw found in an open area in a residential district. Since the skull appeared to be that of a female approaching adulthood, Dr. Angel's immediate reaction was that it must have rolled away from the rest of the skeleton hidden nearby. Acting on this hunch, the investigators searched the surrounding underbrush and cleared up the mystery of a girl missing from a neighboring home for about two years.

Since it is frustrating while examining skeletal remains to find that some of the bones are missing, a forensic anthropologist should make sure that he or she has not overlooked anything in the packing material that may have surrounded the bones during their transportation to the laboratory. If the missing parts cannot be accounted for in that way, the forensic anthropologist should urge that further search be carried out at the find site in the likelihood that they were overlooked there.

AVOIDING BIAS

Failure to see skeletal remains *in situ* and to participate in their removal from the find site to the laboratory is an advantage in a way to a forensic anthropologist, for it forces him or her to characterize the decedent objectively on the basis of the bones alone. Realizing how easy it is to become biased in such matters, I made it a rule in participating in forensic cases always to avoid so far as possible receiving any information about them until I had examined the bones and committed my determinations to writing.

Following this course is not as easy as it may seem. Every agent arriving with a box or bag of bones wants to tell you all about them, if he has not already tried to do so when he called for an appointment. With a little experience one can detect when a phone caller or a visitor is about to begin on the case history. At this point it is important to head off the flow of words with an interjection such as "Don't tell me what you think the remains are, because that will give me a bias, and I want to be able to handle the remains as an unknown!" By establishing this policy at the beginning of the relationship and sticking to it, the investigative agencies with which the forensic anthropologist usually deals will soon come to appreciate the latter's point of view and will automatically withhold the unwanted information until they have had their questions answered.

The one bit of information about the proffered remains that a forensic anthropologist usually cannot avoid learning is the place from which they came. Even this knowledge can set up a subtle bias in one's mind, because an anthropologist tends to think of regional populations in terms of racial composition. Speaking for myself, I have never received skeletal remains from the Deep South without thinking that most likely they would turn out to be those of a black. Being uncomfortable with this propensity, I always tried in such cases to "lean over backwards" to keep it from influencing my determinations.

I recall once seeing two sets of remains in the same week, one from Massachusetts and the other from Mississippi. The old bias in the back of my mind grew as I determined that the remains were those of teen-age females. My examination led me to conclude, however, that the remains from Massachusetts were those of a black, and the remains from Mississippi were those of a white. To be right under these circumstances, as I was in this instance, is especially gratifying.

PROCESSING THE BONES

Since, as explained in the Introduction, the human remains that are presented to forensic anthropologists for examination are more or less skeletonized, often the removal of tissue remnants and adherent extraneous matter is necessary both for convenience in handling and for exposure of the details that provide the basis for the required determinations. It is a serious mistake to clean the bones without noting carefully the location and amount of the tissue remnants (including adipocere), the intensity of the odor of decay, and the different kinds of adherent extraneous matter (mud, sand, loam, moss, grass, leaves, insect remains, etc.). Everything of the sort associated with the bones is evidence as to how the remains reached their particular state and how long this took (see Chapter 6).

Besides the extraneous matter mentioned, remnants of the decedent's head and body hair may also be adherent to the bones. Upon closer examination these could well turn out to be the best indicator of race (see Chapter 11).

Because of all this, I am unhappy with Adelson's recommendation to forensic pathologists (1974, p. 137) that they clean skeletal remains in advance of forwarding them to forensic anthropologists. As we shall see in Chapter 6, a forensic anthropologist needs to see the bones as collected in order to form his own opinion of the duration of time since death.

Cleaning of the bones needs to be carried only to the point where the necessary measurements and observations can be made. However, during this process the investigator should make a special point of looking for unnatural marks penetrating the cortical surfaces. These marks usually indicate either the postmortem chewing efforts of scavenging animals or contact with some sort of metal cutting instrument. The two are readily distinguishable; if made by rodents, tooth marks tend to occur as parallel rows of two or three grooves, each U-shaped in cross-section. The tooth marks of carnivores, on the other hand tend to appear mainly as ragged cone-shaped holes, having been made by the raised canine teeth. By contrast, cut marks most often are single and V-shaped in cross-section.

Cut marks can represent the cause of death (see Chapter 6) or be part of the indications of dismemberment (other parts of which may be represented by saw marks). It is extremely difficult to disarticulate a body without leaving cut marks on the

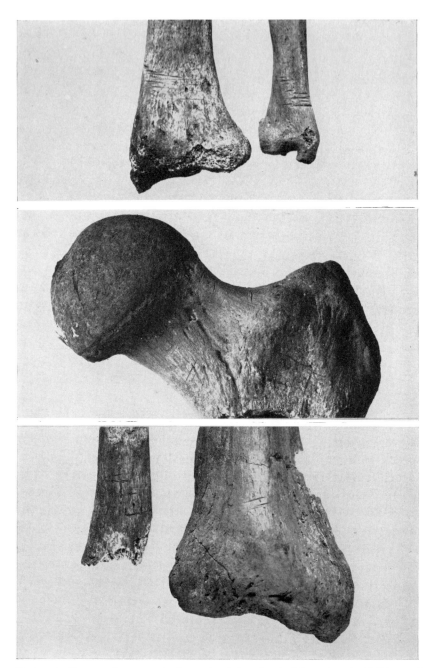

Figure 4. Cut marks around the wrist joint (*top*), hip joint (*middle*), and ankle joint (*bottom*) made by prehistoric Virginia Indians in the course either of defleshing or dismembering the corpse. (Courtesy Smithsonian Institution.)

bones. Figure 4 shows how inconspicuous such marks can be. All cut marks should be carefully plotted on an outline of a skeleton to see what the pattern suggests as regards the intent of the yielder of the cutting instrument.

Even natural bony detail sometimes requires preparation for proper observation. A good example of this is the pubic articular surfaces, which provide one of the best means of estimating age. While I was in Japan examining the remains of the war dead from Korea, I was asked to review a case which one of the anthropologists had estimated to have an age of ca. thirty years. This age was some ten years older than that of the individual to whom all other evidence pointed.

Upon looking closely at the pubic symphyses in this case I got the impression that in an effort to expose the articular surfaces someone had shaved down the cartilage there with a knife until they resembled the plateau stage of metamorphosis. Hence the estimated age of ca. thirty years. Following up on this observation, I soaked the articular surfaces in boiling water for a few minutes, after which I was able to strip off the loosened remaining cartilage and reveal billowed surfaces characteristic of an age in the early twenties.

In addition to cleaning, the bones sometimes need restorative work on account of postmortem breaks and separation of parts normally in apposition. The latter include teeth and epiphyses. Upon drying, single-rooted teeth tend to drop out of their alveoli, and unattached epiphyses tend to drop away from their sites of attachment. Although there is no prohibition against gluing these separated parts back together again, it is unwise to do so until a full record has been made of the state of ossification of the roots of the teeth and the state of fusion of the epiphyses. Once an incompletely ossified tooth is glued back into its alveolus it looks like a mature tooth, and once an epiphysis has been glued to its growing point on the body of a bone it can be confused with one that has begun to fuse. Too much haste in these instances can lead to erroneous impressions of physiological age.

Loose teeth are easily lost, and therefore, I always make it a practice, unless there is a counter indication, to glue them back into their alveoli. Occasionally this reveals some otherwise unimpressive anomaly of alignment that offers a means of personal identification, as explained more fully in Chapter 13.

Bone breaks certainly must be given careful scrutiny to ascertain whether they represent fractures caused by forceful blows delivered at the time of death, but the decision about rejoining broken bones depends on what purpose, if any, this serves.

When the bones are ready for closer and more orderly examination, or perhaps even before they are cleaned and restored, a record of their receipt should be made. An advisable practice is to have a special logbook for forensic cases and to enter therein any numbers assigned by investigative agencies, the dates of receipt of the remains, the condition of the remains as received, and ultimately the dates of return shipments. The need for such careful and detailed record-keeping relates to the chain of possession of forensic evidence explained in the preceding chapter.

Another advisable practice is to carefully guard all remains from forensic cases against loss. Except when being worked on, these remains should be kept under cover, preferably in a locked cabinet. Loss of even a small part of the evidence in a forensic case could be very embarrassing.

FALSE ALARMS

Occasionally a forensic anthropologist quickly detects that the skeletal remains submitted for examination by an investigative agency are not human, or, if human, can be accounted for on some other basis than a crime. In either case as soon as the true nature of these remains is recognized, usually the investigation can be brought to an end. Since the matter of distinguishing between animal and human bones is covered in the next chapter, I shall consider here only such human remains as are apt to arouse suspicion of being crime related, but which, like animal bones, can be shown to be "false alarms."

Probably the most common encounters with bones that are not crime related are those connected with excavations for various kinds of constructions. In my experience the bones in these excavations pertain most often to American Indians from prehistoric

times or American Negroes from the slave period. By and large
they represent burials that had no permanent markers and, therefore, disappeared from general knowledge. Undoubtedly many of
these encounters go unreported because of the reluctance of con-
tractors to suspend operations so that an investigation can be
carried out. On the other hand, when a medical examiner or
coroner is called in he may recognize that the remains are too old
to come within his purview and may content himself with collecting a sample for a forensic anthropologist to verify, or he may
ask a forensic anthropologist to continue the investigation (the
investigation of the Nacotchtanke ossuaries by Stewart and Wedel
(1937) came about in this way). Faced with either situation, the
forensic anthropologist is referred to Chapters 6 and 11 for help.

It is worth mentioning in connection with long-buried remains
that more than once I observed a small green stain on some part
of the vault of the skull. Having read somewhere that in the
American colonies it was a common practice to enclose a dead
body in a "winding sheet" before placing it in a coffin, I have
attributed the stain to the copper in the pin used to hold together
the folds of the upper end of the sheet. Recently Dr. Angel
showed me skulls from Colonial Williamsburg, Virginia, exhibiting one or more green stains on some part of the skull. Quite
likely, therefore, the stain is a good indication of the antiquity of
the burial.

Another extraneous bit of evidence of antiquity sometimes
recovered with the skeletal remains are coffin nails. Machine-cut
nails began to supplant handwrought nails in the period 1790-
1830. The former were largely replaced by wire nails beginning
in the 1850s (Nelson, 1968). The commercial coffins that replaced the simple coffin made by local carpenters included distinctive metal handles. When these are recovered with the
skeletal remains, sometimes cultural historians can assign them
to particular time periods. Other cultural objects found with the
buried remains of whites and blacks are less reliable for dating
purposes.

Among the unusual "false alarms" likely to come to a forensic
anthropologist's attention are lost or discarded anatomical speci-

mens and travel souvenirs. I have examined numerous skulls and
a few bones that had all the appearance of having been used by
doctors and/or medical students for study purposes. The surfaces of such specimens exhibit the characteristic polish and dis-
coloration imparted through much handling. Also, they show
little evidence of exposure to the elements and give the impression, unlike remains from burials, of still retaining organic
matter.

By contrast, the souvenirs are more likely to be skulls derived
from archeological sources. For instance, in Peru ancient cemeteries along the Pan-American highway can be seen to be strewn
with skulls and bones tossed aside by grave looters. Thus it is no
great feat for a tourist to acquire a skull and smuggle it from the
country in his baggage. This is not very different from the activities of some of the American soldiers in World War II. Those
stationed in the Aleutian Islands, for instance, formed hobby
clubs that collected and traded skulls and other objects extracted
from the ancient occupation sites that dot those islands. On two
occasions during the 1950s I identified a skull as that of an Aleut
and accounted for it in this way. One was found along the George
Washington Memorial Parkway near Alexandria, Virginia, the
other in Florida.

One must be well versed in morphological traits to undertake
to determine from where in the world such souvenirs came. The
skulls of Peruvian Indians usually can be recognized by their
artificial deformities (Stewart, 1943) ; those of Aleutian islanders
by their thickened tympanic plates (Stewart, 1933) .

COMMINGLED REMAINS

Up to this point my discussion of bone handling has assumed
that the bones submitted for examination in forensic cases belong
to one and the same individual. This is usually the case. Occasionally, however, for one reason or another, the submitted bones
are those of two or more individuals that have become commingled. They present, of course, a sorting problem. But, if in addition already commingled bones have been gathered up without
any record of their relationships and possibly incompletely re-

covered, the problem of sorting is compounded. Furthermore, sorting becomes still more complicated when any of the bones are broken.

The first thing to do under such circumstances is to separate the bones into kinds and then separate those that exist bilaterally by side. At this point a fairly clear indication of the maximum number of individuals involved should emerge. Beyond this it is a matter of assembling the bones into individuals. The success of the latter operation depends mostly upon the combinations of sex and age represented in the remains and the examiner's ability to determine what Kerley (1972, p. 355) calls the "positive articulation" between the bones of each individual. The articulation of bones like those of the spinal column and pelvis are rather readily determined, but the matching of arm and leg bones is apt to be uncertain.

A number of physical anthropologists have gained bone-sorting experience in working with the commingled remains encountered in Indian ossuaries and other types of mass burials. Two recent publications along this line that offer helpful procedural guidelines are those of Ubelaker (1974) and Finnegan (1976).

Physical anthropologists constantly have been on the lookout for reliable objective sorting methods. During my stay in Japan in 1954-55 I had occasion to visit the University of Fukuoka where some of the professors in the Anatomy Department were experimenting with the use of short-wave ultraviolet rays in distinguishing between the bones of different individuals. I became disillusioned with this method when I learned that the past environment of the bones—actually the accumulated dust on them in this instance—rather than the bones themselves was determining the nature of the fluorescence (cf. McKern, 1958).

A somewhat comparable, but much more complicated, sorting method involves the process of neutron activation (Guinn, 1970). To the best of my knowledge it has not yet been applied to commingled human bones.

This brings us to another objective sorting method which at one time seemed to have great promise, namely, blood grouping.

Today its utility in this direction would seem to be limited to fresh uncontaminated bone (cf. Thieme and Otten, 1957). Heglar (1972) gives a useful historical review of this subject, along with an outline of procedures, but has little to say on the matter of forensic applications. Considering that blood group 0 occurs in approximately 50 percent of American blacks and whites, the chances of commingled remains containing at least two individuals of that group are fairly high.

For the use of bone weight in sorting commingled remains see Chapter 10.

PREPARATION OF REPORTS

All of the handling of the skeletal remains in forensic cases culminates in the determinations which, taken together, determine the nature of the reports to the investigative agencies. The questions asked in these cases by any agency are fairly standard. If the bones are small, fragmentary, or burned, usually the first question is "Are they human?" If they are human, the next question is "Can you tell the sex and age?", or "Do they represent one or more individuals?" If the remains are complete or nearly so, obviously human, and likely to be from one individual, the questions extend to "What is the stature?" "What is the race?" "Do the bones show any traits that might be peculiar to the individual?" "How long ago did death occur?" and "Is the cause of death determinable?"

Helpful information and advice for determining the answers to these questions are set forth in succeeding chapters, so here I shall limit my further remarks to the general aspects of the reports.

My policy in preparing a report on remains received for identification was to describe the state of the remains and to reply in as direct and succinct a fashion as possible to whichever of the above questions were asked. This means that I rarely took photographs and rarely took more measurements than were needed to estimate stature and/or demonstrate some asymmetry. Fortunately, perhaps, I always found my minimal record to be sufficient on the occasions when I appeared in court as an expert witness. This is not to say that now I would not use more of the objective methods to be described in the following chapters.

Since turning over this operation to Dr. Angel, I have noted that he prepares much longer and more detailed reports, and that for his personal record he measures and photographs the bones, just as he is accustomed to doing when working with the Ancient Greeks. His reason for going to such lengths in forensic cases involves personal interests that need not concern us here. In citing his plan of operation my intent simply is to make the point that one has considerable leeway in this matter. However, I must admit that Dr. Angel has accumulated an enviable amount of data that stands him in good stead when he lectures on forensic anthropology.

51–7A
Rev. 2–70

SMITHSONIAN INSTITUTION

Washington, D.C., U.S.A. 20560

A LETTER HAS, HAS NOT, BEEN WRITTEN   **SHIPPING INVOICE**   REGISTRAR FILE NO._____

INITIATING OFFICE
INVOICE NO._____

INSTRUCTIONS TO RECIPIENT:
Loans are made for two months unless stipulated below. When returning material, please mention the Registrar File Number. Types sent on loan must be returned by Registered mail.

DATE _____

TO:

LOAN PERIOD _____

INITIATED BY _____

UNIT _____

APPROVED _____

THIS MATERIAL IS SENT AS:
(1) An open long-term exchange   (4) A loan for examination at our request   (7)
(2) A loan at your request   (5) Return of material borrowed
(3) In exchange   (6) Return of material sent for identification

MATERIAL *(As appropriate, state locality, collector, catalog numbers, etc. Total each distribution category)*

RECEIVED IN GOOD ORDER

NO. OF PACKAGES _____ DATE SHIPPED _____

SHIPMENT _____ PAYMENT _____
    (Express, parcel post, etc.)   *(Prepaid, collect, etc.)*   *(Name)*

SHIPPING NO. _____ SHIPPING CLERK'S INITIALS _____

(Date)

RETAIN THIS COPY

U.S. GOVERNMENT PRINTING OFFICE : 1970 OF—378–716

Figure 5. Recipient's copy of the Smithsonian letter-size shipping invoice.

Being on the staff of a Smithsonian museum, Dr. Angel and I have found it convenient to forward each of our forensic case reports on a Smithsonian shipping invoice (Figure 5). The wording shown in the figure occurs in duplicate on two letter-sized sheets, one white and the other yellow. The only modification needed is to cross out the line reading "Material (etc.)" and substitute "Report." Both sheets go to the addressee with the request that the white copy be signed, dated, and returned to the sender upon receipt of the covered material. This procedure is followed even though the transaction is handled for the addressee by an agent in person (in which event, of course, the method of transportation is stated to be "hand carried"). A form of this sort provides each party with a copy of the report giving all of the data needed to establish the chain of possession of the remains should the case be taken to court.

Finally, this is a convenient point to bring up one detail of the reports that has not been mentioned, namely, the manner of designating the teeth. Physical anthropologists generally use the following simple method for distinguishing each of the elements of the deciduous and permanent dentitions:

Deciduous:

$$\text{Right} \quad \frac{m^2 \ m^1 \ c \ i^2 \ i^1 \ \big| \ i^1 \ i^2 \ c \ m^1 \ m^2}{m_2 \ m_1 \ c \ i_2 \ i_1 \ \big| \ i_1 \ i_2 \ c \ m_1 \ m_2} \quad \text{Left}$$

$$\text{Upper}$$
$$\text{Lower}$$

Permanent:

$$\text{Right} \quad \frac{M^3 \ M^2 \ M^1 \ Pm^2 \ Pm^1 \ C \ I^2 \ I^1 \ \big| \ I^1 \ I^2 \ C \ Pm^1 \ Pm^2 \ M^1 \ M^2 \ M^3}{M_3 \ M_2 \ M_1 \ Pm_2 \ Pm_1 \ C \ I_2 \ I_1 \ \big| \ I_1 \ I_2 \ C \ Pm_1 \ Pm_2 \ M_1 \ M_2 \ M_3} \quad \text{Left}$$

$$\text{Upper}$$
$$\text{Lower}$$

Although this system is perfectly understandable, forensic anthropologists should realize that the following system is now in use among dentists:

Deciduous:

Upper right	Upper left
E D C B A	A B C D E
E D C B A	A B C D E
Lower right	Lower left

Permanent:

Upper right	Upper left
8 7 6 5 4 3 2 1	1 2 3 4 5 6 7 8
8 7 6 5 4 3 2 1	1 2 3 4 5 6 7 8
Lower right	Lower left

Another system in use, mainly in military record keeping, also uses letters and numbers, but in continuous serial order running clockwise from the right, as follows:

Deciduous:

```
                Upper
       A B C D E  |  F G H I J
Right ------------|------------ Left
       T S R Q P  |  O N M L K
                Lower
```

Permanent:

```
                    Upper
      1  2  3  4  5  6  7  8  |  9 10 11 12 13 14 15 16
Right ----------------------- | ----------------------- Left
      32 31 30 29 28 27 26 25 |  24 23 22 21 20 19 18 17
                    Lower
```

Recommended, but not yet widely adopted (Anonymous, 1971), is the following two-digit numbering system:

Deciduous:

Upper

$$\text{Right} \quad \frac{55\ 54\ 53\ 52\ 51 \quad | \quad 61\ 62\ 63\ 64\ 65}{85\ 84\ 83\ 82\ 81 \quad | \quad 71\ 72\ 73\ 74\ 75} \quad \text{Left}$$

Lower

Permanent:

Upper

$$\text{Right} \quad \frac{18\ 17\ 16\ 15\ 14\ 13\ 12\ 11 \quad | \quad 21\ 22\ 23\ 24\ 25\ 26\ 27\ 28}{48\ 47\ 46\ 45\ 44\ 43\ 42\ 41 \quad | \quad 31\ 32\ 33\ 34\ 35\ 36\ 37\ 38} \quad \text{Left}$$

Lower

A suggested modification of this newly recommended system, intended to reflect the fact that the deciduous dentition comes before the permanent dentition, is to interchange the initial digits so that $\frac{1/2}{4/3}$ stands for the quadrants of the deciduous dentition, and $\frac{5/6}{8/7}$ stands for the quadrants of the permanent dentition. Such a system has the advantage over the systems in use of being more readily communicable in print and by wire and more easily translatable into computer input.

Chapter 4

HUMAN VS. ANIMAL REMAINS

IN THE PRECEDING chapter I mentioned that the question "Are they human?" arises mainly when the skeletal remains recovered under suspicious circumstances are "small, fragmentary or burned." Dr. Angel states (1974, p. 20) that in his experience "about 10 percent of the bones brought in as 'possibly human' turn out to be animal." A forensic anthropologist should have little difficulty in at least recognizing whether or not small intact bones and bone fragments that include joint surfaces are human. Pieces of bone that lack joint surfaces are seldom identifiable simply by inspection. I was never satisfied to say only that bone fragments were not human, so, being in a natural history museum, I always took all of the non-human bones to a mammalogist or ornithologist for specific identification.

The biologists in our museum did not relish doing this sort of work, especially when they had little more to go on than, say, a foot bone or a portion of a joint from a long bone. The work of comparing a small fragment with this bone and that bone in one skeleton after another is a time-consuming and tedious process which in the end may yield only a qualified answer, such as "probably sheep." Unsatisfactory though this answer may seem, it provides confirmation that the fragments are nonhuman.

Unfortunately, the recent guides to animal-bone identification prepared for archeologists (Cornwall, 1956; Olsen, 1964; Gilbert, 1973), one of which at least is probably available to every physical anthropologist, are of limited use in the forensic setting, because they deal almost exclusively with wild animals and then only with a selection of bones from these animals. Most of the fragmentary animal bones sent to forensic anthropologists for identification constitute the more promising finds from habitation areas encountered during searches for missing persons. And since one of the common ways of disposing of a human body is by burning,

45

searchers tend to give primary attention to the contents of furnace fireboxes, ash heaps, garbage dumps, etc. In such places most of the encountered bone material represents food debris.

Krogman's (1943) case, called "The Cobbler's Basement," illustrates this point perfectly. A Cincinnati shoemaker, whose shop was located in a basement with an earthen floor, allegedly had lured a young girl downstairs and killed her. Since in a crime of this sort the suspect is presumed to be guilty of having done the same thing before (cf. Sir Sydney Smith, 1960, Chapter I), the investigators dug up the floor of the shop and in the process recovered 18 identifiable bones, mostly pieces, and a number of unidentifiable rib fragments. Krogman's detailed analysis of the identifiable bones (pp. 21-23) indicates that they represented at least ten animals as follow:

> Five sheep: innominate (with signs of cleaver stroke), five ribs (one with signs of saw cut), two cervical vertebrae (one with signs of saw cut)
> One rat: innominate
> One cow: cervical vertebra, scapula, tibia (?)
> One pigeon: tibia
> One barn owl (?) : thoracic vertebra
> One goose or turkey: humerus, sacrum (in 3 pieces)

He added this comment (p. 23) :

> Fundamentally the collection represents the usual detritus marking the living-place of human beings. It is typical of the 'kitchen-midden' refuse heaps of any population. The inclusion of relatively uncommon bones, e.g., barn-owl, rat, et cetera, can be accounted for by the action of rodents burrowing in the earth. It is my opinion and has been my experience that any area of earth chosen at random will yield a most varied assortment of bones representing the accumulation of years . . .

Here was a case which showed no further guilt, but rather one which established innocence of suspicion of multiple guilt.

GROSS DIFFERENCES

More or less complete skeletons of small animals are sometimes sent to forensic anthropologists for identification under the mistaken impression that they are the remains of human fetuses or newborns. I once received a skeleton of this sort which had been found, carefully wrapped in a towel, in a shoebox on the side of a parkway. A local physician who probably never had handled baby bones, judged them to be just that. Actually, the skeleton was the remains of a puppy dog, probably a child's pet.

In the absence of actual bones of human fetuses and newborns for direct comparison with unknowns, a forensic anthropologist will find the illustrations in Bass' *Human Osteology* (1971) helpful in reaching a decision. However, he or she will do well to acquire as early as possible enough experience in handling the actual bones so that recognition comes almost instantaneously.

As would be expected, the bones of anthropoid apes show the closest resemblance to those of man. Although the chance of the bones of a nonhuman primate turning up in a forensic situation is remote, the point of their close resemblance to human bones is worth making by means of an illustration (Figure 6). After examining this figure readers probably will agree that the bones of newborn humans and gorillas are nearly indistinguishable, except in the case of the ilium and perhaps also the mandible. The gorilla's ilium lacks any modification for upright posture; the mandible lacks even a suggestion of a chin. Note, however, that the human and gorilla long bones differ in their relative lengths; that is, whereas the bones of the human upper extremity are somewhat shorter than those of the gorilla's fore extremity, the reverse is true for the lower (or hind) extremity. These differences reflect, of course, two very different postures.

Most animal bones comparable in size to those of adult humans would not ordinarily fool a well-trained forensic anthropologist. Yet under special circumstances skinned bear paws (both hands and feet) have proved to be a rather frequent exception (Stewart, 1951, 1959; Angel 1974). The special circumstances are three in number: (1) the time of year when these specimens come to attention (bear-hunting season); (2) the place of recovery (disposal area remote from bear country); and (3) the manner in which the paws have been skinned (terminal phalanges with their claws removed with the skin).

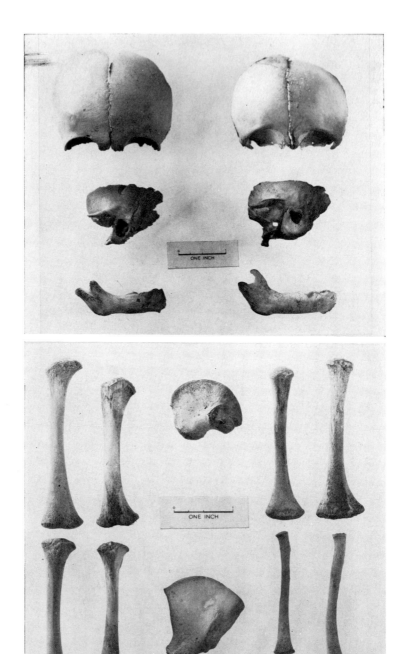

ONE INCH

ONE INCH

There is a simple explanation for this combination of circumstances. Upon killing a bear some hunters do a rough skinning job at or near the kill site. They do not take the time then to dissect out the paws, but simply disarticulate them at the wrist and ankle joints. This is because of the tediousness of skinning the individual fingers and toes and of the intimacy of the connections between the palms and soles and the structures underlying them. So, later on at more leisure, usually at home and remote from the bear country, the hunters finish the skinning of the paws, leaving the terminal phalanges connected with the claws in the skin. Thereupon, they tend to treat the skinned paws as garbage.

The chances of these skinned paws being noted because of their resemblance to their human counterparts depend upon the care given the lot of garbage to which they have been consigned. Since there are records of such specimens having been picked up in city alleyways, the scavenging activities of cats, dogs, and rats seem implicated. Be this as it may, every once in a while law-enforcement agencies are confronted with the need to account for the presence of "mutilated human hands and/or feet" in unexpected places.

Figures 7 and 8 show how the skeletonized bear paws compare with their human counterparts. The general resemblance is such as to explain why laymen are so easily misled under the special circumstances described. Yet at first glance even a human anatomist would be apt to think that, while the human hand and foot are obviously from the right side, in part because of the separation of the first two fingers for opposability, the bear's hand and foot seem to be from the left side. This mirror-image illusion results in large part from the fact that the bear's longest metapodium is number 4 both in the hand and foot, whereas man's is number 2 or 3 in the hand and number 2 in the foot.

Figure 6. Comparison of selected bones of human and gorilla newborns. *Top* —cranial (left, human; right, gorilla); *bottom*—postcranial: *Upper row* (left to right)—femur (h), femur (g), ilium (h), humerus (h), humerus (g); *lower row*—tibia (h), tibia (g), ilium (g), radius (h), radius (g). (Courtesy Smithsonian Institution.)

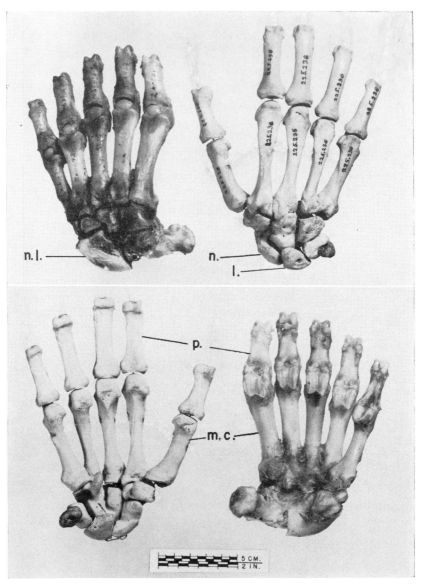

Figure 7. Comparison of bear and human hands in the skeletonized state (minus last two rows of phalanges). *Upper left* and *lower right*—bear; *upper right* and *lower left*—human. The back of the hand is shown above, the palm below. Abbreviations: l. = lunate, mc. = metacarpals, n. = navicular, n.l. = naviculo-lunar, p = phalanges (proximal row). (From Stewart, Bear paw remains closely resemble human bones *FBI Law Enf Bull, 28 (11)*:18-21, Figure 3, (1959). Courtesy of The Federal Bureau of Investigation.)

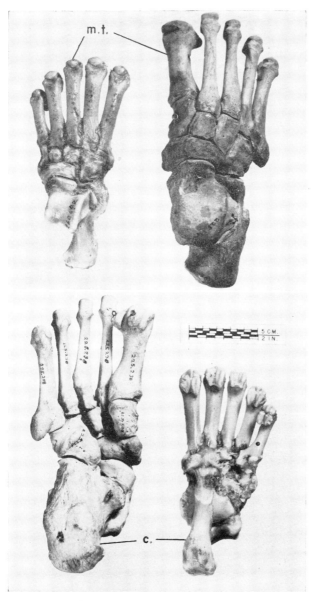

Figure 8. Comparison of bear and human feet in the skeletonized state (minus all phalanges). *Upper left* and *lower right*—bear; *upper right* and *lower left* —human. The upper or dorsal side of the foot is shown above, the under or sole side below. Abbreviations: c. = calcanei, m.t = metatarsals. (From Stewart, Bear paw remains closely resemble human bones, *FBI Law Enf Bull, 28 (11):* 18-21, Figure 4, 1959. Courtesy of The Federal Bureau of Investigation.)

On closer inspection of the bear's bones other differences from the human state are recognizable. Among them, the distal joint surfaces of the phalanges and metapodials are more sculptured, the calcaneous is much narrower, and the generally larger carpals are reduced in number by one through fusion of the navicular and lunate (naviculo-lunar).

Two reports of other animal bones that fooled searchers for missing persons, one by myself (Stewart, 1961) and the other by Dr. Angel (1974), show how bizarre such specimens can be. The one that I reported consisted of a mass of fatty tissue containing several ribs, part of a sternum and what appeared at first sight to be a clavicle. It was found along a public thorough-fare. Any hope that it would prove to be human and through its indications of developmental age would tie in with one or the other of two missing persons evaporated when the supposed clavicle proved to be a cartilagenous artifact and an X ray showed the ribs to be of the sternal rather than vertebral variety. Subsequent comparisons with museum specimens led to the identification of the bones as sheep. Presumably the fresh sheep remains had been lost from a truck carrying them from a slaughter house.

Sheep and other ungulates differ from humans in having separate well-formed rib elements between the ventral ends of the vertebral ribs and the sternum (Figure 9). In humans the connections between the vertebral ribs and sternum are cartilaginous and only occasionally become ossified to any extent. The fact that a human anatomist assisting me in the examination of the sheep specimen did not know about sternal ribs led me to report the case.

Dr. Angel's case referred to above is another example of the resemblance under bizarre circumstances of animal foot bones to those of humans. What made this case really bizarre was the fact that the bones in question were abnormal; actually, from a polydactylous pig. An X ray showed doubling and shortening of the usual two main metapodials (Figure 10). Dr. Angel tells me that he has been unable to discover the frequency of occurrence of polydactylous pigs, but that he suspects it is high.

A reminder of an even more bizarre resemblance is in order,

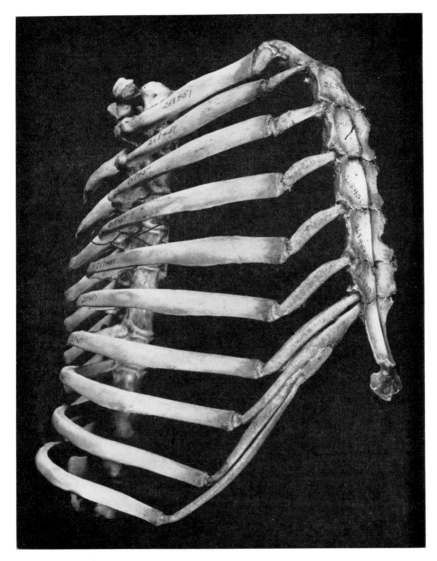

Figure 9. Right side of the thoracic skeleton of a domestic sheep (*Ovis aries;* U.S.N.M. No. 268,451) with well-ossified sternal ribs. (From Stewart, Sternal ribs are aid in identifying animal remains. *FBI Law Enf Bull, 30 (7):* 9-11, Figure 2, 1961. Courtesy of The Federal Bureau of Investigation.)

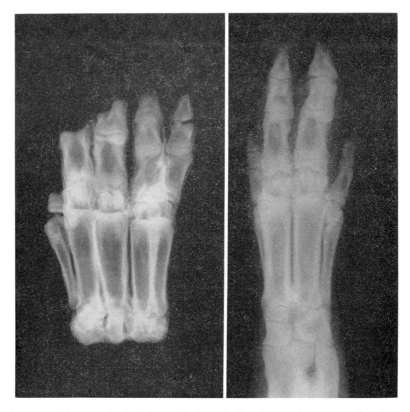

Figure 10. X rays of pigs' feet: *Left*—polydactylous; *right*—normal.   (From Angel, Bones can fool people. *FBI Law Enf Bull 43 (1):* 17-20,30, Figure 6, 1974. Courtesy of The Federal Bureau of Investigation.)

namely, that of the terminal vertebrae of a horse's tail to certain human finger bones. In Figure 11 the equine caudal vertebrae picked to illustrate this point match rather closely proximal phalanges of human thumbs. However, close inspection of the ends of the equine vertebrae shows the unmistakable flat, circular structure of a centrum. Besides, the vertebrae have a circular cross-section at the middle, whereas the human hand bones have a semilunar cross-section.

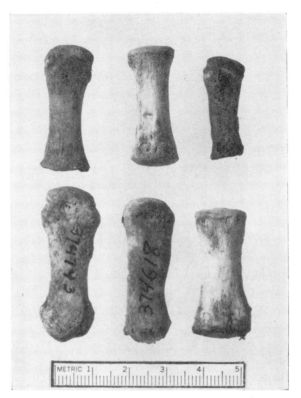

Figure 11. Comparison of terminal vertebrae of a horse's tail with human finger bones. *Middle of top row* and *right end of bottom row*—horse; *others* —human (proximal thumb phalanges, all but one immature). (Courtesy Smithsonian Institution.)

MICROSCOPIC DIFFERENCES

In all of the foregoing the main consideration has been the elimination of animal bones from further consideration in forensic situations. Although, as already indicated, there is some personal satisfaction in pursuing the identification of animal remains to the genus and species this is seldom required and, if only small pieces of shaft are available, may not be possible by gross morphology alone. In the event, however, that it becomes necessary to make further efforts to decide the nature of some small pieces of bone, it is best to resort to microscopic examination.

The microscopic examination of bone sections has been pursued by a number of physical anthropologists since Kerley's introduction of the technique for aging purposes in 1965. This does not mean that these anthropologists have looked also at sections of animal bones and therefore have developed a feeling for the structural differences between genera. Indeed, if one is not experienced in the complicated technique involved, it is best to turn for help to someone who is.

The first American in this century to make extended comparisons of this sort seems to have been J. S. Foote, Professor of Pathology at Creighton Medical College. The usefulness of his publication (1916) today resides mainly in the 453 drawings of complete femoral sections as viewed at low magnification. The coverage includes amphibians, reptiles, birds, and mammals—including man (as seen at different ages and in different racial groups.) The mammals also include cat, dog, sheep, and bear. (For photomicrographs of sections from many of these forms see Amprino and Godina, 1947.)

From Kerley's work physical anthropologists know of the structural components of bone called lamellae and Haversian systems. Rarely seen in human bone, but often in the bones of other animals, is another component consisting of concentric layers called laminae by Foote and plexiform bone by Enlow (1963, p. 65). Figure 12 shows that the presence of laminae in a microscopic section can give a different appearance from that usually seen in sections from human bone.

Foote reported (p. 17) the following relative frequencies of the three components:

	Mammals other than man	*Adult man*
Number of femora examined	133	139
Lamellae as important bone structures	48%	92%
Laminae as important bone structures	50%	8%
Haversian system, complete differentiation	82%	100%

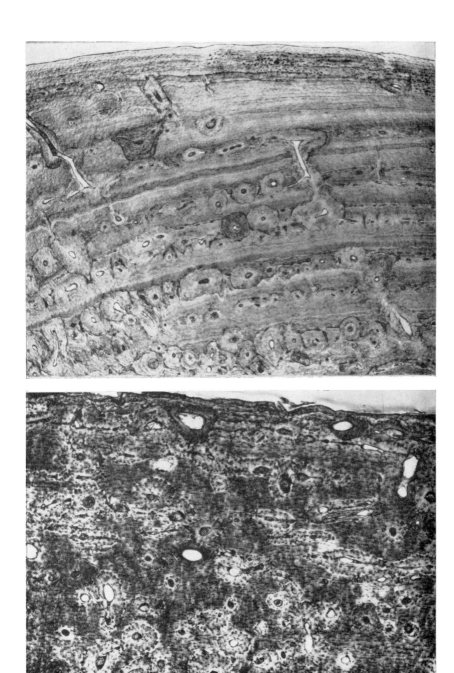

Figure 12. Micrographs (X45) of tibial cortex. *Top*—bear; *bottom*—human female, age 49 (Case No. 67-917). (Courtesy Donald J. Ortner.)

Commenting on the full table, of which only the above portion concerns us here, Foote said (p. 17) :

> . . . lamellae, in some stage of differentiation, form an important part of the majority of all femora, and, therefore, may be considered as the simplest, oldest, and most universal bone units; . . . laminae—incomplete or complete—are found in the smallest number of femora, and . . . Haversian systems, in some stages of differentiation, are found in the largest numbers of femora and to the greatest extent in man.

At the present state of knowledge of this subject there appears to be no way of telling the degree of certainty with which bits of animal and human bone can be differentiated microscopically. Enlow (1963, p. vii) cautions that "marked variations are found in the microscopic structure of bone between different species, between different bones in the same individual, and between different areas in the same bone." In view of all this, about all there is to say is that the finding of a considerable area of laminae or plexiform bone in a section of cortex very likely warrants a diagnosis of "nonhuman."

Chapter 5

BURNED BONES

THE INFORMATION most useful in the interpretation of burned (ashed, incinerated, calcinated, calcined, or cremated) bones was produced by a few anthropologists working independently. Their efforts in the main were not directed toward forensic problems, but rather toward archeological problems. As it happens, however, information applicable to the latter is applicable also to the former. The problems in this area with which both archeologists and forensic anthropologists deal can be put in the form of the following questions: Is it possible to tell from the appearance of burned bones whether they were in the fleshed state or in the dried-bone state when exposed to the fire? If in the fleshed state, do they indicate whether the body had been disarticulated before exposure to the fire? Do signs of differential burning indicate the position of the remains during firing and the intensity of the heat? How reliable are estimates of sex and age made from burned bones?

EXPERIMENTAL CREMATIONS

Krogman seems to have been the first anthropologist in the United States to extend an interest in burned bones to the point of seeking answers to one or more of the above questions through experimental cremation. I base this supposition on the following quotation from one of his early forensic publications (1943, p. 12):

> In 1926 while excavating an Indian Mound in Ohio I uncovered a cremated burial. The bones were very fragmentary, but carbonized muscle tissue still clung to them; muscle fibers could be discerned and, from their position on the bone fragments, I could deduce the muscles involved . . .
>
> As a result of this type of archeological experience I undertook to study the effect of various degrees of heat on dry bones, 'fresh' bone, and the cadaver.

59

In a later version of this statement (Krogman, 1949, p. 72), he added: ". . . using varying degrees of heat ranging from an acetylene torch to a hickory wood fire."

Although Krogman left out of both accounts all further details of his experiment, he did offer (1943, p. 13) the following statement of "general principles":

> Wherever [in a body subjected to cremation] soft tissues surrounding a bone are scant or thin, the bone shows sharp, clear-cut heat fractures (looking somewhat like the patina of age on an old painting), charring, calcination and splintering; where the bone is deeply embedded in muscle tissue or protected by a large muscular mass (e.g. lower $\frac{1}{2}$ of femur), the action of heat on a bone is to produce a molten condition, characteristic of fusion by heat.

Sometime around 1945, when Webb and Snow were summarizing the burial customs of the prehistoric Adena people who lived in the general vicinity of the Ohio River, they found that they needed to specify in which ways the customs of the Adena people differed from those of the prehistoric Hopewell people of the same region. In order to find out what it was that was cremated—i.e. whether a body in the flesh or dried bones—they appealed to Krogman for an opinion and to aid him in his decision sent him bone samples from both Adena and Hopewell cremations. Krogman's conclusion (Webb and Snow, 1945, p. 189) was that the Hopewell people practiced cremation mainly of defleshed and dried bones, whereas the Adena people practiced cremation mainly of fleshed bodies.

Some ten years later Raymond Baby decided it was time to have another look at Hopewell cremation practices. In addition to examining the cremated remains of 128 individuals from four Hopewell sites, he carried out his own cremation experiment, using the gas-fired crematory in the Department of Anatomy at Western Reserve University for the purpose. As he tells it now (Personal communication, 18 February, 1976) :

> The human material, consisting of a whole, unembalmed, fleshed body, an almost completely defleshed cadaver from the dissecting room, and dry bone (macerated, degreased and in use by students for some ten years), was provided by the department . . .
> Briefly this is what was done: The three-jet furnace was preheated

to 1500° F [816° C] before the remains were pushed into three separate areas of it. The gas was increased, bringing the temperature up
to 2100° F [1149° C], and maintained for two and one half hours,
completely reducing the remains. The following day the burnt residue
was carefully removed and examined.

The dry bones [described in detail on page 4 of *Hopewell Cremation
Practices* (Baby, 1954)] remained nearly intact, with little or no reduction in size or alteration in form. In contrast, the fleshed body and
the dissected cadaver exhibited deep checking, warping, reduction of
compact bone, and transverse and diagonal fractures ("hinging").
There was absolutely no observable difference between the two types
of green bone, both fleshed and defleshed.

The description of the dry bones referred to in the above
quotation (Baby, 1954, p. 4) is as follows:

Burnt dry bones exhibit superficial checking, fine longitudinal striae,
deep longitudinal fracturing, or splintering, and no warping. None
of the [ancient] material examined in this study suggested the burning
of dry bones. The few [ancient] cremations that were completely
burnt represented remains burnt in the flesh. In these cases there
was simply a longer period of burning.

Baby's disagreement with Krogman over what the Hopewell
people cremated led Binford (1972) to undertake two further
experimental cremations. Using "a very hot charcoal fire," he
consigned to it first (as "dry bone") selected parts of a burial
approximately 1500 years old and matching recently-macerated
bones from the Anatomy Department of the University of Michi-
gan, and second (as "flesh or green bone") the head, left arm and
feet of a partially dissected green monkey cadaver. Reasoning that
the way in which hot bone was cooled might affect its subsequent
appearance, he cooled half of the bones abruptly by dousing them
with water. As a result of all this he concluded (p. 376) that:

. . . the degree of bone calcining is a function of the length of time
in the fire, the intensity of the heat, the thickness of the protecting
muscle tissue, and the position of the bone in relation to the point of
oxidation of the consuming flame. In both experiments the findings
support Baby's conclusions. Differences are observable between bone
which was dry when burned as opposed to flesh cremation. Dry bone
tends to show predominantly longitudinal fractures, an absence of
warping, and superficial angular cracking; cremations of green bone

or bone with flesh attached show deep transverse fractures, frequently
curved, much warping, and the occasional presence of endosteum.

and that (p. 375):

Water cooling caused the bone to break up, splitting along the heat-
produced fractures and longitudinal strae, although there was no increase in the amount of checking.

Figure 13 contrasts Indian bones judged to have been
cremated in the flesh with modern bones cremated ("ashed") in
the dry, fat-free state (Trotter and Peterson, 1955). As can be
seen, the Indian bones were less uniformly and intensively
burned. Note the presence of transverse cracks in the Indian
bones and their absence in the modern bones, features which ac-
cord with the findings of the earlier investigators described above.
In spite of all surface changes, pathological lesions, if present,
would still be visible. Note, too, that the breaks in the bones are
clean and sharp, making restoration possible when some or all of
the pieces are recovered. I saw Dr. Angel restore an entire skull
that had been shattered into many small pieces by the heat.

STATE OF THE BODY AT FIRING

Going back to Baby's observations on Hopewell cremations,
it is noteworthy that he was able to detect signs of dismemberment
of bodies before exposure to the fire. The signs consisted of
marked differences in the degrees of bone destruction on the two
sides of certain joints. The parts often separated were the head,
lower legs, and (perhaps) the entire upper extremities.

Information about detecting the position of the body in relation to the heat sources has been supplied by Wells (1960) in
connection with his study of Early Saxon cremations in England.
He noted that the less-completely fired skeletal parts often were
the scapulae, sacrum, the spinous processes of the vertebrae, and
the occipital bone. He interpreted this as lending support to the
view that the Saxons placed the body on its back on or close to the
ground and heaped the pyre over it. As further support for this
view he reported having observed the same differential burning
of bones in modern commercial crematoria where "the body (in
the coffin) rests on the floor of the oven and the gas jets are

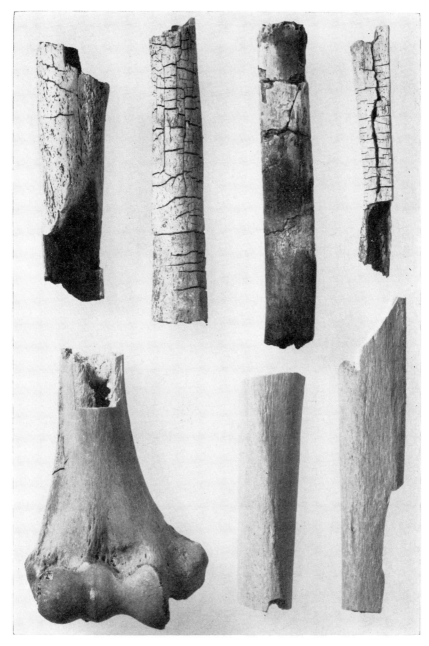

Figure 13. Burned human long bones. *Top row*—Virginia Indian burned in the flesh in an open fire; *bottom row*—Trotter's and Peterson's (1955) study sample No. OS-970, burned in the fat-free state in a furnace. (Courtesy Smithsonian Institution.)

directed downward and laterally upon it" (p. 34).

Under the heading of "A curious clinker" Wells reported (1960, p. 36) another observation that everyone dealing with burned bones should keep in mind. Among his Early Saxon cremated burials he occasionally found a lump of brown, crystalline-like substance rarely larger than a hazelnut (ca. 45 gm. or $1\frac{1}{2}$ oz.). Subsequently in examining modern cremations sometimes he found the same thing, but always beneath the head. He suggested (p. 30) that

> . . . basically it is a transformed keratin from the hair. It was not found during the course of cremating bald or closely cropped males. A full head of hair seems to be necessary to produce it and it is highly probable that some infiltration of fat or tissue fluids into the hair is needed before it transmutes to this curious type of clinker. A large mass of hair placed in a crucible away from the body disintegrated without producing anything like this substance. Another mass of hair (a 20-in, plait wound into a compact ball) was based under the thoracic spine of a young man. At the end of the cremation about 30 gm. of this characteristic clinker was recovered from the same site.

FIRING TEMPERATURES

European anthropologists, unlike their American counterparts, rarely have considered the possibility of prehistoric cremations involving anything but flesh-covered bodies. Their main concern has been to correctly interpret, for demographic purposes, the sex and age of each of the cremated individuals. Sexing of the burnt fragments in particular has been of considerable concern because of the unusually high percentage of females reported in cremations and the possibility that this could be due to failure to recognize the amount of bone shrinkage from the heat. In approaching this problem they have looked at the burned bones from the standpoint of the degrees of heat to which they were subjected.

The most carefully controlled experiment along this line was that of van Vark (1970). He placed cortical fragments of femur, along with fragments of spongy tissue from the mandible and patella, in an electric oven and measured their dimensions after every 100° C (212° F) rise in temperature, starting at 200° C

(372° F) and going up to 1500° C (2732° F). Small pieces of each specimen were set aside at each measuring for macro– and microscopic examination. The results, including amounts of shrinkage expressed in percentages of the original length of the fragments, are shown in Table I.

Van Vark took the further step of comparing his burnt test specimens with similar bone fragments from prehistoric crema-

TABLE I

SHRINKAGE OF FRAGMENTS OF FEMUR, PATELLA, AND MANDIBLE
(MEASURED 5 MIN. AFTER THE GIVEN TEMPERATURE WAS REACHED)*

Temp. Celsius	Mean and s.d. of shrinkage†			Microscopic picture	Macroscopic picture
	Femur (40)	Patella (54)	Mandible (10)	Femur	All 3 bones
0°					
200				V. little	More
300	No	No	No	change	and
400	shrinkage	shrinkage	shrinkage	Questionable	more
500				because of	brittle
600				brittleness	
700	1.75 ± 0.40	2.53 ± 0.53	2.14 ± 0.50		
800	11.56 ± 4.12	14.14 ± 3.16	16.42 ± 4.55		Extensive changes ‡
900					
1000				Completely	
1100	No	No	No	changed;	No
1200	further	further	further	only traces	further
1300	shrinkage	shrinkage	shrinkage	of lacunae	changes
1400				left	
1500					

* From Van Vark, *Some Statistical Procedures for the Investigation of Prehistoric Human Skeletal Material.* Thesis, p 100, 1970. Courtesy of Rijksuniversiteit de Groningen.

† Expressed in percentage of original length of the fragments.

‡ Simultaneous shrinkage, hardening and whitening.

tions. Most of the latter agreed closely, both macro– and micro-scopically, with test specimens which had been heated to a temperature of more than 800-900° C (1472-1652° F). Pre-historic burnt bones of a blue-gray color appeared to agree in macro– and microscopic structure with test specimens exposed to temperatures of 500-800° C (932-1472° F). Wells (1960), Gejvall (1963), and Dokládol (1971) agree that prehistoric cremations reached a temperature of at least 800° C.

Wells' method of reaching this conclusion is especially inter-esting. Many of the Early Saxon cremated burials available to him had glass beads associated with them. Due to the heat of the cremations almost all of these beads showed some degree of fusion, but never complete liquefaction and puddling of the glass. This fact enabled him to determine, by means of a pyrometer furnace, the degree of heat required to reach this stage of melt. It turned out to be between 850° and 940° C depending on bead size.

While on the subject of crematory temperatures, it is impor-tant to include Krogman's findings (1949) for a home furnace. In 1945 a Chicago man by the name of Nischt was tried for the alleged murder of an elderly woman. Since he confessed to hav-ing burned her body in a certain furnace, the latter was searched and some 18,000 recovered bone fragments sent to Krogman for identification. Although he could surely attribute some of them to cow, sheep, goat, dog, chicken, turkey, and goose, in his opinion, none was human.

In a test firing of the same furnace, which had a blower, the "core heart" i.e. at the point directly over the blower's air blast, was found to reach up to 3017° F (1711.6° C). Krogman says that he consigned about 25 lbs. of human bones to this test firing and then "as the test progressed, we agitated the fire, shifting bones centrally, less and less" (p. 81). Although the duration of the test is not stated, Krogman goes on to say (pp. 81-82):

> The initial rapid deterioration of the bones in the central core of heat convinced us that the furnace could destroy human bones, pro-vided they were in the area of maximum heat. *All of the bones recov-ered by us* [three postcranial, eighteen cranial] *came from the periph-ery of the central core* . . .

Krogman attributed the recovery of so many cranial fragments to his unsuccessful efforts to move them from the back of the furnace to the core area.

I feel it is important to stress one point that emerges from all these studies, namely, that a good number of skeletal parts often survive the firing with characteristic features intact enough to be recognizable as human. In most cases of suspected murder where a search has turned up burned bones, actually the most important consideration is whether or not they are human. I would rate the general age period indicated by the bones as next most important. This places the indications of sex in third place. In two different murder trials I had only a handful of burned bones about which all I could say with certainty was that they were human and adult. Aside from burned bones likely being somewhat shrunken in size and sometimes warped, they offer no extra difficulties over unburned broken bones in the matter of aging, sexing, and the commingling of remains of different individuals. As regards sexing, one should remember van Vark's findings (Table I) about the shrinkage of bone under firing.

ANTEMORTEM VS. POSTMORTEM FRACTURES

Since the cause of death is one of the concerns of a forensic anthropologist during skeletal identification, the question arises as to whether some of the fragmentation of a skull that has been burned occurred prior to, and hence was the cause of, death. This question arose in the famous Webster-Parkman trial in the middle of the last century (Bemis, 1850). As part of his efforts to dispose of Dr. Parkman's body, and especially the most recognizable parts of it, Prof. Webster burned the head, forearms, and lower legs in a furnace located in his part of the medical school building. Jeffries Wyman, Hersey Professor of Anatomy there, studied the fragments of burned bone recovered from the furnace and at the trial testified that they represented all the parts missing from the unburned remainder of the body. Being aware that Prof. Webster might have killed Dr. Parkman by hitting him over the head, Prof. Wyman inspected the fragments of the skull vault for signs of fracture. On this point he testified (Bemis, 1850, p. 96):

Some of the fragments of the bones of the skull had the appearance of having been broken previous to calcination, or being burnt in the fire. Calcination removes the animal matter which gives the bones its tenacity; before this is removed, it breaks, with sharp angles, and is more likely to splinter. Common surgical experience shows this. I do not consider the sign as absolute, but only presumptive evidence.

The court also heard an opinion on this point from Oliver Wendel Holmes, occupant of the Chair of Anatomy named in honor of Dr. Parkman. He said (Bemis, 1850, p. 256):

The condition of a fracture of a bone after calcination, would depend upon the degree of calcination. If the calcination had been very complete, the bone would easily crumble. If only partially calcined, the bone might split and break in any direction. In either case, one could not give a very reliable opinion upon the point, whether the fracture was before, or after calcination. Such, at least, has been the respect of my observations.

Although I doubt that either of these distinguished anatomists knew from first-hand experience the variety of changes in bone resulting from burning, so far as I have been able to discover, the problem they were dealing with still is unresolved.

Chapter 6

JUDGING TIME AND CAUSE OF DEATH

As the preceding three chapters make clear, bones submitted for identification in forensic cases often require considerable handling before the major determinations to be considered here-after—sex, age, race, stature, etc.—can be undertaken. Growing naturally out of this preliminary bone handling (animal and burned bones aside), should be two impressions that have little to do with these major determinations, namely, those about the probable time and cause of death. For this reason, the closing chapter of this section is an appropriate place to consider them.

TIME INTERVAL SINCE DEATH

The impression on this score comes principally from observing the presence or absence of: (1) odor, and its intensity; (2) soft parts, and their locations; (3) adherent earth (clay, loam, or sand) ; (4) adherent vegetation (twigs, leaves, grass, or moss) ; (5) adherent insects, living or dead, including immature stages; (6) tooth marks; (7) stains and/or bleaching; and (8) adipocere.

Generally speaking, the odor of decay persists beyond the loss of the soft parts, of which the last to disappear usually is the joint cartilage. Any joint cartilage that remains after the disappearance of odor usually is dry and hard. Hair, which does not produce decay odor, lasts a long time, even in the grave, but is not always collected with the bones. The rest of the observations listed above serve mainly to help establish where the process of skeletonization took place and the level of temperature during the period prior to the date when the remains were recovered (or, for all practical purposes, when they were delivered to the examiner) .

Necrophagous Insects

The place where, and the temperature under which, skeletonization takes place are important because, more than any other

69

factors, they determine the number and variety of the necrophagous insects that are attracted to the corpse and thereupon become the main agents of tissue decomposition. According to
Leclercq (1969, Chapter 13), the changes in an exposed corpse
that follow rapidly on the disappearance of *rigor mortis* involve
autolysis and putrifaction. The former is a biochemical degradation process brought about without the intervention of bacteria
or other agents foreign to the individual; the latter is a decomposition process brought about by the action of the individual's own
microorganisms. The "emanations" from these two processes both
attract the insects to, and condition the sequence in which they
establish themselves on, a corpse (sometimes in as many as six to
eight waves).

Also influential in this situation are the richness of the local
insect fauna, the upper range of the temperature, and the eco-
logical niches represented by the corpse at different stages of its
deterioration. On the other hand, the activities of necrophagous
insects are much curtailed by low temperatures, limited access to
the corpse prescribed by closed structures or underground burial,
and by the prompt conversion of the soft parts to adipocere.

Entomologists have had some success in estimating the time
since death from the infesting insects, and especially from the
rates at which these insects reproduce (see, for example, Nuorteva
et al., 1967; Easton and Smith, 1970). However, apparently the
success of this method of estimating time since death diminishes
rapidly after the first wave of infestation has been established for
three weeks or so.

Insect remains recovered with buried human remains usually
reflect only the time that elasped between death and burial because, except before and during the process of burial, such a
corpse is inaccessible to insects. This is best illustrated by the
finds of some of the physical anthropologists who excavated the
early cemeteries of the Arikara Indians in South Dakota (Gilbert
and Bass, 1967; Ubelaker and Willey, 1978). Summarizing these
finds, Ubelaker and Willey report that fly pupal cases were present
in from 16.4 to 38.3 percent of the burials at five sites. In addition, at four of these five sites elements of the beetle *Trox* were

present in from 1.0 to 2.0 percent of the burials. All burials were over two feet deep.

Since flys and beetles do not burrow more than a few inches below the surface of the ground, the likely explanation of the Arikara finds is that the corpses with the insect remains had been exposed above ground in favorable weather long enough to receive the initial insect infestation, but not long enough to receive the further successions of insects. The beetle *Trox* may even have been attracted solely to the dry buffalo-skin covering. Be this as it may, these insect remains had been underground for over 150 years. In the case of burials, obviously, the accompanying insect remains do not always tell the true length of time since death.

Forensic anthropologists are likely to encounter insect remains mainly in cases that are still incompletely skeletonized after exposure in the open. But whatever the situation, every forensic anthropologist should make it a rule to keep an eye out for insects and save any found for forwarding to a qualified entomologist for possible identification and interpretation as regards the duration of the time since death.

Minimum Time of Skeletonization

There is no escaping the fact that, for most skeletonized remains, estimation of time since death usually is little more than an educated guess. Although undeniably the remains that stink because the bones are still partly flesh covered represent more recent death than those with less odor and with no soft parts still present other than traces of cartilage, the problem is to translate these and other stages of advanced deterioration into specific intervals of postmortem time. By way of help in this connection I can offer only a few guidelines, some of them from my own experience.

Of foremost importance here is the established fact that *under the most favorable circumstances* a corpse will be almost completely skeletonized by the end of two weeks from the time of death. I base this statement primarily on the case from Mississippi mentioned in Chapter 2. The remains of this homicide victim, whose remains were accepted by the court as those of a twelve and

one half-year-old female who had been missing for ten days
(August 13 to 23,) had in this short time become almost completely skeletonized. Since the crime had been committed in the hurri-
cane season and the body hidden under a discarded, vinyl-covered
sofa, in effect the postmortem environment of the remains was that
of an incubator. Under such favorable circumstances the necrophagous insects undoubtedly flourished and quickly disposed of
the soft parts.

Varying Frequency of Carnivores

If large predators were not present in the vicinity of, or lacked
access to, the corpse in the Mississippi case, as the absence of tooth
marks on the bones suggested, their presence was much in evidence in a case from New Mexico with which I was involved. Not
only had these animals (mainly coyotes) destroyed the parts of the
bones (usually the ends) where the cortex is thin, but they had
scattered the remaining parts over a wide area. One foot, still
in a shoe, was reported to have been found in a tree, carried there
perhaps by a carrion bird. As in the Mississippi case, all of this
had taken place within two weeks following the death of the
victim.

Free-ranging carnivores are less likely to occur in urban than
in rural areas. The truth of this generalization was brought home
to me after the New Mexico case when I was asked to examine a
completely articulated, undamaged, and odorless skeleton that
had been found fully clothed on the tree-covered floodplain of the
Potomac River just above Georgetown in the District of Columbia.
This individual had been missing for one year. Because of its
proximity to the river, this area is subject to flooding and hence
may lack native carnivores. Also, the existence of a canal parallel-
ing the river on the city side effectively keeps out roaming dogs.

Shielded Remains

Unlike remains that are exposed to the elements, and to
predators, those shielded therefrom become skeletonized at slower
rates, depending on the circumstances. A good example is a case I
had in Kentucky involving the remains of two women that had

been buried for about four years under a coal pile in a cellar. Although essentially skeletonized, the remains still had a strong odor of decay and still retained liquefied brain tissue sealed off by the meninges within the skulls. As I recall, I had no basis at that time for thinking that in this particular environment human remains might still be in this incomplete stage of deterioration so long after death.

Adipocere Formation

The almost complete absence of adipocere in the remains of the two Kentucky women made little impression on me because I had not yet seen much of it. Later when I was in Japan examining the remains of the American soldiers killed in the Korean War I was impressed by the fact that so many of the bodies of the deeply buried soldiers had been converted in different degrees to this soft, whitish substance, whereas many others found in close association were completely skeletonized. That this is not a new observation is evident from the fact that Wetherill reported it in 1860 (p. 5) when he had occasion to observe the removal of a cemetery in Philadelphia.

Early chemical studies of adipocere (for example, Wetherill, 1860) led to the belief that this material is a form of soap that depends for its formation on long emersion of a corpse in water. According to Mant and Furbank (1957), however, adipocere is now known to consist mainly of fatty acids formed by the post-mortem hydrolysis and hydrogenation of body fats. This new explanation accounts for the fact that adipocere is often admixed with remains of the non-fatty soft parts.

Adipocerous change begins to occur only a few days after death, but does not become visible for about three months. The presence of moisture is still regarded as a prerequisite for the change, although the quantity need not be as great as earlier thought necessary. Running water might even retard the process, whereas a well-nourished body alone might contain enough water to permit the transformation to be carried forward. Since adipocere, once formed, is relatively permanent, its extensive formation may preserve the surface features of a body for years.

An extreme example of this, the almost complete body of a man who died in 1792, is on exhibit in the Hall of Physical Anthropology in the National Museum of Natural History.

I said above that not all of the deeply-buried bodies of the American soldiers killed in Korea had been transformed into adipocere. When cleaned, the bones from these exceptional cases looked very much like those of macerated dissecting-room skeletons; in other words, they were completely free of soft parts and odor, but appeared still to contain considerable organic matter.

Effect of Shallow Burial

In comparison with the skeletons from the deep burials, those recovered from the shallow graves of the American soldiers who had been held for varying lengths of time in prisoner-of-war camps were virtually indistinguishable in appearance from prehistoric skeletons recovered archeologically; that is, they gave little if any visible evidence of containing organic matter and were beginning to show breakdown of the cortical surfaces.

These Korean POW skeletons reminded me of similar-looking bones from a mass grave in Europe that American anthropologists had been asked to give opinions on around the end of World War II. The consensus was that probably they had been in the ground many years. Later I learned that investigators had been so intent on connecting the grave with the war atrocities then much in the news that they had dismissed as intentionally misleading the denials of recency by the local inhabitants. The grave actually dated from the War of 1870.

Residual Bone Nitrogen

According to Knight and Lauder (1969) there are a number of objective ways of getting at the relative age of archeological-looking bones. Perhaps the best is to measure their residual nitrogen. Ortner *et al.* (1972) point out that at death the protein in the bones begins to hydrolyze to peptides, which in turn break down to their constituent amino acids. The rate at which the degradation process takes place depends to a large extent upon the prevailing temperature, the amount of water present, and the pH of this water. Anyway, since of the bone constituents only protein contains nitrogen, many investigators have found that the quantity of this element remaining in dead bone at any time offers a rough measure of the length of time since death.

Cook and Heizer (1947), for example, found a normal human femur from a fresh cadaver to contain 4.08 percent N, whereas archeological bones from California believed to be around 500 years old had an average 1.87 percent and much older bones (1000 years old?) from the same state had on average 0.49 percent. Although such findings are impressive, they give little assurance that the bones of a particular individual dead anywhere up to fifty years can be reliably dated by this method. Moreover, the chemical procedures involved are anything but simple.

Root Penetration

Turning now to a very different aspect of estimating the time since death, no studies to my knowledge have been made on the rate of root penetration into buried bones, much less bones left on the surface. As opposed to the situation in the tropics, where plants grow prolifically and rapidly destroy any bones within reach (Warren, C.P., 1975), in areas of temperate climate the penetration of plant roots into bones is seldom observed, unless a burial turns out to have been within the reach of certain rapidly-growing trees, such as locusts. For these reasons rarely, if ever, is it possible to estimate postmortem time from roots, and especially if all one has to go on is the severed ends of the roots protruding from the excavated bones. Needless to say, if one gets a case in which roots are involved, it is best to seek the advice of a botanist.

Staining and Bleaching

Finally, how long does it take for bones to become discolored? I have seen bones that had been recovered from river and/or swamp mud (muck) and were of the color of this muck. Although undoubtedly some of these bones were ancient, I have never discovered criteria for judging from the color alone how long the bones were in the muck, much less whether this time corresponds to that since death.

On the other hand, I am under the impression that bones can become bleached fairly rapidly, but not until all organic matter has been lost from the cortical surfaces. Bleaching is sometimes seen in the skeletal parts that have become exposed in shallow graves. In such cases the exposed and bleached parts contrast with the more-deeply buried and possibly soil-stained parts and thereby bear witness to the position of the body in the grave. However, since in a shallow grave exposure of the uppermost bones to sunlight often is accidental, the bleaching is a better measure of exposure time than of time since death.

CAUSE OF DEATH

When a forensic anthropologist has finished his examination of a skeleton he is likely to be asked: "Did you learn the cause of death?" Seldom can this question be answered in the affirmative with any assurance. Individuals can survive massive bone damage and then die or be put to death in some way that leaves no sign on the skeleton. For this reason a forensic anthropologist should simply describe any evidence of bone damage, point out its location in relation to vital centers, explain the possibility of its having been sustained at the time of death or otherwise, and discuss the likely types of objects that produced the damage. After all, some one has died and the reason for the investigation is to learn whether or not a crime was committed, whatever the cause of death.

Signs of Blows

One can usually speak more confidently of the way in which bone damage was inflicted than of the effect this damage had upon the individual's vitality. In general, the nature of bone damage depends on the shape of the object that struck the body and upon the force with which the object was propelled. In the case from Mississippi described above the left side of the victim's lower jaw had been broken into two or three pieces, probably by a right-handed assailant striking with the fist (or some other blunt object such as a revolver butt). Also there were signs on the occiput and in the right temporal fossa that a bullet had passed through the skull. Since a bullet is a relatively small object and is propelled at high velocity, it makes a circular, sharp-edged entrance hole, but a much larger and more ragged exit hole.

Examination of the interior of the skull showed that, as usual, on the side where the bullet entered, the inner table had been carried away from the edge, leaving it beveled. Owing to the dispersal of the bullet's force by the brain, the side of the skull opposite the entrance hole showed not only an irregular area of bone loss (much of it involving the outer table), but also a number of radiating fracture lines. With experience one can judge whether the bullet was of large or small caliber, and from what distance it was fired, but this is not the province of the forensic anthropologist.

A blow from a blunt object to the vault of the living head will produce different effects depending mainly on the location of the center of impact and the force of the impact. In the dried skull evidence that a blow had been received will not be seen unless the force of the blow was great enough to fracture the bone. An understanding of the mechanism of skull fracture will help a forensic anthropologist in forming an opinion about the location of the point of impact. Any further opinion about the extent of the associated brain damage is not in the forensic anthropologist's province.

In the late 1940s E. S. Gurdjian and associates in Detroit provided the first clear understanding of the patterning of skull fractures through experiments on dried skulls painted with "stresscoat" (a brittle lacquer) and on cadaver heads. Some of their main findings are summarized in the following statement (Gurdjian *et al.,* 1950, p. 313) :

> At impact, the area around the point of application of the blow is inbended. Simultaneously there is an outbending of the bone peripheral to the inbended area. This outbending is selective and may be localized to a certain part of the skull, where a linear fracture is initiated due to the resultant tearing-apart forces. The fracture then extends toward the point of impact and in the opposite direction. Extension is directly toward the region of impact rather than to one or the other side, because, although initially this area is in compression (bent in), it rebounds immediately after the energy of the blow has

been absorbed and becomes an area of tensile stress. A fracture which has started at a considerable distance will, of course, propagate in a direction normal to the greatest tensile stress.   Therefore it must travel toward the center of the area of impact. If insufficient energy was expended in the blow, the fracture may remain limited and not reach the point of impact.

The fracture lines at a distance from the point of impact are frequently referred to (but not by Gurdjian *et al.*) as fracture by *contre-coup*. This reflects the earlier belief that the force of the blow was transmitted from the point of impact directly through the head to the areas of bone breakage, thereby simulating a counter blow. Gurdjian *et al.* (1950, p. 336) caution that the fracture pattern can be modified by such "chance characteristics" as thickened diploë, enlarged Pacchionian bodies, aberrant venous channels between the inner and outer tables, and thickened tables. An X ray may tell whether any of these characteristics had affected the course of the fracture line(s).

In a body that has been struck by the blast from a shotgun the bones sometimes show small depressions where they were struck by the metal pellets. Usually in such cases some of the pellets are still present in the bone, either visible to the naked eye or detectable by X ray. By comparison, a pointed object, such as an ice pick, produces a deeper, smoother, and more-conical hole in bone. On the other hand, a flat-bladed object, such as a knife, hatchet, or axe, usually produces an elongated cut mark that is V-shaped in cross-section. Yet Kerley (1973, p. 183) has shown that when a long bone receives a glancing blow from an axe the result can be a smoothly-concave cut "on the side of entry, combined with a series of rippled cuts in the side of exit, where the blade 'chattered' as it was deflected by the bone itself."

From the locations on the bones of any of these types of marks often one can deduce whether or not the object causing them had been directed at a vital center, or represents efforts toward dismemberment. Dismemberment is done sometimes in part with a saw, which leaves a cut surface that is distinctively roughened.

Simple breaks in the bones do not always have such lethal connotations. This is true especially when the bones in question have been exposed on the ground for some time. A heavy animal can break a bone by stepping on it. In pointing this out to investigators, it is well to raise the question of accessibility of the find site to hoofed farm animals. In this connection it is noteworthy that scavenging animals rarely, if ever, cause bone damage that would be confused with the kinds mentioned here.

Signs of Strangulation

An exception to the simple bone breaks in the matter of lethal connotation is one that involves the hyoid bone and/or the variably ossified thyroid cartilage, both located in the anterior neck (Figure 14). Interruptions to the normal continuity of these bony structures discovered after death may mean that a constricting force was applied to the neck and caused death by strangulation.

Most anthropologists pay little attention to these structures, and some may be unaware even that the thyroid cartilage can become ossified to the point where it is recoverable after death like any other dried bone. The hyoid is situated above the thyroid cartilage, with which it is connected by ligaments. Made up of an internally-concave, ovoid-shaped body from which on each side an elongated horn (greater cornu) extends postero-superiorly and in front of this a short stubby horn (lesser cornu) extends superiorly, the mature bone is U-shaped. Maturity in this instance comes sometime in middle life when the two greater cornua unite with the body. Since the lesser cornua seldom fuse with the body, their free state should not be mistaken for evidence of fracture.

The thyroid is the largest of nine cartilages making up the so-called "laryngeal skeleton." This "skeleton" moves up and down during swallowing in such a way as to be visible because of the prominence of the conjoined thyroid laminae (known popularly as the "Adam's apple"). Attached posteriorly to each of these laminae are two cornua, a long one superiorly and a short one inferiorly. Ossification of the thyroid cartilage is said to begin about twenty years of age (a little later in females) and to continue erratically into old age. Because the thyroid is located lower in the neck than the hyoid and hence is less protected, it would seem to be more prone to fracture when ossified. As yet, however, the relative frequency of fracture of the two bones in

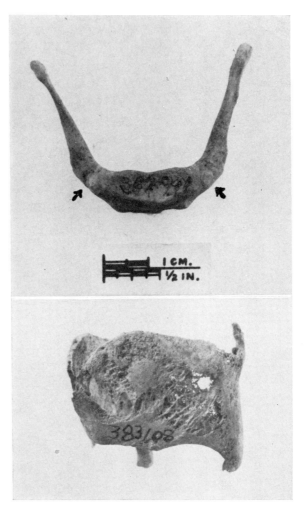

Figure 14. Two bones of the throat subject to fracture.   *Upper*—hyoid (Arikara Indian, U.S.N.M. No. 382,991) in ventral view;   *lower*—ossified thyroid cartilage (Arikara Indian, U.S.N.M. No. 383,108) in left ventral view. Arrows point to facets on the hyoid for missing lesser cornua. (Courtesy Smithsonian Institution.)

forensic cases is not clearly established.

The rare reports of fracture in one part or another of these two bones of the throat attributed to forceful strangulation include one by Dutra (1944, p. 346) and two by Sydney Smith (1939a, p. 280; 1942, p. 37). In Dutra's case a young woman was judged to have been strangled owing to the fact that her hyoid, found attached to the skull in a mass of adipocere, was broken. Since there is no mention of her thyroid, presumably it had not yet ossified.

In the first of Sydney Smith's cases, involving a woman forty-five years of age, the greater horns of the hyoid had not yet united, but the right one was fractured. Smith noted (p. 280) that "In the fractured ends adipocere had been deposited showing that the fracture was present before the body or head was buried." In his second case, involving a man over sixty, both greater horns of the hyoid had united with the body and the thyroid cartilage was ossified. Fractures were present in both bones. Here, too, adipocere in the broken ends of the bones indicated that breakage had occurred antemortem.

Section II

GENERAL SKELETAL TRAITS

Among the determinations that forensic anthropologists try to arrive at in examining skeletal remains are six—sex, age, race, stature, weight, and handedness—that can be called general, in the sense that each of them does no more than assign the individual to a class within the population at large. For example, if the skeleton of an unknown can be said to be male, the search for identity is narrowed to half of the population; if the age is judged to be around thirty-five, the search is further narrowed to those males of the population who are in the fourth decade of life; etc. Thus, none of these traits alone, nor all six of them together, positively identify the individual. Only when the general traits fit both the description of a missing individual and the circumstantial evidence connected with the recovery of the remains does identification become plausible at most.

In contrast to general traits are some specific or individual traits—healed fractures, dental anomalies, mastoid air-cell patterns and the like—that, as in the case of fingerprints in fleshed remains, are unlikely to be matched in any other individual. However, the identification of a skeletonized individual from one or more specific traits depends, as in the case of finger prints, upon a favorable comparison with a record made during life.

These considerations have led me to give separate treatment in this book to the procedures used in arriving at each of the two kinds of traits. The general traits to be considered in the present section will be followed by specific traits in Section III. The order of the general traits to be followed here reflects my preference for attributing sex before estimating age and stature (the two sexes age at different rates and grow to different sizes). Stature, on the other hand, is an important factor in estimating weight and in attributing race. Handedness is independent of all the others.

In this section I shall have occasion to begin referring to two documented series of skeletons, the Terry and Todd Collections. Robert J. Terry (1871-1966) and T. Wingate Todd (1885-1938) headed the departments of anatomy at Washington University, St. Louis, and Western Reserve University, Cleveland, respectively. Terry served in that capacity from 1900 to 1941; Todd from 1912 to 1938. During this period each began assembling the skeletons from the cadavers dissected in his department—Todd in 1912 and Terry only two years later. Todd's collection, which at his death totaled 2600 (Cobb, 1952), is now housed in the Cleveland Museum of Natural History. Terry's collection, which was added to until 1965, totals 1636 and is housed in the National Museum of Natural History in Washington (Stewart, 1969). As will appear, these two large samples of the blacks and whites in the American population have provided the basis for much of the research undertaken by American forensic anthropologists.

Chapter 7

ATTRIBUTION OF SEX

E ARLY ARTISTIC RENDERINGS of the human skeleton (Figure 15, for example) demonstrate that anatomists long have recognized the postmortem persistence of sexual dimorphism in the bones of adults and have represented it mainly through distinctions in pelvic conformation. Since the outstanding secondary sex character of the adult female skeleton is the modification of the pelvic girdle for childbearing, the resulting differences between the adult bony pelves of the two sexes have been cited in all forensic textbooks as the best indicators of sex in the skelton. Recogni-

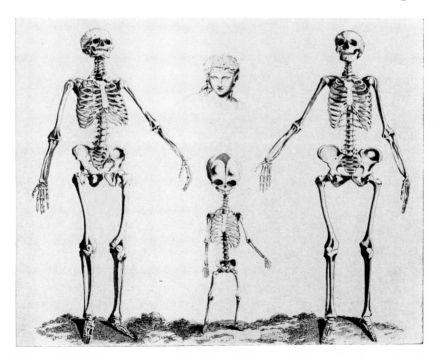

Figure 15. Eighteenth-century drawings of human skeletons by Jean Joseph Sue showing sex and age differences. (From Knox, 1829.)

85

tion of other sex-related characters of the skeleton has come more recently. Today, therefore, forensic anthropologists have at their command a variety of indicators of sex to aid them in their identification efforts, albeit with rare exceptions they are applicable to the post-adolescent period only.

The simplest of these indicators is an observable sex-related detail of a bone, like the little triangle on the inferomedial border of the body of the pubis (Figure 23, arrow), which can be categorized as present (female), absent (male), or indeterminate (sex?). The existence of the third category indicates the limitation of all such present/absent details for use in the attribution of sex.

The next simplest indicator is a single dimension of a bone, say the diameter of the proximal joint surface of the humerus. In order for a dimension to have utility for forensic application it must have been measured on an adequate number of documented skeletons of both sexes and the figures for each sex arranged in a frequency distribution to show by comparison the extent of overlap. Only the figures outside the overlap certainly distinguish a member of one sex from a member of the other sex (usually, but not always, the largest figures indicate maleness; the smallest femaleness).

A slightly more involved indicator is an index, which is the ratio between two differently-directed dimensions selected to express the shape of some part of a bone, say the base of the sacrum. The circumstances governing the utility of an index for the attribution of sex are essentially the same as for a single dimension. And again the result is the same: An overlap in the distributions for the two sexes is always present, so only the extremes of shape are reliable indicators of sex.

Much more complicated to develop and apply is the indicator most recently introduced, known as discriminant function, which most commonly is used to evaluate groups of dimensions. Although, as might be expected, the accuracy of attribution is improved by the increased number of morphological characters taken into consideration, it is never completely fulfilled; that is, one can never feel 100 percent sure that a small fraction of the skeletons of unknowns is correctly sexed, no matter how many skeletal characters are taken into consideration.

As physical anthropologists have become more experienced they have tended to gain confidence in their ability to judge by eye the sex of skeletons, and therefore to hold that the trained eye can more quickly synthesize to this end a wide variety of morphological characters than can any metrical device. I argued in support of this point of view in 1954 when I criticized Hanna and Washburn (1953) for the way they used the ischium-pubis index in sexing Eskimo skeletons. At the same time I recognized the validity of their counter argument that any physical anthropologist who has not had the opportunity to gain experience in sexing skeletons by eye is better off using one of the metrical procedures.

Metric procedures, being objective, also serve as a useful check on one's subjective impression of the sex of an unknown. Although, as pointed out in Chapter 2, an experienced forensic anthropologist may have no doubts about the correctness of his subjective impression of sex in a case headed for court, his position as an expert witness in the case is strengthened if he can testify that the attribution of sex by one or more appropriate objective procedures agreed with his subjective judgment. When a forensic anthropologist does not protect himself in this way the opportunity exists for a canny opposing attorney to ask him questions aimed at discrediting an attribution based solely upon subjectivity.

In considering in more detail the various sex indicators I shall begin with the skull and proceed caudad, taking up in more or less anatomical order each bone for which information oriented toward sex attribution is available. In most cases the information applies primarily to American blacks and whites. For discriminant function sexing of Japanese see Giles (1970b).

SKULL AND LOWER JAW*

As the female moves from puberty into adulthood her skull retains much of the gracility and smoothness characteristic of the prepubertal period, whereas the male's skull during this time be-

*See also BONES AND TEETH at the end of this chapter.

comes less gracile, relatively larger, and much rougher in the areas of muscle insertions. The resulting differences are most notice-able in the orbital borders, supraorbital ridges, mastoid processes, occipital crest (especially its medial protuberance), malar bones, and chin (see Figures 64-67).

Although borders, ridges, processes, and crests are thicker and/ or more prominent in males than in females, the differences are not easily quantified, and hence the establishment of size bound-aries for these features whereby the amount of separation of the two sexes can be evaluated has proved to be impracticable. As re-gards the malar bones and the chin, differences in conformation rather than in size are the important things to look for. The shape of the chin is particularly helpful, since a square chin usually implies a male, whereas a rounded or pointed chin implies a fe-male. Anyone who works with skulls develops an eye for these details and soon becomes able to make a tentative attribution of sex on this basis alone.

Back in 1943 when I spent a short time teaching anatomy at Washington University, St. Louis, I tested my ability to correctly sex the skull and lower jaw by inspecting those of 100 American blacks from the Terry Collection, equally divided between the two sexes. My score was only 77 percent correct (Stewart, 1948, p. 317). In thinking about this test later, I decided that it was a good thing I had not taken the skulls in the order in which they were catalogued (they had been selected by a preparator), be-cause, with females being greatly outnumbered in dissecting-room collections, I could have improved my score whenever in doubt simply by recording my judgment as "male."

If one's record of accuracy in skull sexing by inspection is no better than mine was in 1943 (I hope it has improved since then), it is especially important to back it up with any method claiming to do, if not better, at least as well as the eye. According to Giles (1970b), discriminant function sexing by cranial and/or mandibu-lar measurements meets this requirement, because it has a tested accuracy between 83.2 percent and 88.3 percent for American blacks and whites, depending upon the particular race involved and the combination of measurements used.

TABLE II.

DISCRIMINANT-FUNCTION SEXING BY CRANIAL MEASUREMENTS*

Numbered discriminant functions and their weights

Measurements†	Whites						Blacks					
	1	2	3	4	5	6	7	8	9	10	11	12
1	3.107	3.400	1.800	—	1.236	9.875	9.222	3.895	3.533	—	2.111	2.867
2	-4.643	-3.833	-1.783	—	-1.000	—	7.000	3.632	1.667	—	1.000	—
3	5.786	5.433	2.767	—	—	—	1.000	1.000	0.867	—	—	—
4	—	-0.167	-0.100	10.714	—	7.062	—	-2.053	0.100	1.000	—	-0.100
5	14.821	12.200	6.300	16.381	3.291	19.062	31.111	12.947	8.700	19.389	4.963	12.367
6	1.000	-0.100	—	-1.000	—	-1.000	5.889	1.368	—	2.778	—	-0.233
7	2.714	2.200	—	4.333	—	4.375	20.222	8.158	—	11.778	—	6.900
8	-5.179	—	—	-6.571	—	—	-30.556	—	—	-14.333	—	—
9	6.071	5.367	2.833	14.810	1.528	—	47.111	19.947	14.367	23.667	8.037	—
Sectioning point	2676.39	2592.32	1296.20	3348.27	536.93	5066.69	8171.53	4079.12	2515.91	3461.46	1387.72	2568.97
Percent correct	86.6	86.4	86.4	84.5	85.5	84.9	87.6	86.6	86.5	87.5	85.3	85.0

*From Giles, Discriminant function sexing of the human skeleton. In Stewart, T.D. (Ed.): *Personal Identification in Mass Disasters*, pp. 99-109, Table LI, 1970b, citing Giles and Elliot, 1963. Courtesy of the National Museum of Natural History, Washington.

†See text for measurement descriptions.

TABLE III
DISCRIMINANT FUNCTION SEXING BY MANDIBULAR MEASUREMENT*

Measure-ments†	Numbered discriminant functions and their weights					
	Whites			Blacks		
	1	2	3	4	5	6
10	1.390	22.206	2.862	1.065	2.020	3.892
11	—	—30.265	—	—	—2.292	—
12	—	1.000	2.540	—	2.606	10.568
13	—	—	—1.000	—	—	—9.027
14	—	—	—5.954	—	—	—3.270
15	—	—	1.483	—	—	1.000
16	2.304	19.708	5.172	2.105	3.076	10.486
17	1.000	7.360	—	1.000	1.000	—
Section-ing point	287.43	1960.05	524.79	265.74	549.82	1628.79
Percent correct	83.2	85.9	84.1	84.8	86.9	86.5

*From Giles, Discriminant function sexing of the human skelton. In Stewart, T.D. (Ed.): *Personal Identification in Mass Disasters,* pp. 99-109, Table LII, 1970b, citing Giles, 1964. Courtesy of the National Museum of Natural History, Washington.
†See text for measurement descriptions.

TABLE IV
DISCRIMINANT FUNCTION SEXING BY COMBINED CRANIAL AND MANDIBULAR MEASUREMENTS*

Measurements†	Function No. 6 and weights for blacks
1	1.289
5	—0.100
7	1.489
9	4.289
10	—0.976
12	—0.544
16	3.478
17	1.400
Sectioning point	718.23
Percent correct	88.3

*From Giles, Discriminant function sexing of the human skeleton. In Stewart, T.D. (Ed.): *Personal Identification in Mass Disasters,* pp. 99-109, Table LIII, 1970b, citing Giles, 1970a. Courtesy of the National Museum of Natural History, Washington.
†See text for measurement descriptions.

Tables II, III, and IV give the available basic data needed to apply the discriminant function method of sexing to the skulls and lower jaws of American blacks and whites. The measurements listed by number in these tables are defined (Giles, 1970b, p. 108) as follow:

1. Maximum length of the skull, from the most anterior point of the frontal, in the midline, to the most distant point on the occiput, in the midline.

2. The greatest breadth of the cranium perpendicular to the median sagittal plane, and avoiding the supramastoid crests.

3. Cranial height measured from basion (midpoint on the anterior border of the foramen magnum) to bregma (intersection of the coronal and sagittal sutures).

4. From basion (see 3) to nasion (midpoint of the nasofrontal suture).

5. Maximum width between the lateral surfaces of the zygomatic arches measured perpendicular to the median sagittal plane.

6. From basion (see 3) to the most anterior point on the maxilla in the median sagittal plane.

7. Lowest point on the alveolar border between the [upper] central incisors to nasion (see 4).

8. Maximum breadth of the palate taken on the outside of the alveolar borders.

9. The length of the mastoid measured perpendicular to the plane determined by the lower border of the left orbit and the upper borders of the auditory meatuses (= Frankfort plane). The upper arm of the sliding calipers is aligned with the upper border of the auditory meatus, and the distance (perpendicular to the Frankfort plane) to the tip of the mastoid is measured.

10. Height from the lowest median point on the jaw (menton) to the lower alveolar point (bony process between the [lower] central incisors). If the menton is in a notch, then the measurement is taken from a line tangent to the lowest points on the margins lateral to the notch.

11. Mandibular body height as measured between the first and second molars.

12. From the most anterior point on the mandibular symphysis to an imaginary point formed by the posterior margin of the ramus and the anteroposterior axis of the body, and measured parallel to the axis.

13. The thickness of the mandibular body measured at the level of the second molar parallel to the vertical axis of the body.

14. The smallest anteroposterior diameter of the ramus of the jaw.

15. The distance between the most anterior point on the mandibular ramus and the line connecting the most posterior point on the condyle and the angle of the jaw.

16. Height measured from the uppermost point on the condyle to the middle of the inferior border of the body parallel to the vertical axis of the ramus. (The middle of the ramus on the inferior margin is not a distinct point but can be easily estimated.)

17. Maximum diameter, externally, on the angles of the jaw (gonion).

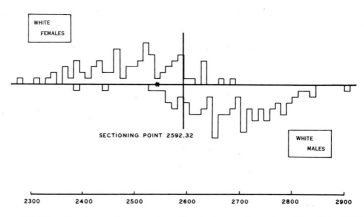

Figure 16. Distribution of scores for discriminant function No. 2 in Table II (108 males and 79 females). Asterisk locates the score from the test-case calculation given in the text. (From Giles, Discriminant Function sexing of the human skeleton. In T.D. Stewart (Ed.): *Personal Identification in Mass Disasters,* pp. 99-109, Figure 24, 1970b. Courtesy of the National Museum of Natural History.)

Giles (1970b) has given an example of how the discriminant function sexing method is applied in a forensic case (a skull of an unknown attributed to the white race). Using function No. 2 in Table II, which has an accuracy rating of 86.4 percent, and noting in Figure 16 how the sectioning point keeps the number of mis-classified specimens to a minimum, one carries out the calculation as follows:

Measurements (see text)	Discriminant function weights		Measurements of unknown (in mm)		Products
1	3.400	×	168	=	571.200
2	−3.833	×	140	=	−536,620
3	5.433	×	128	=	695.424
4	−0.167	×	94	=	− 15.698
5	12.200	×	125	=	1525.000
6	−0.100	×	93	=	− 9.300
7	2.200	×	72	=	158.400
9	5.367	×	29	=	155.643
			Score		2544.049

Giles gives his interpretation of this result in these words (p. 101):

A score for this specimen of 2544 puts it on the female side of the sectioning point of 2592 [as indicated by the asterisk in Figure 16] but . . . . not far from the demarcation line. In fact, this skull, though small, had a number of unmeasurable indicia of maleness, which presumably are reflected in the position of its discriminant function score relative to the majority of females.

Put more succinctly, function No. 2 does not positively tell the sex of the test specimen. Faced with this situation, a forensic anthropologist would be well advised to qualify his attribution of sex.

CLAVICLE

In 1957 Thieme and Schull reported (p. 243) "the results of an investigation designed to find the sex discriminating efficiency of several measurements on the post-cranial skeleton, using specimens of known sex [blacks from the Terry Collection]." One of these measurements was the maximum length of the left clavicle. Their analysis of the distribution by sex (their Figure 3) shows that the total range of the combined sexes (99 males and 101 females) was between 120 and 175 mm, with males overlapping females between 125 and 155 mm. The total number of individuals in the overlap was 156 or 78 percent of the sample. Although this indicates a relatively low sex-discriminating efficiency, the authors included the measurement anyway in one of the discriminant functions they constructed (see Table VI, No. 5).

STERNUM

According to W. Krause (1897), the first known statement in the literature on the sexual dimorphism of the sternum was by an investigator named Wenzel who in 1788 studied 200 specimens in Sömmerring's collection in Mainz, Germany. Krause's version of this statement (which he claimed to be false) is "'. . . das Manubrium sterni beim Manne kürzer ist als die Hälfe des Mittelstückes, beim Weibe aber länger" (p. 21).

Joseph Hyrtl gave wide currency to this statement in his *Handbuch* (1865) by making it one of his anatomical laws. As translated by Thomas Dwight (1881, p. 327), Hyrtl's law reads: "The manubrium of the female sternum exceeds half the length of the body, while the body in the male sternum is, at least, twice as long as the manubrium."

Hubert von Luschka also reported the statement in his *Anatomie* (1863-1869), but with a formulation different enough to be called Luschka's law. Dwight (1881, p. 327) has supplied an English version: "The body [of the sternum] is usually twice as long as the manubrium in woman, and two and one half times as long in man."

Dwight had already begun checking on these laws at the time he wrote his prize essay of 1878. The number of specimens available to him then (6) were too few, of course, to provide an opinion. By 1881, however, he had records of fifty-six known individuals (thirty males and twenty-six females) which showed that, while the laws held good for the means in both sexes, they failed to apply to twelve of the thirty men and to fourteen of the twenty-six women. Taking aim particularly at Hyrtl, he said (p. 328):

"[His law] is certainly of no practical value, and does not justify the assertion [by him] that 'it is hardly possible to err in determining the sex.' Luschka also is quite in error."

Dwight's point is more easily comprehended when each of his sets of measurements is converted into a ratio (length of manubrium × 100/length of corpus) and all of the ratios arranged by sex into frequency distributions (Figure 17). As can be seen, the overlap of the distributions is too great to provide a satisfactory means of separating the two sexes.

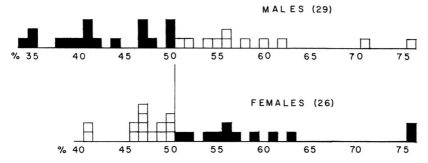

Figure 17. Sex distributions of ratios between the lengths of the manubrium and corpus sterni in 55 documented cases studied by Dwight (1881. One male with a ratio of 94.2 has been omitted to save space). The black squares represent the individuals correctly sexed by Hyrtl's law.

Dwight returned to this subject in 1890, by which time his collection had grown to 142 males and eighty-six females. The individual measurements are not given, but the means show that the earlier sample was fairly representative:

Date	No.	Mean length of manubrium	Mean length of corpus	Mean ratio
		mm	*mm*	*%*
		Males		
1881	30	52.0	106.0	50.6
1890	142	53.7	110.4	48.6
		Females		
1881	26	47.0	89.0	52.8
1890	86	49.4	91.9	53.8

This time Dwight had the forensic application in mind in drawing his conclusions (1890a, p. 529) : ". . . [Hyrtl's] law does not apply to two persons out of five, and thus can be of no value in the case of an individual."

In view of all this, it is noteworthy that one of the female victims in the famous Ruxton murder case had a sternum that yielded the following length measurements: Manubrium, 51.5 mm; corpus, 87.8 mm (ratio—58.6%). Glaister and Brash (1937, p. 81) speak of these figures as "clearly a female proportion." They then go on to say (italics added) :

> The proportion between the two main parts of the sternum (breast-bone) is very definitely influenced by sex. Owing to the certainty of the reconstruction of the trunk, the lower half of which contained a female pelvis, independent proof that the upper half also belonged to a female was not necessary. But it may be of interest to record the fact that *the proportions of the sternum alone would have justified an opinion that it was part of a female body.*

In view of Dwight's findings shown in Figure 17, I shall leave it to the reader to decide whether or not the italicized portion of this quotation needs qualification.

The most recent study of the sternum as a sex determinator is that by Thieme and Schull (1957). They took a width measurement on the manubrium between the estimated center of the surfaces of the sternoclavicular articulation on the two sides and plotted (their Figure 2) its distribution by sex in ninety-nine male and ninety-eight female blacks from the Terry Collection. The total range of the two sexes was from 15 to 45 mm. Within this range the overlap of the sexes was from 26 to 38 mm and contained 164 individuals or 83.2 percent of the sample. This is a poorer showing than that for the clavicular length (see above) and probably for this reason the measurement was not included in any of the discriminant functions constructed by these authors (cf. Table VI).

SCAPULA

In his Shattuck Lecture of 1894 Dwight claimed (p. 74) that "There is no single instance of a [scapula] measuring less than 14 cm [in length] being male, nor of one measuring 17 being female."

He based this claim on a documented series of eighty-four males and thirty-nine females (probably all whites), but failed to state how the length was measured. Judging from the scale of the measurements cited, they can only be maximum lengths between the superior and inferior angles (Martin's No. 1). To check this out, therefore, I took this measurement on the right scapula (usually the larger of the two) in a sample of fifty males and forty females (both blacks and whites) from the Terry Collection. By arranging the measurements by sex into frequency distributions (Figure 18) it appears that the overlap supports Dwight's claim. Also, the racial distributions give reason to believe that the rule applies equally to blacks and whites.

Although the body of the scapula was the main aspect of the bone to which Dwight gave attention in his Shattuck Lecture, he mentioned that he had tested also the sexing ability of the glenoid cavity in sixty-three male and twenty-seven female bones. His

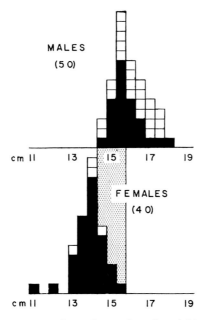

Figure 18. Sex distributions of maximum lengths of 90 right scapulae from the Terry Collection. White squares = whites (24 males, 4 females; black squares = blacks (26 males 36 females); stippling = overlap.

conclusion from this was (p. 75) that "Very few male sockets [glenoid cavities] are less than 3.6 cm [in length] and very few female ones as long." A search of the literature yielded no evidence that Dwight had pursued the matter further. For this reason, and because my respect for Dwight's statements was growing as I studied his investigations into methods of sexing skeletons, I decided to supply supporting evidence here as I did for scapular length, again using documented right scapulae from the Terry Collection.

Dwight did not say how he had measured the length of the glenoid cavity. I found Martin (1928) of little help in this regard, as did Vallois (1932). The latter gives directions (pp. 7-8) which are easy to follow and yield reproducible results. As translated, they read as follows:

> The inferior point is easy to find, for, at this level the articular margin generally is sharp. But the superior point is different, for there, the border of the cavity forms the blunt projection of the supra-glenoid tubercle; I have utilized therefore the most elevated point of this projection, easy to locate when one examines the cavity in profile.

I would add that the arthritic lipping sometimes present at these points should not be included in the measurement.

Figure 19 shows that Dwight's statement is essentially correct: A glenoid-cavity length of 36 mm does serve to separate the sexes in a high percentage of cases.

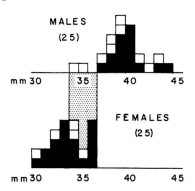

Figure 19. Sex distributions of glenoid-cavity lengths of 50 right scapulae from the Terry Collection. White squares = whites (10 males, 5 females); black squares = blacks (15 males, 20 females); stippling = overlap.

HUMERUS

The head of the humerus was the next articular surface after the glenoid cavity to which Dwight gave attention. He had begun collecting data on the articular surfaces of the long bones prior to his Shattuck Lecture (1894b), but did not publish any details thereon until 1905. In the meantime George A. Dorsey, as explained in Chapter 1, picked up the idea from the Shattuck Lecture and reported in 1897 the maximum diameter of the head of the humerus in 135 skeletons of American Indians. One of Dorsey's conclusions (p. 82) reads as follows: ". . . if the maximum diameter of the head of the humerus of any American skeleton measures 44 mm, the chances are extremely great that it is a male; if it measures 45 mm it is a male to a practical certainty."

Dorsey, of course, took his measurements on dry bones, whereas Dwight took his over the cartilage on dissecting-room specimens. Also, instead of maximum diameter Dwight took vertical (or sagittal) and transverse diameters separately (Martin's Nos. 10 and 9, respectively). Only his vertical diameter, which approximates the maximum, needs to be considered here. The graph developed by Dwight from this measurement taken on white males and females (200 each) is shown here in altered scale as Figure 20. Commenting on it, Dwight said (1905, p. 24):

> The curve of the vertical diameter of the humerus shows that the smallest male measurement is 41 mm. and the largest female 50 mm. Thus there is an overlapping extending through half the breadth of the two curves. There are 313 individual measurements overlapping (78.25 percent). But the chart shows clearly that this wide spread of overlapping is due to a few aberrant specimens. If we take away only nine male and ten female (4.75 percent), the number of overlapping bones is reduced to 64, or 16.80 percent of the remaining 381. What is most remarkable is that after this elimination of extreme formations, the overlapping is limited to diameters of 45 and 46. [Footnote:] That part of the curves represented by a continuous line shows them as they would be after this elimination.

The question that arises at this point is: How much allowance should be made for the cartilage at the margins of the head of the humerus? To get an answer to this question I took the vertical

diameter on fifty male and fifty female humeri from the Terry
Collection (including those from the same individuals used in the
study of the glenoid cavity) and made a graph (Figure 21) like
those for the scapula. My averages compare with Dwight's as follow: 48 vs. 49 mm in males; 41 vs. 43 mm in females. This suggests that the cartilage adds 2 mm at most to the diameter.

Like Dwight, I found only a small overlap, but centering on 43
to 45 mm instead of 45 to 46 mm. I would say, therefore, that in
the case of the vertical diameter of the humeral head dry-bone
measurements descending from 45 mm probably represent fe-

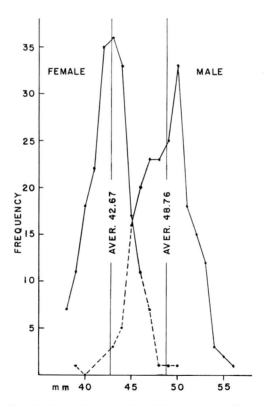

Figure 20. Sex distributions of vertical head diameters of 400 humeri of whites
(200 males, 200 females) from the Anatomy Department, Harvard Medical
School. Measurements taken over cartilage. (Modified from Dwight, The size
of the articular surfaces of the long bones as characteristic of sex; an anthropological study. *Am J Anat, 4:* 19-32 Plate I, 1905. Courtesy of *Am J Anat.)*

males through 44 to 43 mm, and almost certainly females below 43 mm; that measurements ascending from 45 mm probably represent males through 46 to 47, and almost certainly males above 47 mm.

As an afterthought, Dwight (1905, p. 26) measured the maximum length of the humerus in 100 male and 100 female whites to see whether there "is greater discrepancy between the articular heads of the bones than between their lengths." "As a practical anatomist," he said, "I know that no one would think of determining the sex of [the humerus] by its length." The male range in Dwight's series was from 290 to 360 mm, with an average of 324.6 mm; the female range was from 240 to 350 mm, with an average of 299.8 mm. These figures indicate an overlap of the sexes between 290 and 350 mm, involving 179 individuals or 89.5 percent of the sample.

Thieme and Schull (1957) also looked at the sexing ability of humeral length and for the purpose used ninety-nine male and 101 female blacks from the Terry Collection. Their male range extended from 290 to 400 (mean 339.0 mm); their female range

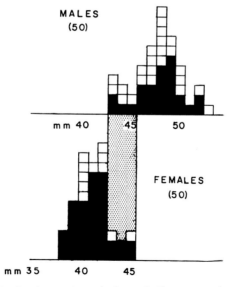

Figure 21. Sex distributions of vertical head diameters of 100 right humeri from the Terry Collection. White squares =whites (24 males, 11 females); black squares = blacks (26 males, 39 females); stippling = overlap.

from 270 to 350 mm (mean 305.9 mm). The overlap of these ranges, from 290 to 350 mm, included 172 individuals or 86.0 percent of the sample. Unlike Dwight, Thieme and Schull had no compunction about using humeral length for sexing purposes, in spite of its unimpressive showing in their study, and therefore included it in two of the discriminant functions they constructed (see Table VI, Nos. 5 and 6).

Thieme and Schull (1957) went further and looked into the ability of the epicondylar width of the humerus to discriminate between the sexes. Using ninety-eight male and one hundred female blacks from the Terry Collection, they found the male range to be from 55 to 74 mm (mean 63.9 mm); the female range from 49 to 65 mm (mean 56.8 mm). Within the overlap of the sexes (55 to 65 mm) were 143 individuals or 72.2 percent of the sample. On the basis of this showing the epicondylar width found its way into two of the discriminant functions constructed by these authors (see Table VI, Nos. 5 and 6).

SACRUM

Edward Fawcett (1867-1942), Professor of Anatomy of the University of Bristol in England, appears to have been the first to recommend the corporobasal index of the sacrum (S1-corpus width $\times$ 100/basal width) as a means of sexing the skeleton. The comparison, in other words, is between the widths of the body of the first sacral vertebra and of the basal part of the sacrum. Although Fawcett became convinced of the utility of this index in 1931, not until 1938 did he publish supporting figures on 242 males and 167 females (213 whites, 196 blacks) from the Todd Collection in Cleveland based on measurements taken by William Sassamen, Todd's assistant.

The ranges and means for the two sexes derived from Sassamen's measurements are shown in Figure 22 as separate lines below the rows of figures (percentages). Commenting on the figures which these lines represent, Fawcett said: "It is quite clear . . . that the surmise as to the sexing value of a corporobasal index is justified." This is surprising because, as can be seen, the overlap of the ranges of the sexes is too great to be of much help, forensically speaking.

Since the margins of the body or corpus of S1 are subject to considerable arthritic distortion from about forty years of age onwards (Stewart, 1958) , and Fawcett makes no mention as to how Sassamen dealt with such cases, I measured an additional series of fifty males and fifty females from the Terry Collection to clarify this point. I eliminated not only specimens showing arthritic distortion, but those with sacroiliac fusion. In presenting the results in Figure 22, I have distinguished the cases forty years of age or under (black squares) from those over forty (white squares) so that the reader can judge whether or not evidence of degenerative changes still is present. Noteworthy is the closeness of the ranges and means of the Todd and Terry samples. Again I have to say that this index is not a good discriminator of sex; its use is not recommended except as a last recourse.

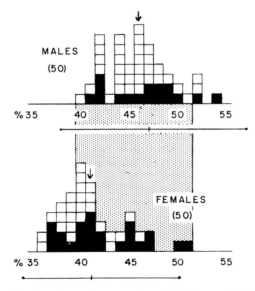

Figure 22. Sex distributions of corporo-basal indices of 100 sacra from the Terry Collection. Arrows indicate the means. White squares = individuals over 40 years of age; black squares = those 40 years of age and under; stippling = overlap. The lines below the rows of numbers (percentages) give the ranges and means for a larger sample from the Todd Collection (Fawcett, 1938).

INNOMINATE

As mentioned earlier, forensic textbooks from the early nineteenth century onwards place reliance fairly consistently upon the pelvis, and especially upon the knowledge thereof gained from the practice of obstetrics, for the attribution of skeletal sex. In addition to measurements of the pelvic inlet, two features often are mentioned: (1) The subpubic angle (acute in males, obtuse in females), and (2) the greater sciatic notch (contracted in males, open in females). Anthropological textbooks add a number of other features, most of which are summarized in my chapter in the two editions of Gradwohl's *Legal Medicine* (1954a, 1968). Rather than simply repeat that listing here, I shall direct attention to, and illustrate, the following six features which I regard as the most helpful in rapidly attributing sex. After that I shall take up more complicated sexing methods involving the innominate.

Shape of the Body of the Pubis

As part of the enlargement of the pelvic inlet for childbearing, the body of the pubis is broader in females than in males. Also, the inferomedial angle of the body of the pubis is much more prominent in females than in males. Together these features give the body of the pubis a rectangular shape in females, as compared with a triangular shape in males. Figures 23 and 24 show this sex difference as viewed both ventrally and dorsally. Sydney Smith (1939b, p. 404) may have been the first to describe this sex difference.

Ventral Arc

In the ventral view of the body of the female pubis shown in Figure 23 the character of the bone bordering on the symphyseal articular surface has a different appearance (partly due to beveling) from that lateral to a curving line which Phenice (1969) called the ventral arc (indicated by arrow in the figure). In effect, since the inferomedial angle is especially prominent in females, the arc creates a triangle at this point in females. Males lack this triangle or show only traces of it. Cleland (1889, p. 95) may have been the first to call attention to this characteristic feature of females.

Figure 23. The anteromedial parts of two right innominates viewed from in front. *Above*—male (Terry Collection No. 614); *below*—female (Terry Collection No. 1188R). (Courtesy Smithsonian Institution.)

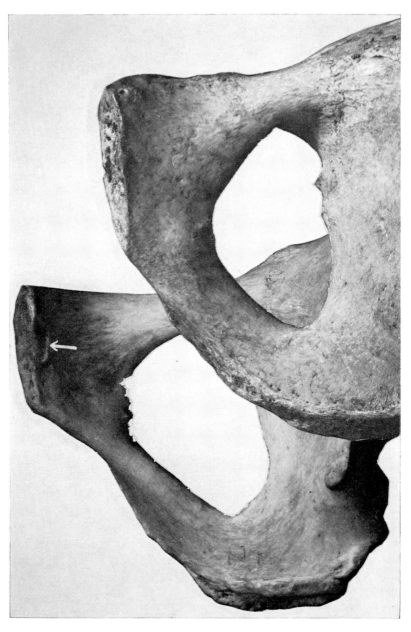

Figure 24. Same innominates as in Figure 23 viewed from behind. Arrow points to a pit-like scar of parturition undermining the dorsal margin of the articular surface of the pubis in the female. (Courtesy Smithsonian Institution.)

Scars of Parturition

Signs of childbearing sometimes, *but not always,* appear in two places on the innominate: (1) On the dorsal side of the symphysis pubis near the margins of the articular surfaces (Figure 24), and (2) in the preauricular grooves or sulci of the ilia (Figures 25 and 26). The preauricular scarring occasionally extends a little ways across the sacroiliac joint onto the sacrum. In all these places the scars take the form of pits, sometimes in a row. Houghton (1974, pp. 382-383) explains this phenomenon as follows:

> From the fourth month of pregnancy a hormonally-mediated softening of the ligaments of the pelvic joints occurs in preparation for birth, while rupture and haemorrhage at the site of attachment of the joint ligaments have been demonstrated following birth . . .
>
> Both the pubic symphysis and the sacro-iliac joints are subject to these hormonally-mediated changes. However, the sacro-iliac joint is

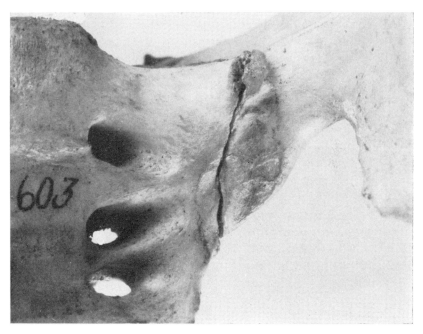

Figure 25. Pit-like scars of parturition in the pre-auricular groove of a left ilium (Terry Collection No. 603, 50 years of age). Note the extension of the scarring inferiorly across the sacroiliac joint onto the sacrum. (Courtesy Smithsonian Institution.)

in the direct line of transfer of body weight and its ligaments are under greater stress at all times, and especially during pregnancy, than the pubic symphysis . . . It seems therefore reasonable to postulate that the bony imprint of pregnancy will be more evident at the site of attachment of the sacro-iliac ligaments than at the attachment of the ligaments of the pubic symphysis.

As evidence of the correctness of this view, Houghton reports that in forty-six female innominates with both pubic and iliac scars those in the latter location tended to be more apparent. For further details on this subject see Putschar (1931, 1976) and Stewart (1957, 1970).

Inferior Pubic Curvature

The medial border of the inferior ramus of the pubis tends to be concave or convex depending upon the prominence of the inferomedial angle of the body of the pubis (Figure 23); in other words, the rectangular shape of the female pubic body goes along with an inferior ramus having a concave medial border, whereas a triangular shaped male pubic body goes along with an inferior ramus having a convex medial border. Sydney Smith (1939b, p. 404) may have been the first to describe this sex difference.

Iliac Articular Surface

The joint surface on the ilium for articulation with the sacrum tends to be more elevated in females than in males. Like the widening of the pubic body, this elevation contributes to the enlargement of the pelvic inlet. The difference between the two sexes in this instance appears mainly along the margin of the joint surface that is posterosuperior as anatomically oriented (Figure 26, arrow). St. Hoyme (1963) is the only one to my knowledge who has described this sex difference.

Sacroiliac Osteophytosis

Occasionally in individuals over forty years of age ossification of the anterior sacroiliac ligaments may be observed. Since these ligaments bridge the sacroiliac joint, the development of osteophytes here, which always begins on the iliac side superiorly, eventually may produce fusion of the joint (Figure 27). Evidence from

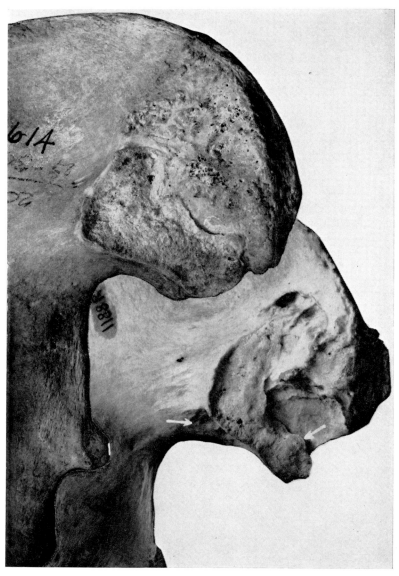

Figure 26. The posteromedial parts of the same innominates as in Figures 23 and 24. Arrows indicate two female features: (1) Scars of parturition in the pre-auricular groove, and (2) the raised posterior margin of the articular surface. Also, the female has a wider sciatic notch. (Courtesy Smithsonian Institution.)

skeletal collections (Stewart, 1976b) indicates that 90 percent of cases with any degree of sacroiliac osteophytosis are males. Unlike males, females often develop bony spurs at the point of the joint margin to which the arcuate line is directed.

Pelvic Indices

St. Hoyme (1957) attributes the earliest use of indices for sexing pelves to Matthews and Billings (1891, pp. 220-222, 262-263). The index that gave them the best results they called the *pubo-ischium index* (pubo-ischium depth × 100/maximum width of the superior strait). This index is not to be confused with the ischium-pubis index discussed below. In eighteen skeletons from what was then known as Arizona Territory the ordering of this

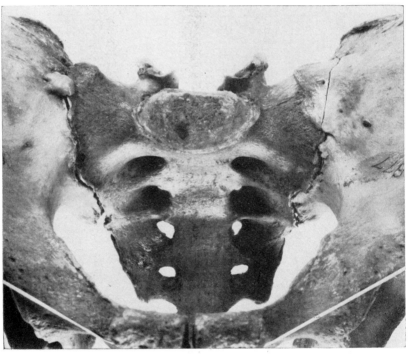

Figure 27. Sacroiliac osteophytosis in a male white, aged 58 (Terry Collection No. 887). *Right side*—beginning lipping; *left side*—partial fusion, secondarily broken. (Courtesy Smithsonian Institution.)

index showed, in Matthews' and Billings' words, "very prettily the natural grouping of the sexes," i.e. only one appeared to be out of place. However, the use of skeletons of unknown sex does not provide an adequate test of an index as a sex indicator. For this reason, and because no one seems to have followed up on this matter in the meantime, I decided to find out how satisfactorily the pubo-ischium index works on documented specimens from the Terry Collection.

First, there was the problem of how to interpret the definition of pubo-ischium depth given by Matthews and Billings (p. 221), namely, "from the smooth level surface on the pubic side of the ilio-pectineal suture [sic] above to the lowest part of the tuber ischii." This seemed to me most likely to describe the distance shown in Figure 28 as line DE. Second, there was the problem of what Matthews and Billings did when the dorsal margin of the upper surface of the superior pubic ramus took the form of a prominant ridge known as the "pecten." I decided that the easiest thing to do in such cases was to include the pecten.

Acting on these decisions, and using much the same series as for the length of the glenoid cavity of the scapula, I obtained the results shown in Figure 29. As can be seen there, the overlap between the sexes is restricted only enough for one to say that the index accurately identifies the sex in about 60 percent of the cases. In addition to this limitation the pubo-ischium index requires the whole pelvis for its determination. The operation of assembling the pelvis in order to measure the width of the superior strait is both difficult and time consuming.

These disadvantages are lacking in the case of the *ischium-pubis index* (length of pubis × 100/length of ischium), which expresses the same secondary sex changes but more simply, because it can be determined from a single innominate. The two measurements involved are defined in Figure 28 as lines AB (length of ischium) and AC (length of pubis). There is but one difficulty here and that is caused by frequent uncertainty about the location of point A after complete fusion of the three original elements of the innominate. This is the reason for representing in Figure 28 an innominate in which the lines of union between the three original elements are still visible. Undoubtedly there is some personal error involved in taking the two measurements used in this index.

Washburn (1948) was the first to apply to humans the ischium-pubis index devised by Schultz (1930, pp. 346ff.) and applied by

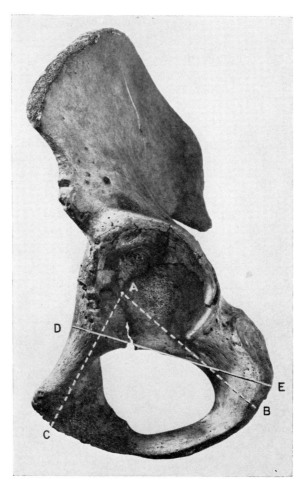

Figure 28. Immature left innominate showing the location of point A in the acetabulum from which the lengths of the ischium and pubis (lines AB and AC, respectively) are measured for the ischium-pubis index. Line DE defines the pubo-ischium depth used in the pubo-ischiatic index. (Courtesy Smithsonian Institution.)

him to nonhuman primates. To test the sex-discriminating ability of this index Washburn measured 300 documented skeletons in the Todd Collection (100 male and 100 female whites; fifty male and fifty female blacks). His findings are shown in Figure 30. In whites the overlap for the two sexes is from 91 to 94 and contains 18 individuals or 9 percent of the sample; in blacks the overlap is from 84 to 88 and contains 17 individuals or seventeen percent of the sample. However, if Washburn's 100 blacks are combined with Thieme's and Schull's 200 blacks (1957, Figure 5), the overlap of the sexes in this racial group is extended from 84 to 91 and contains 79 individuals or 26 percent of the sample. Whatever the cause of this change, it is important to note that the overlap for the whites remains distinct from that for the blacks. In using this index for sexing purposes, therefore, the accuracy of sex attribution is improved by knowledge of the race of the decedent under investigation.

In his enthusiasm for the ischium-pubis index Washburn claimed (1948, p. 202) that it "alone will sex skeletons with more accuracy than all the traditional measurements, indices, and observations together." The next year he combined the index with the maximum width of the greater sciatic notch and thereby claimed (for Bantus) an accuracy in sexing of over 90 percent. And in 1953 he and Hanna added to these two traits still another—

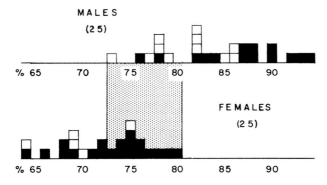

Figure 29. Sex distributions of pubo-ischiatic indices of 50 pelves from the Terry Collection. White squares = whites (11 males, 5 females); black squares = blacks (14 males, 20 females); stippling = overlap.

the interiliac index (the ratio of upper to lower iliac heights: overlap 71 percent)—and claimed (for Eskimos) an accuracy in sexing of 100 percent. At this point I protested (Stewart, 1954b) such high claims for this type of procedure, mainly on the evidence that the two sexes overlap in every trait studied up to that time. I still hold this opinion (Stewart, 1977a).

Sciatic Notch

In concluding this subsection on the innominate it is desirable to expand on the use of the greater sciatic notch in sexing. Wash-

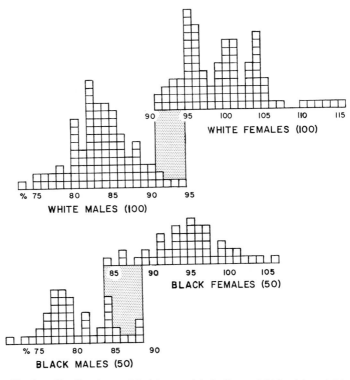

Figure 30. Sex distributions of ischium-pubis indices of 200 whites (100 males, 100 females) and 100 blacks (50 males, 50 females) from the Todd Collection. Stippling = overlap. (From Washburn. Sex Differences in the pubic bone. *Am J Phys Anthropol, 6:* 99-207, Figure 1, 1948. Courtesy of Am J Phys *Anthropol.*)

burn (1949) found the maximum width of the notch in Bantus of known sex to range from 17 to 38 mm in males and from 21 to 45 mm in females, which makes the overlap 17 mm. Letterman (1941), on the other hand, measured the width of the notch in a slightly different way in 426 documented specimens from the Terry Collection (114 male and 106 female whites; 104 male and 102 female blacks), but ended up with much the same sort of overlap for the sexes: 19 mm on average in whites and 18 mm in blacks. Letterman, like a number of earlier workers, judged the overlap of notch size in the two sexes to be great enough to make sexing uncertain in a high percentage of cases. Thieme and Schull (1957) appear to have held the same opinion.

In view of this evidence of the relatively poor showing of the greater sciatic notch as a sex discriminator in adults, it is surprising that already in the last century von Fehling (1876) and Thomson (1899) recognized that the shape of the notch was different in the two sexes in the fetal stage. Perhaps because these investigators, fearing distortion of the fetal bones during drying, worked with wet preparations, they did not attempt to support their observations with measurements.

The person responsible for the first tested method of sexing the fetal notch was Barbara Boucher, an English investigator. Her method (Boucher, 1955, 1957) is to mark the point of contra-flexure on each side of the notch (Figure 31) by looking down with one eye from a height of twelve inches. Next, she positions a thin brass taper gauge, calibrated in millimeters (Figure 32), upright on a table and determines from the scale of the gauge the distance between the horizontally-aligned points. Then, with the points on the notch still in contact with the vertical gauge, she determines the depth of the notch by running a second taper gauge (Figure 32), held at a right angle to the first, down between the width scale and the apex of the notch.

Boucher's findings on specimens of known sex are summarized in Table V. Notice that she was more successful in sexing females than males, and that her blacks had larger notches than her whites. In my opinion the procedure should not be undertaken in forensic cases without taper gauges of the kind described and without assurance from practice on documented specimens that results comparable to Boucher's can be attained.

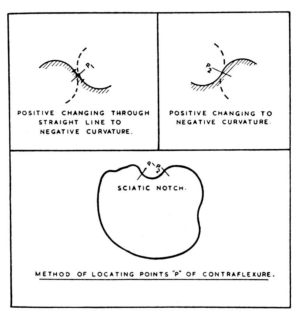

Figure 31. Diagram showing method of determining the two measuring points on the sides of the fetal sciatic notch as the first step in attributing sex. (From Boucher, Sex differences in the foetal pelvis. *Am J Phys Anthropol, 15:* 581-600, Figure 2, 1957. Courtesy of *Am J Phys Anthropol.*)

FEMUR

In his 1878 essay Dwight had the following to say (pp. 33-34) about the role of the femur in skeletal sexing:

> Two points in the femur are usually mentioned as of sexual signifi-
> cance. They are, that in the female the long axis of the neck forms
> more nearly a right angle with the shaft, and the other that when the
> femur is held with its condyles resting on a level the shaft inclines fur-
> ther outward than in man. It is evident that these phenomena arise
> from the same cause, viz., that woman having a broader pelvis, and at
> the same time shorter legs, this arrangement is necessary in order to
> bring the knees together. Nevertheless, its importance has been very
> much exaggerated. There is no doubt that a short man with a broad

pelvis would have femora in this respect more of the female type than a tall woman, and there is great individual variation . . . We may conclude that though the usual statement is theoretically correct, it is by itself of no diagnostic value.

Dwight returned to this subject in his Shattuck Lecture of 1894 (p. 75), by which time he had studied sixty-four documented cases and could say, "My own observations taken with others, convince me that there is probably no sexual significance in the angle [of the neck of the femur] . . . "

The Shattuck Lecture also gave Dwight the opportunity to comment on the importance of the greatest diameter of the femoral head as an indicator of sex. He said (p. 76) that " . . . but

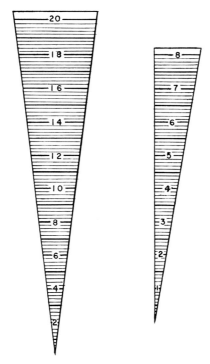

Figure 32. Millimeter taper gauges designed for measuring the width and depth of the sciatic notch in fetuses and "stillbirths." (From Boucher. Sex differences in the foetal sciatic notch. *J For Med, 2:* 51-54, Figure 1, 1955. Courtesy *J For Med.*)

TABLE V
DATA ON THE SCIATIC-NOTCH INDEX IN MACERATED FETUSES AND
"STILLBIRTHS" OF KNOWN SEX FOR USE IN SKELETAL SEXING*

Racial group	No.	Mean ± S.E.	Range	Percent correct
Whites		*Males*		
Great Britain	46	4.57 ± 0.091	3.65 — 6.0	80.43†
United States	19	4.81 ± 0.436	3.9 — 6.0	57.8 †
Blacks				
United States	49	4.84 ± 0.0085	3.38 — 6.8	73.3 ‡
Whites		*Females*		
Great Britain	61	5.64 ± 0.096	4.0 — 7.3	88.52†
United States	14	5.41 ± 0.23	4.9 — 6.68	71.4 †
Blacks				
United States	47	5.81 ± 0.021	4.35 — 8.77	95.1 ‡

*From Boucher, Sex differences in the foetal pelvis. *Am J Phys Anthropol, 15:*
581-600, Table I and p. 589, 1957. Courtesy of *Am J Phys Anthropol.*
†4.9 and below = male, 5.0 and above = female.
‡5.0 and below = male, 5.1 and above = female.

two of the male bones have a diameter of less than 4.5 cm and but two of the female a greater . . . Thus it would seem that the actual measurement of the head of the femur is a pretty good criterion of the sex." As in the case of the head of the humerus (see above), George A. Dorsey (1897) confirmed this observation on American Indian skeletons.

Dwight's definitive pronouncement on the subject did not come until 1905 when he listed his individual measurements of the greatest diameter of the femoral head on 200 males and 200 females, all whites. The femora were measured in the fresh state, i.e. over cartilage, and without regard to side. As in the case of the vertical diameter of the humeral head (Figure 20), I have converted Dwight's graph (Figure 33) to a more convenient scale.

When Karl Pearson and Julia Bell studied the English femur (1919) they tended to belittle Dwight's contribution because Dwight did not measure the heads of both femora; did not take both the vertical and transverse diameters; did not investigate the effect of the presence of cartilage on the measurements; and did not

seem to appreciate that it was a mistake for sexing purposes to reduce the overlap by removing from consideration a few extreme
cases.   The fact remains, however, that Dwight was the first to
provide basic data on the femoral head for use in sexing.

Dwight explained the adjustment of his curves (1905, pp. 24-
25, italics added) thusly:

> The curve of the head of the femur . . . is interesting inasmuch as
> there are fewer aberrant bones to remove [than in the case of the head
> of the humerus] *and yet greater ultimate overlapping.*   Originally 313
> bones (78.25 percent), (precisely the same as in the vertical diameter

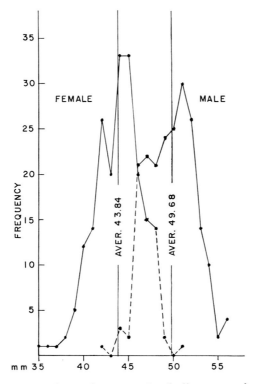

Figure 33. Sex distributions of greatest head diameters of 400 femora of
whites (200 males, 200 females) from the Anatomy Department, Harvard
Medical School. Measurements taken over cartilage. (Modified from Dwight,
The size of the articular surfaces of the long bones as characteristic of sex;
an anthropological study. *Am J Anat, 4:* 19-32, Plate III, 1905. Courtesy of
Am J Anat.)

of the humerus) overlap, but of these only six male and three female (2.25 percent) are sufficiently isolated to justify their removal, after which 113 (28.90 percent) of the remainder still overlap. Moreover, the overlapping includes three millimeters, namely 46, 47 and 48 mm, instead of only two, as in both diameters of the humerus.

Even the last is far from a bad result and shows that the size of the head of the femur has a great sexual significance, *but distinctly less than that of the head of the humerus.*

Pearson and Bell (1919, p. 43) restored the "aberrant" cases and recommended the following subdivisions of Dwight's total range for sexing purposes:

♀	♀?	Sex ?	♂ ?	♂
< 44.5	44.5 - 45.5	45.5 - 48.5	48.5 - 49.5	49.5 <

This interpretation does not take into account the effect of the presence of cartilage on the measurements. I have attempted to settle this matter, as I did for the head of the humerus, by measuring a series of specimens from the Terry Collection. Indeed, the series for the humerus and femur are essentially the same. My averages for the greatest diameter of the femoral head compare with Dwight's as follow: 48 vs. 50 mm for males; 42 vs. 44 for females. This indicates that an allowance of 2 mm probably should be made for cartilage. With this in mind, and taking into account that my overlap for the two sexes (Figure 34) differs only slightly from Dwight's after his removal of the "aberrant" cases, I feel reasonably safe in recommending the following adjustment in Pearson's and Bell's range subdivisions for use in sexing the dry bones of American Whites:

♀	♀?	Sex ?	♂?	♂
< 42.5	42.5 - 43.5	43.5 - 46.5	46.5 - 47.5	47.5 <

Additional information on the diameter of the head of the femur (left) is available from the work of Thieme and Schull (1957). These authors tested the ability of this measurement to discriminate sex in 200 Blacks (99 males and 101 females) from the Terry Collection. Assuming that they took the maximum diameter, they obtained a wider range for each sex than I did for my racially-mixed sample: Males—40-53 vs. 43-54; females—37-47 vs. 38-46. Also, their overlap is from 40 to 47, whereas mine is only from 44 to 46. Thus their overlap represents 72 percent of their sample, whereas mine represents only 17 percent of my sample. Perhaps these differences are of a racial nature. Whatever, I am inclined to agree with Dwight that the humeral head is a better discriminator of sex than the femoral head (see also Stewart, 1977a).

Bicondylar femoral length (left) also received attention from Thieme and Schull (1957) in their study of the sex-discriminating efficiency of measurements. They took this measurement on 99 male and 101 female blacks in the Terry Collection. The range in males was from 420 to 540 mm and in females from 380 to 490 mm. This means that the overlap of the sexes was from 420 to 490 mm and included 73 percent of the sample. Judging from these

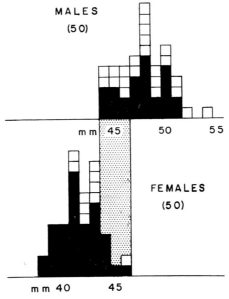

Figure 34. Sex distributions of greatest head diameters of 100 left femora from the Terry Collection. White squares = whites (23 males, 10 females); black squares = blacks (27 males, 40 females); stippling = overlap.

findings, bicondylar femoral length is not as good an indicator of
sex as maximum humeral length (see above). Nevertheless,
Thieme and Schull used bicondylar femoral length in all four of
the discriminant functions they constructed (see Table VI, Nos. 5,
6, 7 and 8).

MULTIPLE LONG BONES

Earlier in this chapter I explained how to sex a skull through
discriminant function analysis of selected cranial measurements.
The same procedure is followed with postcranial measurements.
Historically, the first time this method was applied to cranial measurements was some years after it had been applied to long-bone
measurements. José Pons of Barcelona, Spain, tried out the
method first (1955) on several dimensions of the femur and sternum. He was followed by Thieme and Schull (1957) and Howells
(1964), each varying the measurements and/or bones used—femur,
innominate, humerus, clavicle—in an effort to find the combination most discriminatory of sex.

Table VI gives eight discriminant functions applicable to the
long bones of whites and blacks as assembled from these sources by
Giles (1970b). Included with each function is the percentage of
correct sex attributions which that function yielded in a trial.
Comparison of Table VI with Tables II-IV shows, not surprisingly,
that post-cranial measurements analyzed in this way yield higher
percentages of correct sex attributions than do cranial and/or
mandibular measurements alone (93.1-98.5 percent vs. 83.2-88.3
percent.

Giles' (1970b, pp. 108-109) definitions of the measurements referred to by numbers in Table VI are as follow:

18. Femur length taken maximally, but perpendicular to a
line defined by the distal-most points of the two distal condyles
(so-called oblique or standing length).

19. Greatest diameter of femur head.

20. Least transverse diameter of shaft of femur.

21. Width of the distal end of the femur (epicondylar
breadth).

22. Ischial length measured from where the long axis of

TABLE VI

DISCRIMINANT FUNCTION SEXING BY POSTCRANIAL MEASUREMENTS*

Measure-ments†	Numbered discriminant functions and their weights							
	Whites				Blacks			
	1ᴿ	2ᴸ	3	4	5	6	7	8
18	1.000	1.000			0.070	1.000	1.000	—
19	30.234	30.716	—		58.140	31.400	16.530	1.980
20	—3.535	—12.643	—		—	—	—	—
21	20.004	17.565	—		—	—	—	—
22	—	—	—	0.607	16.250	11.120	6.100	1.000
23	—	—	—	—0.054	—63.640	—34.470	—13.800	—1.390
24	—	—	—0.115	—0.099	—	—	—	—
25	—	—	—0.182	—0.134	—	—	—	—
26	—	—	0.828	0.451	—	—	—	—
27	—	—	0.517	0.325	—	—	—	—
28	—	—	—	—	2.680	2.450	—	—
29	—	—	—	—	27.680	16.240	—	—
30	—	—	—	—	16.090	—	—	—
Section-ing point	3040.32	2656.51	9.20	7.00	4099.00	1953.00	665.00	68.00
Percent correct	94.4	94.3	93.1	96.5	98.5	97.5	96.9	93.5

*From Giles, Discriminant function sexing of the human skeleton. In Stewart, T.D. (Ed.): *Personal Identification in Mass Disasters,* pp. 99-109, Table LIV, 1970b, citing Pons, 1955 (functions 1-2); Howells, 1964 (functions 3-4); Thieme and Schull, 1957 (functions 5-8). Courtesy of the National Museum of Natural History, Washington.

†See text for measurement descriptions; R and L indicate appropriate for right or left side.

the ischium crosses the ischial tuberosity to a point in the acetabulum that is defined as the intersection of the long axes of the pubis and the ischium.

23. Pubic length measured from the point in the acetabulum defined in 22 to the upper extremity of the symphyseal articular facet of the pubis.

24. Height of the sciatic notch, taken as a perpendicular dropped from the point on the posterior inferior iliac spine, where the upper border of the notch meets the auricular surface, to the anterior border of the notch itself.

25. Acetabulo-sciatic breadth, taken from the median point on the anterior border of the sciatic notch (half way between

the ischial spine and the apex of the notch) to the acetabular border, and perpendicular, as far as possible, to both borders.

26. Taken from the most projecting point on the pubic portion of the acetabular border perpendicular to the innominate line, and thus to the plane of the obturator foramen.

27. The distance from the anterior iliac spine to the nearest point on the auricular surface, and subtracted from the distance from the anterior iliac spine to the nearest point on the border of the sciatic notch.

28. Maximum length of the humerus.
29. Maximum epicondylar width of the humerus.
30. Maximum length of the clavicle.

TARSAL BONES

Attribution of sex can be made also from smaller elements of the skeleton than those considered up to this point. The main effort in this direction is that of Gentry Steele (1970a, 1976), using the left talus and calcaneus singly and together. His sample consisted of 116 whites (58 males and 58 females) and 123 blacks (60 males and 63 females) from the Terry Collection. Selection ensured that they were young enough to be free from arthritic changes.

From various measurements on this sample Steele developed a series of discriminant functions, and then, after testing them, selected the five given in Table VII as the most reliable. The seven measurements needed to apply these functions are explained in Figure 35. Opposite the name of each measurement in Table VII is the coefficient(s) or weight(s) by which it is to be multiplied. A discriminant function score is the sum of the multiplications in a column. If a score is greater than the sectioning point, the individual is likely a male; if the score is equal to or less than that sectioning point, the individual is likely a female. The claimed accuracy of the attribution is given at the bottom of the table as a percentage of the sample correctly sexed.

In connection with the claimed accuracy of the functions, Steele (1976, p. 587) expressed reservations in answering two questions: (1) Can these functions be used for present-day

TABLE VII

DISCRIMINATE FUNCTION SEXING BY FOOT-BONE MEASUREMENTS*

Measurements (Martin's No.)†	Numbered discriminant functions with weights				
	1	2	3	4	5
Calcaneus:					
Body height (4a)‡	0.36061	—	—	—	0.23126
Load-arm width (2)	0.41828	—	—	—	—
Talus					
Maximum length (1)	—	0.42002	0.84693	0.38368	0.31859
Maximum width (2)	—	0.41096	—	0.42741	0.51311
Body height (3a)	—	—	27.92377	0.13722	—
Width/length index (2/1)	—	—	—	—	—
Trochlear width/ length index (5/4)	—	—	10.35583	0.29162	—
Male mean	33.57	40.87	79.09	52.41	49.88
Sectioning point	32.00	38.75	75.44	50.05	47.30
Female mean	30.42	36.62	73.84	47.68	44.72
Percent accuracy	79	83	86	88	89

*From Steele, The estimation of sex on the basis of the talus and calcaneus. *Am J Phys Anthropol,* 45:581-588, Table 4, 1976. Courtesy of *Am J Phys Anthropol.*

†Martin, 1928, II, pp. 1053-1055, 1059. See also Figure 35.

‡Martin's No. 4 modified to include posterior facet.

American black and white populations? and (2) Can the functions determine sex of individuals of unknown racial origin? Regarding the first question he cautioned that "there is no way to measure the effect of socioeconomic differences or continuation of secular changes in America [since the 1920s and 1930s when most of the Terry Collection was formed]." In answering the second question he was thinking particularly of forensic cases in which the skeletal finds are limited to individual bones. Rightly, he was more outspoken here: " . . . the investigator must be cautious if the race of the subject is unknown."

BONES AND TEETH

With the exception of the shape of the greater sciatic notch, all of the osteological sex indicators considered above apply to adults. Inability to sex most subadult skeletons is frustrating. It is due, of course, to the fact that documented skeletons from shortly after birth to seventeen years of age, unlike the skeletons of adults, are virtually impossible to come by for study purposes.

Being aware of this situation, Hunt and Gleiser (1955) realized while working at the Forsyth Dental Infirmary for Children in Boston that some of their developmental data secured radiographically had potential for distinguishing sex in preadolescent children. Specifically, they noted that the sex difference in dental maturation is far less than that occurring in the postcranial skeleton. This finding led them to formulate (1955, p. 481) the following sexing procedure:

On the dental radiograph [a lateral jaw film], the developmental stage

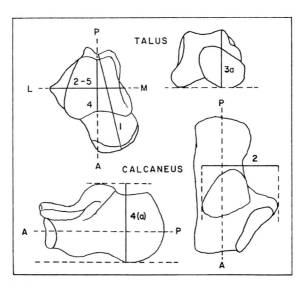

Figure 35. Outline drawings of a right talus and calcaneus to show the location of the measurements listed in Table VII. Abbreviations: A = anterior, L = lateral, M = medial, P = posterior. (From Martin, *Lehrbuch der Anthropologie*, Rev. 2nd ed. in 3 vol. ed. by Stephanie Oppenheim, II, Figures 482-484, 486-487, Wien, 1928.)

of the permanent mandibular first molar is recorded [following the system of Gleiser and Hunt, 1955, Table 4]. For a tooth with 'two-thirds of the root completed,' for example, the mean age for boys of our Boston series would be 84.3 months (7.0 years). For girls, the estimate would be 80.7 months (6.7 years). An assessment of bone age should be made from the atlas of Greulich and Pyle (1950) on male standards, and another from female standards. In [such a case], if the 'male bone age' were seven years, the equivalent 'female bone age' would be about 5.6 years.

For this imaginary child, the dental and osseous ages by male stand-ards agree closely; while by female standards they diverge by more than a year. Its sex would therefore be diagnosed as male, and its age as seven years.

Unfortunately, it is seldom possible to apply this ingenous method of sexing to skeletonized material, mainly because the de-rangement and/or loss of the small bones of the hand that occurs with the decay of the soft tissues usually renders comparison with standards in a radiographic atlas impossible, or virtually so. Hunt and Gleiser thought that the knee might serve as a substitute, especially since a radiographic atlas for this region (Pyle and Hoerr, 1955) also is available. So far as I can discover, however, no one has tested this suggestion.

Chapter 8

ESTIMATION OF AGE

F ROM CONCEPTION to adulthood growth and development are two different processes that constitute a major part of the phenomenon of aging. Following the cessation of growth and development, which signifies adulthood and occurs around age twenty-three to twenty-five, depending on sex, aging continues in the form of degenerative change. The latter manifests itself more and more, especially from around forty years onward (Stewart, 1958). All of this means that the estimation of age in the skeleton depends upon different sorts of evidence in each period of life. For this reason, the methods of age estimation to be considered in this chapter cannot be arranged meaningfully by skeletal parts as in sexing; instead they must be arranged, first, by the amount of growth, and then, by the sequence of the processes constituting development and degeneration.

Practically, however, it is still necessary to keep in mind that, because of the physiological change involved, birth is an even more noteworthy event in an individual's life than arrival at adulthood; it will thus be necessary to distinguish between the prenatal (fetal) period and the postnatal (pre– or subadult) period. In the absence of firm conventions and nothing to go on but the skeleton, I shall leave to the discretion of the individual investigator whether or not to apply to a preadult age determination one or other of the terms "infant," "child," "juvenile," or "adolescent."

BY AMOUNT OF GROWTH
In the Fetal Period

The fetuses that come to the attention of forensic anthropologists are usually in such a deteriorated state that only after reducing the remains to clean, dry bones can a safe estimate of size, and hence age, be made. It is possible in the fetus to approximate age from long-bone size (diaphysial length) because (1) long-bone size has a high correlation with stature (between 0.968 and 1.0, according to Olivier and Pineau, 1960); and (2) the increase in mean stature and in mean crown-rump length through the entire period of gestation is linear.

Figure 106 in Stewart (1954a) shows a plot of femoral length against crown-rump length and the corresponding fetal months for sixty-five fetal skeletons that had been assembled over the years in the National Museum of Natural History. My initial effort in this direction was extended first by Olivier and Pineau (1958, 1960) and then by Fazekas and Kósa (1966). Since there is relatively little difference between the findings of these two pairs of investigators, I have chosen those of Olivier and Pineau to present here. As Figure 36 shows, Olivier and Pineau took 50

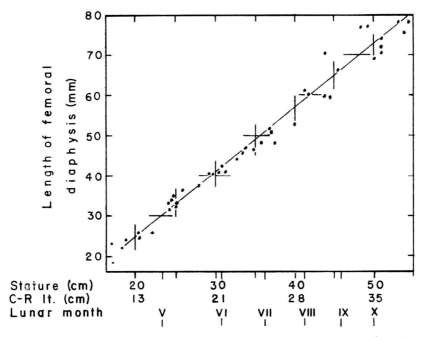

Figure 36. Lengths of the diaphyses of 44 fetal femora plotted against the corresponding statures. Mean crown-rump lengths and ages in lunar months added. (From Olivier and Pineau, Nouvelle détermination de la taille foetale d'après les longueurs diaphysaires des os longs. *Ann Méd Lég, 40:* 143, 1960. Courtesy of *Ann Méd Lég.*)

cm as the mean stature at birth. The corresponding crown-rump length is 35 cm and the corresponding length of the femoral diaphysis is about 73 mm.

From these data and those for the other long bones Olivier and Pineau (1960 p. 142) arrived at the following regression equations:

$$
\begin{aligned}
\text{Fetal stature} &= 7.92 \text{ Humerus} \quad -0.32 \pm 1.8 \quad \text{cm} \\
'' \quad '' &= 13.8 \ \text{ Radius} \quad\ -2.85 \pm 1.62 \ '' \\
'' \quad '' &= 8.73 \text{ Ulna} \quad\quad -1.07 \pm 1.59 \ '' \\
'' \quad '' &= 7.85 \text{ Fibula} \quad\ +2.78 \pm 1.65 \ '' \\
'' \quad '' &= 7.39 \text{ Tibia} \quad\quad +3.55 \pm 1.92 \ ''
\end{aligned}
$$

These authors also give the correspondences between the means of fetal age, stature, and crown-rump length shown in Table VIII.

At Birth

All demographic records show high rates of mortality at birth and slowly declining rates thereafter. Forensic anthropologists should take these facts into account whenever they deal with small human skeletal remains recovered under suspicious circumstances. Beyond looking for evidence as to the cause of death, they should make a special effort to establish as closely as possible the age at death. In this setting, knowledge of bone size at birth becomes especially important.

In Figure 36 bone growth through the usual time of birth is shown as a regression line of femur length against stature rising through a time period corresponding to the latter months of pregnancy. The average femur length at birth thus arrived at varies according to the size and composition of the series studied (both sexes are usually included). Thus in 1954 I judged average femur length to have reached 80 mm at the end of ten lunar months. Olivier and Pineau, as noted above, found this length to be near 73 mm for their series. Fazekas and Kósa (1966, Table 1) placed it at 74.3 mm in theirs. Obviously, these figures, besides having a range of 7 mm, give no indication of the variability in bone length that accompanies such a variably-timed event as birth.

TABLE VIII
FETAL GROWTH (IN CM)*

Age in lunar months	Stature	Crown-rump length
4¼	17.65	11.60
4½	19.81	13.17
4¾	21.88	14.65
5	23.80	16.05
5¼	25.64	17.39
5½	27.40	18.67
5¾	29.08	19.88
6	30.69	21.05
6¼	32.23	22.17
6½	33.72	23.24
6¾	35.15	24.28
7	36.52	25.27
7¼	37.85	26.23
7½	39.13	27.16
7¾	40.37	28.06
8	41.58	28.93
8¼	42.74	29.78
8½	43.84	30.59
8¾	44.97	31.39
9	46.03	32.16
9¼	47.07	32.91
9½	48.08	33.64
9¾	49.06	34.35
10	50.02	35.05

*From Olivier and Pineau, Détermination de lâge du foetus et de l'embryon. *Arch Anat (La Semaine des Hopitaux)*, 6:21-28, Table II, 1958. Courtesy of *Arch Anat*.

Upon pondering this situation it occurred to me to see what could be learned from a frequency distribution of the lengths of each kind of long bone from all the buried late fetuses and newborns encountered in an American Indian cemetery. I picked for this purpose the cemetery at the protohistoric Arikara site (39WW1) near Mobridge, South Dakota, excavated by D. H. Ubelaker in 1971. Among the reasons for picking this cemetery

was that the skeletons recovered therefrom were all well preserved and the bone lengths of most of the immature ones had
been measured already by Ginger Merchant for her masters thesis
(1973; see also Merchant and Ubelaker, 1977).

Table IX shows that, of ninety-six femora in the 62.5-100 mm
size range, 71 or 74 percent fall in the interval between 73.5 and
81.5 mm in length, giving an average length of 77.5 ± 4 mm. The
concentration of specimens immediately around this average
length is impressive. Applying the same procedure to the other
long bones, I obtained data with which to produce drawings
(Figures 37 and 38) of all six long limb bones of the skeleton of a
newborn showing how they fit within the narrow ranges of the
birth-size concentrations.

TABLE IX

FREQUENCY DISTRIBUTION OF
FEMUR LENGTHS IN THE 62.5-
100 MM RANGE: ARIKARA

Class intervals	No.	%
62.5- 65	3	3.1
65.5- 70	1	1.0
70.5- 75	19	19.8
75.5- 80	50	52.1
80.5- 85	12	12.5
85.5- 90	5	5.2
90.5- 95	3	3.1
95.5-100	3	3.1
Totals	96	99.9
73.5- 75.5	21	
76 - 78.5	27	74.0*
79 - 81.5	23	

* Average = 77.5 ± 4 mm.

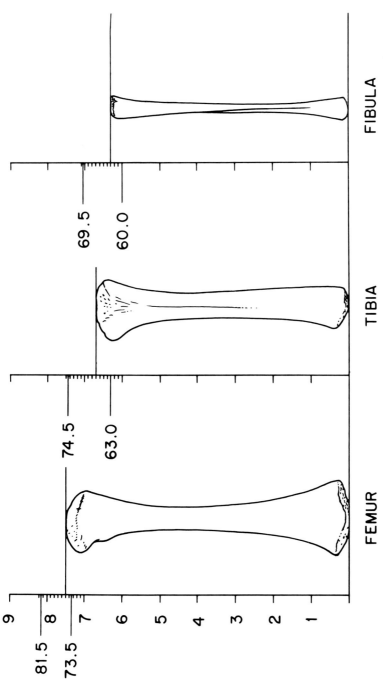

Figure 37. Lower limb long bones of an Arikara Indian Newborn (U.S.N.M. No. 383,155) drawn to natural size against a scale in mm showing the size range at birth.

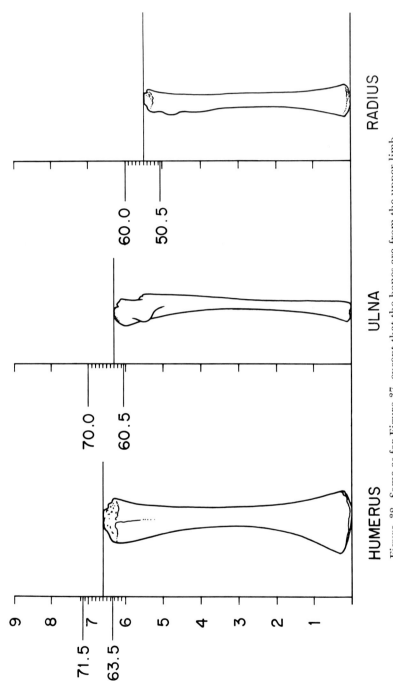

HUMERUS ULNA RADIUS

Figure 38. Same as for Figure 37, except that the bones are from the upper limb.

These drawings offer the investigator a means of quickly determining the likelihood of a specimen being in a reasonable range of birth size. All that is needed is to hold a long bone against the proper drawing and to note whether the upper extremity falls within the range indicated. Since the Arikara were fairly large people, it seems likely that the scale applies as well to modern American populations of European and African origins.

From Birth Through Preadult Years

Documented skeletons from this age period are impossible to come by at least in numbers adequate to establish an accurate relationship throughout the period between dry long-bone length and age. In 1954 the best I could do in the way of solving this problem (Figure 107 in Stewart 1954a) was (1) to construct an approximate growth curve for femoral length in Eskimos based on a few specimens judged to be newborn, 3, 6, 12, and 18 years old, and (2) to parallel the Eskimo curve with another representing larger-sized preadults, thereby hopefully approximating the true growth curve for femoral length in whites.

Merchant's study of Arikara preadults now provides a good means of evaluating the accuracy of this contrived growth curve for whites. Whereas I limited myself mainly to tooth eruption in judging the ages of the few Eskimo skeletons I examined for the purpose, Merchant judged the ages of her 140 Arikara by the more comprehensive Schour and Massler (1944) and Moorrees *et al* (1963) methods of assessing dental development. Then, having constructed growth curves for the Arikara femora according to the indications of the two aging methods employed, she used Maresh's (1955) mean femoral measurements, made on large numbers of radiographs of living preadult whites, to construct a growth curve for whites. These curves are reproduced here as Figure 39. Anyone who takes the trouble to compare this figure with the one I published in 1954(a) will see that the Arikara curves are at a greater distance from the Eskimo curve than my white curve is from the Eskimo curve. For this reason it now seems to me that the white curve resulting from Maresh's measurements is preferable to the one I published earlier.

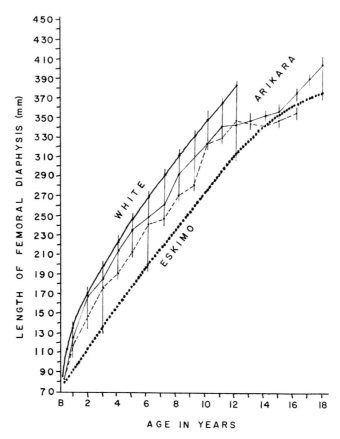

Figure 39. Curves showing growth in length of the femoral diaphysis between birth and 18 years of age in three racial groups. The two curves for the Arikara are explained by the use of different methods for assessing age from dental development. (From Merchant and Ubelaker, Skeletal growth of the protohistoric Arikara. *Am J Phys Anthropol, 46:* 61-72, Figure 4, 1977, Courtesy of *Am J Phys Anthropol.*)

Merchant did not construct comparable curves for the other long bones, although the data to do so are set forth in her thesis and in Maresh's 1955 publication. To take this further step here would use up too much space in proportion to its utility, so I shall continue my practice (begun in 1954) of simply stating the lengths of the other long bones in approximate percentages (newly adjusted) of femur length:

	Birth (%)	Birth to 6 years (%)	6 years to 12 years (%)	Adult (%)
Tibia	88	83	83	80
Fibula	84	82	82	80
Humerus	87	75	73	71
Radius	70	58	57	53
Ulna	83	64	63	57

Lacking a femur to use in estimating stature, one can compute its probable length from some other bone by means of these percentages.

I cannot emphasize too strongly that an estimate of age by this method is liable still to considerable error. The major source of this error is likely to be the measurements on the whites, which reflect distortions recorded in the radiographs. On this point Maresh (1955, pp. 725-730) comments as follows:

> No correction of the measurements has been made for distortion. We have calculated this magnification from roentgenograms of dried bone specimens of infants, children, and adults as between 1.0 and 1.5% at a focal-film distance of $7\frac{1}{2}$ ft. (2.3 m) with the bone in direct contact with the cassette surface. However, the distortion, because of the object-film distance in the living state, varies considerably from areas such as the femoral head and neck, where in chubby adolescents the distance may be from as much as 10 cm. to the cassette surface, to as little as 1 cm. for the distance from the lower end of the radius to the cassette.

BY STAGE OF DEVELOPMENT

The signs of development available in preadult skeletal remains to appraise and to relate to age consist of ossification centers of three kinds: (1) those, known as primary centers, that unite to give major elements of bones their ultimate characteristic form; (2) those, known as secondary centers, that appear at certain articular ends and/or margins of many bones and develop into epiphyses; and (3) those, known as dental germs, that appear in special crypts (alveoli) in the jaws and develop into deciduous and permanent teeth. Since these signs denote events that overlap in time, they will be taken up here as nearly as possible in the order in which they are most useful in the estimation of age.

Appearance of Primary Centers of Ossification

One of the new contributions to anatomical knowledge that Krogman brought to the attention of forensic anthropologists in his *Guide* (1939) was an improved listing of the ages between birth and five years when the primary centers of ossification make their appearance. Francis *et al.,* from whose publication (1939) the list had been taken, were working on the problem in Todd's laboratory at Western Reserve University during Krogman's sojourn there.

Although I followed Krogman's example and included the list in my chapter in Gradwohl's *Legal Medicine* (1954a, 1968), I realize now that I have never had occasion in a forensic case to apply the information. This is understandable when one considers that these ossific centers are very small and amorphous to begin with and therefore are most unlikely to be recovered once the soft parts have decayed.

For this reason I am not including here the dates of appearance of the primary centers and instead simply pointing out where they may be found in the rare event that one has a case to which they apply. Additionally, in such a case I recommend consulting the radiographic atlases of Flecker (1942), Greulich and Pyle (1950, 1959), and Pyle and Hoerr (1955).

Union of Primary Centers of Ossification

Anyone who has studied osteology will be aware that the skeleton of a newborn includes many bones still separated into two or more parts derived from primary ossification centers. For example, the lower jaw and frontal bone are still divided along the midline; each vertebra, with the exception of the axis or epistropheus, consists of a central and two lateral parts; and each innominate is represented by the forerunners of the ultimately conjoined ilium, ischium, and pubis. Also, he or she will be aware that the bones of the skull of an infant are so thin that they tend to warp on drying, but that even when not warped they articulate imperfectly, exhibiting gaps (fontanelles) in the areas where three or more bones will eventually come together. All of these features are well illustrated in anatomy textbooks (see also Figures 110 and 111 in Stewart, 1954a).

With two notable exceptions, the primary centers that have not yet united at birth will do so during the first six to eight years of postnatal life. The exceptions are the primary elements of the innominate and the spheno-occipital synchondrosis (sometimes erroneously, but conveniently, referred to as the "basilar suture"). These two exceptional events do not take place until the end of the second decade of life, a fact which has made it possible to date them rather accurately, as will appear.

As for the timing of the earlier events, it is still necessary to depend upon the general statements given in anatomy textbooks. The following statements by Robert J. Terry (1942) about the timing of the more useful of the earlier events are typical and probably as reliable as any:

Fontanelles (p. 171)

Sphenoid and mastoid	Close soon after birth
Occipital	Closes during first year
Frontal	Closes during second year

Mandible (p. 169)

Symphysis	Union completed in second year

Frontal bone (p. 135)

Metopic suture	Said to remain open in 8 to 9 percent of whites. When closure takes place, it begins in second year

Atlas (p. 99)

Posteriorly	Union occurs in third year
Anteriorly	Union occurs about the sixth year

Axis (p. 100)

Dens, body and two sides of arch	Union of all four parts occurs during third or fourth year

Occipital bone (p. 130)

Squamous with lateral parts	Union completed in fifth year
Lateral parts with basilar parts	Union completed before seventh year

Returning to the two exceptional maturational events mentioned above, it is noteworthy that Terry (1942) gives the impression of not being positive about when they terminate. Of the primary elements of the innominate he says that they become united by the eighteenth *or* twentieth year. And of the spheno-occipital synchondrosis he says ossific union begins about the twentieth year and is completed *in the course of two or three years.* My observations on the well-documented remains of the American soldiers killed in North Korea (McKern and Stewart, 1957) show clearly that neither statement is correct. The pertinent parts of the report on the war dead read as follow:

> The terminal stage of union between the primary elements of the innominate was observed in only two cases in the seventeen-year age group and in none of the eighteen-year age group. This stage consisted of fissures occurring at two sites: 1) the posterior superior angle of the obturator foramen (marking the line of union between the ischium and the pubis) and 2) in the sciatic notch (marking the line of union between the ilium and the ischium). The significance of this finding is that seventeen years represents the final age for union of the primary elements of the innominate [in males]. (P. 57)
>
> . . . active closure of the [spheno-occipital synchondrosis is in process in males] up to and including the age of eighteen years. In the following age groups (nineteen to twenty) activity practically ceases and by twenty-one years the [synchondrosis] is closed. (P. 34.)

Tooth Formation and Eruption

Unlike the centers of bone growth, most, if not all, of the developing teeth are likely to remain in place during the process of skeletonization. Also, as compared with epiphysial development, dental development is less variable (Lewis and Garn, 1960) and offers a more reliable means of estimating age in the skeleton through the first dozen or so years of postnatal life.

Tooth eruption or emergence is, of course, the traditional easy way of translating dental development into chronological age. By itself the method has limited reliability, especially as regards the deciduous dentition on account of the latter's great variability of eruption time. However, the general outline of the process is useful to have for reference. Meredith (1946, 1951) summarized the eruption of the deciduous teeth as shown in Table X.

TABLE X
USUAL ORDER AND TYPICAL RATE OF ERUPTION OF THE
DECIDUOUS DENTITION IN THE UNITED STATES*

Order of eruption	Rate of eruption†			
	$7\frac{1}{2}$ months	1 year	2 years	3 years
i_1	+	+	+	+
i^1		+	+	+
i^2		+	+	+
i_2			+	+
m^1 and m_1			+	+
c (upper and lower)			+	+
m_2				+
m^2				+
Number erupted	1	6	16	20‡
Zone of 98%	—	1 to 11	10 to 19	—

*Modified from Meredith, Order and age of eruption for the deciduous dention, *J Dent Res,* 25:63-64, 1946; A chart on eruption of the deciduous teeth for the pediatrician's office, *J Pediatr, 38:*483, 1951. Courtesy of *J Dent Res* and *J Pediatr.*

†Two weeks earlier in the average male than in the average female.

‡Mean age of completion of eruption is 28.2 months.

The sequence of eruption of seven permanent teeth is given in Table XI. Keep in mind that these data were derived from the living and therefore that it was the eruption of the teeth through the gums that was timed. Also, note that the permanent teeth of the girls erupt ahead of those of the boys.

Dentists have long known in a general way the sequence of developmental events that the teeth undergo in the depths of the jaws, and yet it was not until 1935 that convincing documentation was provided. In that year Rudolf Kronfeld of the Dental Depart-

	Boys		Girls	
Tooth	Mean age	Range	Mean age	Range
Maxilla				
M1	6.40	5/ 7 - 7/ 2.5†	6.22	5/ 5- 7/0
I1	7.47	6/ 8 - 8/ 3	7.20	6/4.5- 8/0
I2	8.67	7/ 8 - 9/ 8	8.20	7/2.5- 9/2
Pm1	10.40	8/11 -11/10.5	10.03	8/ 7-11/6
Pm2	11.18	9/ 7.5-12/ 9	10.88	9/ 4-12/5.5
C	11.69	10/ 4 -13/ 1	10.98	9/ 7.5-12/4
M2	12.68	11/ 4 -14/ 0.5	12.27	10/11 -13/7.5
Mandible				
M1	6.21	5/ 5 - 7/ 0	5.94	5/ 1.5- 6/9
I1	6.54	5/ 9 - 7/ 4	6.26	5/ 6 - 7/.05
I2	7.70	6/10 - 8/ 7	7.34	6/ 5.5- 8/2.5
Pm1	10.79	9/ 6 -12/ 1	9.86	8/ 7 -11/1.5
Pm2	10.82	9/ 4 -12/ 3.5	10.18	8/ 8.5-11/8
C	11.47	9/ 9.5-13/ 2	10.89	9/ 2.5-12/7
M2	12.12	10/ 9 -13/ 6	11.66	10/ 3.5-13/0

*From Hurme, Standards of variation of the eruption of the first six permanent teeth. *Yrb Phys Anthropol (1948)*, *4*:181-200, diagram, 1949. Courtesy of *Yrb Phys Anthropol*.

†Read 5 years, 7 months to 7 years, 2½ months. This is equivalent to plus or minus one standard deviation.

ment of Loyola University in Chicago presented in convenient form the histologic and roentgenographic findings of W. N. G. Logan and himself on the timing of several aspects of tooth formation for both the deciduous and permanent dentitions. Although based on small samples, the Kronfeld standards were so superior to those then in use that they were widely adopted (for a reprint nineteen years later see Stewart and Trotter, Eds., 1954).

The Kronfeld standards are no longer used. As noted above, Merchant (1973) used the standards of Schour and Massler (1944) and of Moorrees *et al.* (1963) in her study of skeletal growth in Arikara Indians. Yet according to Figure 38 she obtained with the former (interrupted line) a somewhat lower estimate of mean age over the preadult years as compared with the result she obtained with the latter (solid line). In part this was due to some errors in the Schour and Massler chart to which she calls attention, and in part to the oversimplification of the facts that is unavoidable in the type of drawings used by Schour and Massler. Provided that one takes into account the possibility of underestimation of age, availability and ease of use do make the Schour and Massler chart attractive. Whether or not one uses it depends upon the requirements for accuracy in age estimation indicated for the forensic case at hand.

There is every indication that Moorrees *et al.* (1963) used approved methods, adequate samples, and rigid controls in developing their standards relating to the formation of the mandibular deciduous canine and molars. In addition, they calculated the error of estimation. For these reasons, and because their publication may not be readily available to some readers, I am reproducing in Figures 40-43 the stages and norms applicable to their method. The stages provide a means of classifying the images of the developing teeth seen in a lateral jaw radiograph; the norms give for each stage the mean age in years plus and minus one and two standard-deviation limits. The authors recommend averaging the findings for different teeth, and, in the absence of sex identification, averaging the chronologic ages obtained from the male and female norms.

Abbreviations used in the figures are explained as follow:

C_{co}	= Coalescence of cusps	$R_{1/4}$	= Root length 1/4
C_{oc}	= Cusp outline complete	$R_{1/2}$	= Root length 1/2
$Cr_{1/2}$	= Crown 1/2 complete	$R_{3/4}$	= Root length 3/4
$Cr_{3/4}$	= Crown 3/4 complete	R_c	= Root complete
Cr_c	= Crown complete	$A_{1/2}$	= Apex 1/2 closed
R_i	= Initial root formation	A_c	= Apex closed
Cl_i	= Initial cleft formation		

Instead of including the lengthy Moorrees *et al.* charts on resorption and exfoliation of the deciduous mandibular canines and molars I give in Figure 44 and Table XII the data of Garn *et al.* (1958) on the calcification and eruption of the permanent mandibular premolars and molars. The latter authors give for each sex simply the mean age at which each of five stages of calcification and two stages of eruption appear in radiographs. These stages are defined (p. 562) as follow:

Stage   I. Stage of the full-follicle, immediately preceding the first evidence of cusp calcification, and therefore systematically six months earlier than the latter in each case.

Stage II. Crown completion and beginning root formation, especially as characterized by the "floor" in molar teeth.

Stage III. Alveolar eruption, i.e. elevation of the crown above the alveolar margin. This stage is reasonably comparable to alveolar eruption as commonly deter-

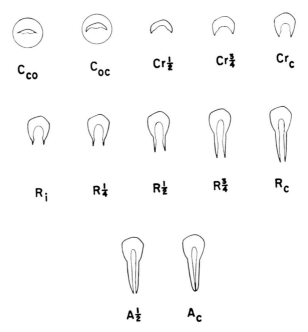

Figure 40. Stages of tooth formation for the deciduous mandibular canine. See text for abbreviations. (From Moorrees *et al*, Formation and resorption of three deciduous teeth in children. *Am J Phys Anthropol, 21:* 205-213, Figure 1, 1963. Courtesy of *Am J Phys Anthropol.*)

mined in skeletonized material (cf. Garn *et al.,* 1957).

Stage IV. Attainment of the occlusal level (cf. Garn and Lewis, 1957).

Stage V. Apical closure.

Although the combination of data on dental development between birth and about fifteen years given here from the two sources was derived radiologically on the living, often it can be used in forensic cases to arrive at an age estimate without X-raying the jaws. I am referring, of course, to cases in which the developing teeth either are visible naturally in their crypts or have been made visible through breaks. The young girl from Mississippi mentioned in Chapters II and VI whose lower jaw had been frac-

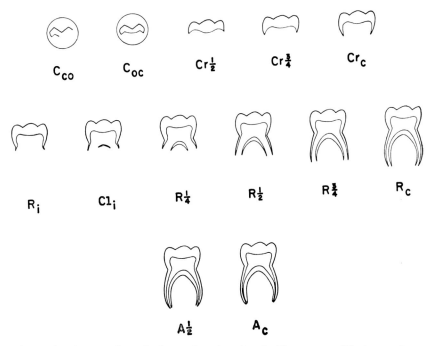

Figure 41. Stages of tooth formation for the deciduous mandibular molars. See text for abbreviations. (From Moorrees *et al.* Formation and resorption of three deciduous teeth in children. *Am J Phys Anthropol, 21:* 205-213, Figure 2, 1963. *Courtesy of Am J Phys Anthropol.*)

tured, probably just before she was shot through the head, is a case in point. The fracture revealed that the calcification of the root of the permanent second molar had reached Stage IV of Garn *et al.* (1958), which by reference to Table XII indicates a mean age of 11.8 years. The girl's actual age was 12.5 years.

When it comes to estimating age from radiographs of skeletonized jaws I would expect very few forensic anthropologists to be able to qualify as experts, in the sense that Garn and Hunt, say, are experts along this line. However, from a general knowledge of developmental anatomy any forensic anthropologist should be able to apply the information given here and to come up with an

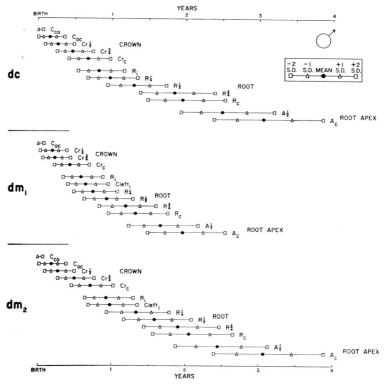

Figure 42. Male norms of tooth formation for the deciduous mandibular canine (dc) and molars (dm$_1$, dm$_2$). From Moorrees *et al.* Formation and resorption of three deciduous teeth in children. *Am J Phys Anthropol, 21:* 205-213, Figure 4, 1963. Courtesy of *Am J Phys Anthropol.*)

age estimate that is close enough for all practical purposes, if qualified in terms of a range. On the other hand, if the reliability of the age estimate is especially important, someone with this special expertise should be consulted.

Union of Epiphyses

During the terminal stages of the formation and eruption of the permanent teeth some of the epiphyses reach their full size and begin to unite. For forensic purposes it is customary to give more attention to the epiphyses of the larger bones than those of the smaller bones, because the former are more likely to be re-

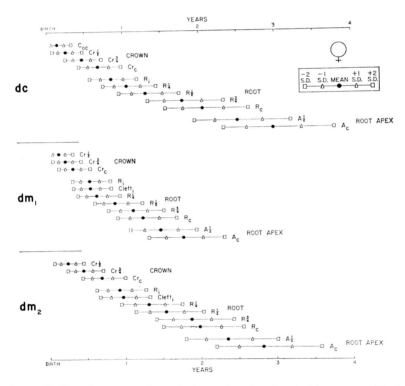

Figure 43. Female norms of tooth formation for the deciduous mandibular canine (dc) and molars (dm₁, dm₂). (From Moorrees *et al.* Formation and resorption of three deciduous teeth in children. *Am J Phys Anthropol, 21:* 205-213, Figure 5, 1963. Courtesy of *Am J Phys Anthropol.*)

covered, and in any event, provide sufficient developmental details for evaluation. The progression of union of the major epiphyses is fairly orderly and in this respect follows a pattern widespread among primates (Schultz, 1944, Figure 20). In so far as the long limb bones are concerned, the order of union begins in the elbow

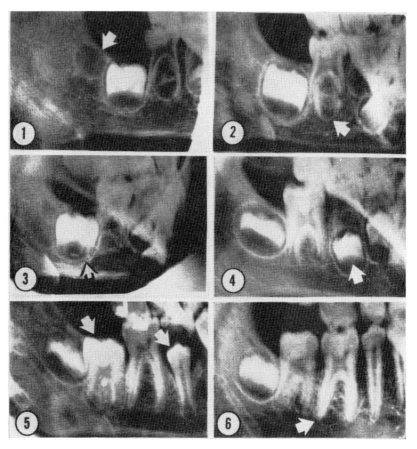

Figure 44. Oblique jaw radiographs showing stages of calcification and eruption of the permanent mandibular premolars and molars. 1. Full follicle stage of M_2; 2. full follicle stage of P_2; 3. beginning root formation of M_2; 4. beginning root formation of P_2; 5. alveolar eruption of P_2 and M_2; 6. attainment of occlusal level by P_2 and M_1 and apical closure of M_1. (From Garn *et al.* The sex difference in tooth calcification. *J Dent Res, 37*:561-567, Figure 1, 1958. Courtesy of *J Dent Res.*)

TABLE XII

MEAN AGES OF FIVE DEVELOPMENTAL STAGES FOR PERMANENT
MANDIBULAR PREMOLARS AND MOLARS: BY SEX*

		Boys		Girls	
Tooth and stage		No.	Mean age	No.	Mean age
P_1	I	98	2.2	66	1.8
P_1	II	97	7.4	75	7.2
P_1	III	46	10.1	47	9.7
P_1	IV	34	10.9	34	10.3
P_1	V	24	13.0	16	12.5
P_2	I	100	3.3	79	3.3
P_2	II	90	8.2	76	8.0
P_2	III	33	11.1	31	10.3
P_2	IV	27	12.2	23	11.3
P_2	V	18	14.1	14	13.4
M_1	II	105	4.3	70	4.0
M_1	III	54	5.8	39	5.7
M_1	IV	46	6.9	24	6.9
M_1	V	48	10.3	39	10.6
M_2	I	113	3.5	83	3.2
M_2	II	89	8.9	88	8.7
M_2	III	40	11.2	39	10.7
M_2	IV	26	12.7	17	11.8
M_2	V	22	15.0	15	14.6
M_3	I	69	9.0	66	9.0
M_3	II	34	14.6	19	15.2

*From Garn *et al.,* The sex difference in tooth calcification. *J Dent Res, 37:* 565, Table I, 1958. Courtesy of *J Dent Res.*

at the distal end of the humerus and terminates in the shoulder at the proximal end of the humerus. In between these events the order of union progresses from region to region as follows: Elbow → hip → ankle → knee → wrist → shoulder. An easy way to remember this succession is to visualize the body in the contracted position diagrammed in Figure 45.

Much confusion exists regarding the time of union of each of the major epiphyses. All too often this has been stated as occurring in a single year, with variation either not stated (cf. Flecker, 1942, p. 103, Table LX) or limited to only a couple of years (cf.

Krogman, 1939, p. 19). The difference in timing between the two sexes also is usually stated in general terms, such as that females are ahead of males by two years or less (Krogman, 1939, p. 18; Flecker, 1942, Table LX).

Disregarding for the moment the true extent of the variation, how is one to interpret an age of union stated as a single year? Is it the mean age of union (50% of cases united)? Or is it the age of latest incomplete union (after which 100% of cases are united)? The distinction is important forensically because, by estimating age on a 50 percent basis, the possibility of a uniting epiphysis indicating an age either above or below the figure given is not ruled out, whereas by estimating age on a 100 percent basis the possibility of this same epiphysis indicating an age older than the figure given is entirely ruled out.

Tables XIII and XIV summarize the best information I have been able to find, relating to the major epiphyses and mainly in whites, on the age of beginning union and of the latest age of incomplete union. Three things about these tables are especially noteworthy: (1) the considerable differences between the results of the several observers; (2) the sex differences, placing females in advance of males by one to two years, found by Flecker and Paterson; and (3) the generally higher ages yielded by inspection of the gross bones. The observer differences, especially those between radiologists, seem to be due mainly to inadequate samples,

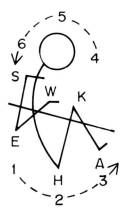

Figure 45. Diagram to aid in remembering the sequence of epiphysial union. E = elbow, H = hip, A = ankle, K = knee, W = wrist, and S = shoulder.

TABLE XIII
AGE OF BEGINNING EPIPHYSIAL UNION AS DETERMINED
(I) RADIOGRAPHICALLY* AND (II) GROSSLY†

	I				II	
Region and epiphysis	Davies & Parsons (1927)	Borovanský & Hněvkovský (1929)	Flecker (1942)		Stevenson (1924)	McKern and Stewart (1957)
	♂ & ♀	♂	♂	♀	♂ & ♀	♂
Elbow						
Dist. humerus	16-4‡	14	14-7	13-4	—	—
Med. epicond.	?	14	12	10	—	—
Prox. radius	14	14	14		—	—
” ulna	15	14	?	13-10	—	—
Hip						
Head of femur	16-4	—	14	13-4	—	—
Gr. troch.	15-10	—	15-10	14-4	—	—
Lsr. ”	16	—	?	?	—	—
Ankle						
Dist. tibia	16	—	14-9	13	18	—
” fibula	17	—	15	14-10	18	—
Calcaneus	—	—	14-6	12-10	—	—
Knee						
Dist. femur	17	—	16	14	18	—
Prox. tibia	15	—	16	14	18	—
” fibula	17	—	16	14	18	—
Wrist						
Dist. radius	17	16	17-3	15-11	18	—
” ulna	?	16?	17·3	15	18	—
Shoulder						
Prox. humerus	18-2	18	16	15-8	19	—
Other						
Acromion	—	—	—	—	18	—
Iliac crest	—	—	—	17-1	19	—
Med. clavicle	—	—	?	?	21	18

*Borovanský and Hněvkovský studied only the upper extremity. They took the age of beginning union to be indicated by the first traces of fusion. Davis and Parsons and Flecker say that they took the age of beginning union to be indicated by the youngest in whom the epiphysis was found fused. In all three studies the number of radiographs examined varied with the epiphysis.

†Stevenson examined 110 skeletons (twenty of them females) in the Todd Collection, of which all but one were between the ages of seventeen and twenty-eight. He says that in the "stage of beginning union a tendency is evident for the distinct superficial hiatus between epiphysis and diaphysis to be replaced by a line. Quite as characteristic of this stage is an occasional bridging over or knitting together of the two margins." McKern and Stewart interpreted beginning union as just that. Their series of 375 male skeletons did not extend below the age of seventeen, and yet in the case of all but one (medial clavicle) of the epiphyses listed here they found a fairly large percentage of the seventeen/eighteen-year group already with complete union.

‡Read sixteen years and four months.

Essentials of Forensic Anthropology

TABLE XIV
LATEST AGE OF INCOMPLETE EPIPHYSIAL UNION AS DETERMINED
(I) RADIOGRAPHICALLY* AND (II) GROSSLY†

	I						II	
Region and epiphysis	Davis & Parsons (1927)	Borovanský & Hněvkovský (1929)	Paterson (1929)		Flecker (1942)		Stevenson (1924)	McKern and Stewart (1957)
	♂ & ♀	♂	♂	♀	♂	♀	♂ & ♀	♂
Elbow								
Dist. humerus	21	18	—	—	16	16	(Before 17)	(Before 17)
Med epicond.	20	19	—	—	17	16	18	19
Prox. radius	19	18	18/19‡	14/15	20-5§	19-10	18	17/18
" ulna	19	18	18/19	14/15	17-6	16	18	17/18
Hip								
Head of femur	19/20	—	18	17	20-2	18-2	19	19
Gr. troch.	18/19	—	18	16/17	17-6	16-10	18	19
Lsr. "	17	—	18	16/17	17-11	16-10	18	19
Ankle								
Dist. tibia	17/18	—	18	16	18	16-4	19	19
" fibula	18/19	—	18	16	18	16-4	19	19
Calcaneus	—	—	—	—	18	16	—	—
Knee								
Dist. femur	19	—	18	16/17	19	19	20	21
Prox. tibia	19	—	18/19	16/17	19	18	21	22
" fibula	21	—	18	16	19-8	18	20	21
Wrist								
Dist. radius	22	19	21	19/20	23	20-5	21	22
" ulna	20	19	21	19/20	23	22	21	22
Shoulder								
Prox. humerus	21	19	21	18	19-2	20-5	21	23
Other								
Acromion	—	—	—	—	19-2	16-1	21	22
Iliac crest	—	—	—	—	22-9	22-9	22	22
Thor. vert. 2-6	—	—	—	—	—	—	—	23
Med. clavicle	—	—	Abt. 20		25	26-4	27	30

*Davis and Parsons, Borovanský and Hněvkovský, and Paterson seem to have given the age when most or all cases of a given epiphysis have completely united. It may not be correct to call this the "latest" age of incomplete union. For Flecker, on the other hand, the late age is that of the oldest subject in whom fusion had *not yet* taken place.

†Stevenson and McKern and Stewart agree that the latest age is the one after which every skeleton shows union of that particular epiphysis.

‡Read eighteen or nineteen years.

§Read twenty years and five months.

but perhaps also to the indifferent quality of many of the radio-graphs. Although the sex difference is not as well documented as could be wished, there can be no doubt about its existence. The higher latest ages of incomplete union yielded by gross inspection of the bones probably can be accounted for by the existence of features at the epiphysial line which, when seen in the actual bones have been interpreted as the last signs of union, but when seen in radiographs have been interpreted as persistent "scars" of previously completed union.

In spite of deficiencies in the available information, the im-portant thing to note is the repeated observation of a considerable interval between the ages of beginning union and of latest ob-served incomplete union. Take the distal epiphysis of the ulna, for example. In any sample of white males between the ages of sixteen/seventeen and twenty-two years there are individuals with this epiphysis both uniting and already united. In support of this statement Table XV gives my observations on the state of this epiphysis in a sample of 239 American soldiers of this age period killed in the Korean War. Because my sample of seventeen-year-olds was limited to ten, I cannot say for sure that union does not

TABLE XV

AGE DISTRIBUTION OF STAGES OF UNION (IN %) OF THE DISTAL EPIPHYSIS OF THE ULNA: MALES*

Age	No.	Stages†				
		0	1	2	3	4
17-18	55	29	1	11	24	35
19	52	7	—	5	32	56
20	45	4	2	—	24	70
21	37	—	—	—	10	90
22	24	—	—	—	8	92
23	26	—	—	—	—	100
Total	239					

*From McKern and Stewart, Skeletal age changes in young American males. Analyzed from the standpoint of age identification. *Environmental Protection Res Div*, Tech. Rep. EP-45, Table 21, 1957. Courtesy of Quartermaster Res. & Dev. Center, U.S. Army, Natick, Mass.

†0 = no union, 1 = ¼ union, 2 = ½ union, 3 = ¾ union, 4 = complete union.

begin in the sixteenth year or even earlier, but I feel reasonably certain that incomplete union does not continue beyond the age of twenty-two. In between these ages, according to the table, the percentages of completely united epiphyses increase fairly regularly year by year through age twenty-one, after which very few are ununited, and none is ununited after twenty-two.

As for females, the evidence of Tables XIII and XIV suggests that the best general rule is to reduce the male ages of beginning union and of latest incomplete union by at least two years to obtain the likely female ages.

Of all the data given in Tables XIII and XIV those derived from the Korean War dead (McKern and Stewart, 1957), having been made on large collections of skeletons of known age, probably are most applicable to forensic cases. In the course of McKern's analysis of the observations I had made on these skeletons he developed what he called the "total pattern of skeletal maturation" to serve as a means of translating into age the numerous maturational indicators available in the Army age range. I will not burden the reader with all the details of this procedure, because I feel that the so-called "Segment III," which is much simpler to use than "Segment I" or "Segment II," serves adequately and is therefore the most practicable.

To employ Segment III in estimating age the first thing to do is to observe the state of union of the following nine epiphyses which McKern considered the best indicators of skeletal age of all those he studied:

Proximal humerus	Head of femur	Medial clavicle
Medial epicondyle	Distal femur	Sacrum ¾ joint
Distal radius	Iliac crest	Lateral sacral joints

The state of union of each epiphysis is rated on a scale of 1 to 5 (instead of my original 0 to 4)* and all of the ratings are added together to get a total score. The total score can then be translated into age by reference to Table XVI or by inserting the score in the following age-prediction equations:

---

*As thus changed, 1 = no union, 2 = ¼ union, 3 = ½ union, 4 = ¾ union, 5 = complete union.

(Scores 18-36) Age = .0758 Score + 16.6146
(Scores 38-46) Age = .5617 Score + 2.1995

From his experience in developing the concept of a total pattern of skeletal maturation McKern offered (p. 171) the following sound advice, which supports what I said earlier about the sequence of epiphyseal union:

TABLE XVI
OBSERVED AGE RANGES AND PREDICTED AGES CORRESPONDING
TO TOTAL MATURATIONAL SCORES FOR "SEGMENT III"
EPIPHYSES IN MALES*

Score	Age range	Predicted Age
18	17-18	17.98
20	17-20	18.13
22	17-20	18.28
24	17-21	18.43
26	17-20	18.59
28	17-20	18.74
30	17-21	18.89
32	17-22	19.04
34	17-22	19.19
36	17-22	19.34
38	18-23	19.15
40	18-24	20.27
42	18-25	21.39
44	19-25	22.52
46	19-25	23.64

*From McKern and Stewart, Skeletal age changes in young American males. Analyzed from the standpoint of age. *Environmental Protection Res Div,* Tech. Rep. EP-45, Table 51, 1957.   Courtesy of Quartermaster Res & Dev. Center, U.S. Army, Natick, Mass.

. . . the innominate bone is the most critical ageing area of the skeleton. The combination of pubic symphysis, iliac crest, ischial tuberosity and ramus will immediately place the skeleton in its proper age group. If the pubic symphysis, which is a good age indicator over much of the life span, is damaged or missing, the remaining age areas of the innominate will give the observer a clue as to his next most reliable source of age information.   For example, if the iliac crest suggests an adolescent age, then the basilar suture [spheno-occipital synchondrosis] and the epiphyses of the elbow can be turned to for both clarification and supportive evidence. On the other hand, if the iliac crest exhibits the pattern of a young adult, the epiphyses of the shoulder, wrist, and knee joints as well as the medial end of the clavicle will help to establish an exact age estimate.

Before leaving the subject of epiphyseal union it will be helpful to add two other pointers provided or reinforced by the Korean war-dead experience. The first pointer concerns the order and timing of union of the epiphyseal rings on the bodies of the thoracic vertebrae. As Table XVII shows the upper seven segments, but especially T4 and T5, are the last to show incomplete union. This stage can persist into the twenty-third year.

TABLE XVII

PERCENTAGE OF COMPLETE UNION OF THE RINGS ON EACH OF
THE THORACIC CENTRA IN MALES BETWEEN THE AGES OF
SEVENTEEN AND TWENTY-FIVE*

Age	No.	Thoracic vertebrae											
		1	2	3	4	5	6	7	8	9	10	11	12
17-18	54	13	13	13	8	4	4	8	13	13	13	13	13
19	50	24	22	14	6	8	8	22	24	24	24	24	24
20	43	100	86	77	70	68	77	96	100	100	100	100	100
21	35	100	92	83	86	83	89	95	100	100	100	100	100
22	24	100	96	84	67	71	91	96	100	100	100	100	100
23	26	100	97	93	81	85	97	100	100	100	100	100	100
24-25	27	100	100	100	100	100	100	100	100	100	100	100	100
Total	259												

*From McKern and Stewart, Skeletal age changes in young American males. Analyzed from the standpoint of age. *Environmental Protection Res Div,* Tech. Rep. EP-45, Table 32, 1957. Courtesy of Quartermaster Res. & Dev. Center, U.S. Army, Natick, Mass.

The second pointer is a warning concerning variations in the appearance of the medial or sternal epiphysis of the clavicle. In their classical study of the clavicular epiphyses, Todd and D'Errico (1928) defined three types of medial end: Plane, sigmoid and concave or excavated. In the excavated type the epiphysis may appear to be protruding from a hole, and especially if it happens to be too small to cover the whole articular surface of the medial end. Also, Todd and D'Errico pointed out (p. 34) that the medial epiphysis does not always ossify. When this is the case,

> . . . the shaft, left bare and naked, does not preserve indefinitely its coral-like texture but, at the date of 'union,' glazes its surface with the same waxy bone as that which grows in the epiphysis itself. Therefore in an adult bone it is sometimes quite difficult to decide whether one is looking at an epiphysis-covered extremity or merely at a shaft-end over which has been poured that deposit of glazed new bone comparable with and indistinguishable from epiphysial bone.

These circumstances make it necessary to place primary reliance on the signs of union of an ossified epiphysis. The evidence is good that this stage occasionally persists until the age of thirty.

Metamorphosis of the Pubic Symphysis: Males

In his study of age changes in the pubic bones of white males Todd (1920) makes the following statements (pp. 326-327) :

> Ossified epiphyses for the symphysial face are rudimentary, erratic in their occurrence and very irregular in form. When they occur they rapidly fuse with the symphysial surface, usually in its upper area, taking part in the formation of the upper extremity and losing their identity very quickly.
>
> . . . there is little actual increase of bone substance at the symphysial end of the os pubis after the eighteenth year, and none at all after the twenty-first. In the main and practically entirely the symphysial change is one of metamorphosis.

It is for these reasons that I am making a distinction here between the change in the pubic symphysis and that in all the other joints. In so doing the inclusion of degenerative changes—the subject of another subsection—in the late stages of pubic metamorphosis is unavoidable.

In the study cited, Todd defined (pp. 313-314; for a more expanded account see pp. 301-313) ten phases of male pubic metamorphosis as follow:

1. Age 18-19. Typical adolescent ridge and furrow formation with no sign of margins* and no ventral beveling.

---

*In "the complete absence of a delimiting margin the symphysial face . . . is nevertheless distinctly marked off from the ventral and dorsal aspects of the pubic bone by a sudden change in surface appearance and bony texture." (p. 301).

2. Age 20-21. Foreshadowing of ventral beveling* with slight indication of dorsal margin.

3. Age 22-24. Progressive obliteration of ridge and furrow system with increasing definition of dorsal margin and commencement of ventral rarefaction (beveling).

4. Age 25-26 (24-26).† Completion of definite dorsal margin, rapid increase of ventral rarefaction and commencing delimitation of lower extremity.

5. Age 27-30 (26-27). Commencing formation of upper extremity with increasing definition of lower extremity and possibly sporadic attempts at formation of central rampart.‡

6. Age 30-35 (27-34). Development and practical completion of ventral rampart with increasing definition of extremities.

7. Age 35-39 (34-38). Changes in symphysial face and ventral aspect of pubis consequent upon diminishing activity, accompanied by bony outgrowths into pelvic attachment of tendons§ and ligaments.

8. Age 39-44 (38-42). Smoothness and inactivity of symphysical face and ventral aspect of pubis. Oval outline and extremities clearly defined but not "rim" formation‖ or lipping.

9. Age 45-50 (42-51). Development of "rim" on symphysial face with lipping of dorsal and ventral margins.

10. Age 50 (51) and upwards. Erosion of and erratic, possibly pathological osteophytic growth on symphysial face with breaking down of ventral margin.

---

*". . . from this stage onwards the porous beveled strip becomes more pronounced, until it is finally obliterated by the superposition upon it of the definitive ventral margin." (p. 303).

†Ages in parenthesis from here on are the so-called Ahmed correction recommended by Brooks (1955, Table 2).

‡"The ventral rampart is often incomplete . . . When a hiatus remains it is almost always in the upper third of the margin, as though the prolongation from the upper extremity had been too weak to complete its union with the upward growth from below." (p. 308).

§". . . the linear prominence appearing on the ventral aspect [of the body of the pubis is] the line of attachment of the gracilis muscle." (p. 311).

‖A "narrow marginal projection . . . comparable to but more distinct than the bony rim which develops round the glenoid fossa on the scapula." (p. 311).

Todd followed this first study on the pubic symphysis with five others (1921) covering white females, Negro-hybrids (male and female), other mammals, and variations from the normal. Unfortunately, the numbers of specimens available to Todd for all but the white males were too small to give sure indications of sex and race differences in the rate of metamorphosis.

It is noteworthy, too, that Todd (1921, p. 40) said: "I do not believe that pregnancy and child-birth leave any permanent stamp upon the skeleton." As pointed out in the previous chapter, this is contrary to present belief. All in all, however, his studies have proved a great boon to skeletal identification, providing a firm basis, both methodological and terminological, upon which to build.

Around fifteen years after the publication of Todd's first study someone selected from the many photographs illustrating that study a series of ten judged to typify the ten phases of pubic metamorphosis (personal communication from Krogman, June 13, 1969). A layout of drawings made from these photographs seems to have been widely distributed (see, for example, Figure 116 in Stewart, 1954a). Then in 1955 Brooks published photographs of casts of the same specimens represented in the drawings. Although the Brooks' photographs leave something to be desired, they are better in some respects than the drawings and therefore are being reproduced here as Figure 46.

Thirty-five years after the publication of Todd's first study McKern and the writer were faced with the problem of analyzing the plaster casts of 349 pubic symphyses obtained from the skeletons of young American males killed in the Korean War. Having noted that Todd had distinguished between the metamorphosis of the ventral and dorsal sides of the symphysial surface until the two formed a plateau, and then had considered the metamorphosis of the surface of this plateau as a whole, I suggested to McKern that he look upon the changes going on in these same three aspects of the surface as separate components of the process of metamorphosis. [Quite frankly, I had Sheldon's (1940) method of somatotype analysis in mind.] The result was that McKern set up six stages (0-5) for each of the three components (I, dorsal demiface; II, ventral demiface; III, whole

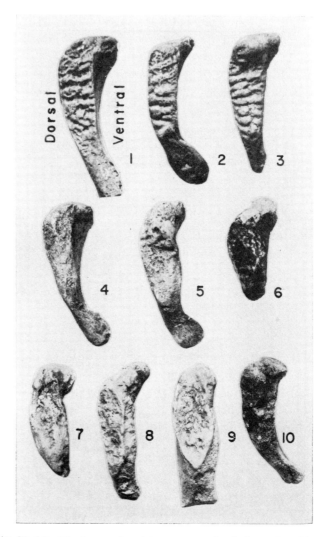

Figure 46. Todd's 10 phases of pubic metamorphosis in male whites. (From Brooks, Skeletal age at death: The reliability of cranial and pubic age indicators. *Am J Phys Anthropol, 13:* 567-597, Plates I and II, 1955 Courtesy of *Am J Phys Anthropol.*)

surface) and typified stages 1 to 5 of each component with casts selected from the collection (Figure 47).*

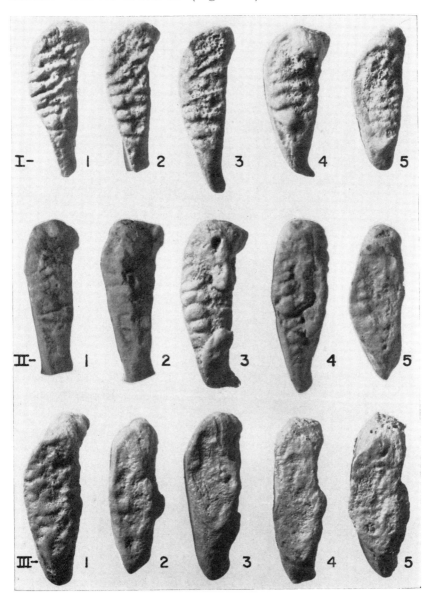

Figure 47. McKern's and Stewart's five phases of each of three components of pubic metamorphosis in male whites. (Courtesy Smithsonian Institution.)

*Until recently sets of these casts, copied in plastic, were produced and sold commercially. Unfortunately, the small demand made the operation unprofitable, and hence production has been discontinued.

The system worked out by McKern is more than just a variation of Todd's phases. In addition to increasing the number of subdivisions of the metamorphosis, it forces the observer to give more attention to the makeup of the articular face of the symphysis.

The definitions of McKern's individual stages (McKern and Stewart, 1957, pp. 75-79) are as follow:

Component I. (Dorsal demiface)

0. Dorsal margin absent.
1. A slight margin formation first appears in the middle third of the dorsal border.
2. The dorsal margin extends along entire dorsal border.
3. Filling in of grooves and resorption of ridges to form a beginning plateau in the middle third of the dorsal demiface.
4. The plateau, still exhibiting vestiges of billowing, extends over most of the dorsal demiface.
5. Billowing disappears completely and the surface of the entire demiface becomes flat and slightly granulated in texture.

Component II. (Ventral demiface)

0. Ventral beveling is absent.
1. Ventral beveling is present only at superior extremity of ventral border.
2. Bevel extends inferiorly along ventral border.
3. The ventral rampart begins by means of bony extensions from either or both of the extremities.
4. The rampart is extensive but gaps are still evident along the earlier ventral border, most evident in the upper two thirds.
5. The rampart is complete.

Component III. (Whole articular surface)

0. The symphysial rim is absent.
1. A partial dorsal rim is present, usually at the superior end of the dorsal margin; it is round and smooth in texture and elevated above symphysial surface.
2. The dorsal rim is complete and the ventral rim is be-

ginning to form. There is no particular beginning site.

3. The symphysial rim is complete. The enclosed symphysial surface is finely grained in texture and irregular or undulating in appearance.

4. The rim begins to break down. The face becomes smooth and flat and the rim is no longer round but sharply defined. There is some evidence of lipping on the ventral edge.

5. Further breakdown of the rim (especially along superior ventral edge) and rarefaction of the symphysial face. There is also disintegration and erratic ossification along the ventral rim.

My reason for reporting both the Todd and the McKern and Stewart systems here is their very different age bases shown in Table XVIII. The McKern and Stewart system would seem to be more reliable for the age period seventeen to thirty, whereas the Todd system would seem to offer more help in cases beyond the age of thirty (cf. Masset, 1976).

TABL XVIII
AGE DISTRIBUTIONS OF WHITE MALE SAMPLES USED IN
ESTABLISHING CRITERIA FOR AGING PUBIC SYMPHYSES

Ages	Todd (1920)	McKern & Stewart (1957)	
17	—	5	
18-20	5	132	
21-25	15	107	85.1%
26-30	23	53	
31-39	52	45	
40-50	95	7	
51-60	57	—	
61-70	40	—	85.9%
71-80	13	—	
81-90	6	—	
Totals	306	349	

Note that the McKern and Stewart definitions, unlike those of Todd, do not include an age for each stage. To derive an age estimate for an unknown with the aid of Figure 47, an examiner must compare the symphysis of the unknown with the pictured five stages of each component noting the numbers of the ones resembling it the closest. By putting together the selected numbers of the three components—say, 4 in component I, 3 in component II, and 1 in component III—a formula is obtained: 431. When added together, the numbers constituting this formula yield a total score of 8. And finally, by looking up the total score in Table XIX the examiner can read off the estimated mean age (24.14 years in this case) and the standard deviation (± 1.93 years).

TABLE XIX

AGE RANGE, MEAN AGE, AND STANDARD DEVIATION CALCULATED FOR EACH TOTAL SCORE OF THE SYMPHYSIAL FORMULA: MALES*

Total score	No.	Age range	Mean age	Standard Deviation
0	7	—17	17.29	.49
1- 2	76	17-20	19.04	.79
3	43	18-21	19.79	.85
4- 5	51	18-23	20.84	1.13
6- 7	26	20-24	22.42	.99
8- 9	36	22-28	24.14	1.93
10	19	23-28	26.05	1.87
11-12-13	56	23-39	29.18	3.33
14	31	29+	35.84	3.89
15	4	36+	41.00	6.22
Total	349			

*From McKern and Stewart, Skeletal age changes in young American males. Analyzed from the standpoint of age. *Environmental Protection Res Div,* Tech. Rep. P-45, Table 27, 1957. Courtesy of Quartermaster Res. & Dev. Center, U.S. Army, Natick, Mass.

At this writing, Hanihara and Suzuki in Japan (Personal communication, April, 1977) are preparing to publish a new method of age estimation from the pubic articular surfaces. What they have done is to develop ratings for a sizable number of symphysial characters and to subject them to multiple regression analysis. The method, which would seem to have great promise, will need to be tested on American population samples before the wisdom of its use in the United States can be appraised.

Metamorphosis of the Pubic Symphysis: Females

I pointed out above that Todd had too small a sample of female pubic symphyses to give a sure indication of the rate of metamorphosis of the articular surfaces in this sex. The combined samples of whites and Negro-hybrids for which he gave ages total 63, and 86 percent of these are more than thirty years old. Although he defined ten phases for the females, as for the males, these have not been widely used. To remedy this situation, Gilbert and McKern (1973) assembled and analyzed 103 female symphyses (mostly whites, age range thirteen to fifty-nine years) obtained at autopsy.

They concluded (p. 31) that "females are absolutely different from males in the rate and locality of age-related metamorphic changes in the *os pubis*." In their opinion the difference is particularly noticeable in two places: (1) the dorsal demiface, where flattening takes place at a more accelerated rate than in males; and (2) the ventral demiface, where the rampart fails to develop to the same extent as in males. The accelerated flattening of the dorsal demiface has the effect of giving a female pubis aged twenty-five the appearance of a male aged thirty-five. As for the different-appearing ventral rampart, they said (p. 36):

> In males, the two demifaces are separated by an imaginary line. In females, the ventral rampart (demiface) is beveled away from the dorsal demiface . . . Because of this structural difference, a female pubis in stage 3 of Component II would be aged about thirty-eight, and a male in the same category of the male standard would be aged about twenty-three.

For use in sexing unknowns Gilbert and McKern presented their findings in exactly the same way as did McKern and Stewart (1957). The following, then, are their slightly edited definitions (pp. 33-34) of the six (0 to 5) stages of each the three components:

Component I. (Dorsal demiface)

    0. Ridges and furrows very distinct, with ridges billowed; dorsal margin is undefined.

    1. Ridges begin to flatten, furrows to fill in, and a flat dorsal margin to appear in the mid-third of the demiface.

    2. Dorsal demiface spreads ventrally, becoming wider as

flattening continues; dorsal margin extends superiorly and inferiorly.

3. Dorsal demiface is quite smooth; margin may be narrow or indistinct from face.
4. The demiface—broad and very fine grained—becomes complete and unbroken, but may exhibit vestigial billowing.
5. Demiface becomes pitted and irregular through rarefaction.

Component II. (Ventral demiface)

0. Ridges and furrows very distinct. The entire ventral demiface forms an obtuse angle with the dorsal demiface.
1. Beginning inferiorly, the furrows of the ventral demiface begin to fill in, forming an expanding beveled rampart, the lateral edge of which is a distinct, curved line extending the length of the symphysis.
2. Fill-in of furrows and expansion of the demiface continue from both superior and inferior ends. Rampart spreads laterally along its ventral edge.
3. All but about one third of the ventral demiface is filled in with fine-grained bone.
4. The ventral rampart presents a broad, complete, fine-grained surface from the pubic crest to the inferior ramus.
5. Ventral rampart may begin to break down, assuming a very pitted and sometimes cancellous appearance through rarefaction.

Component III. (Whole articular surface)

0. The rim is absent.
1. The rim begins to appear in the mid-third of the dorsal surface.
2. The dorsal part of the symphysial rim is complete.
3. The rim extends from the superior and inferior ends of the symphysis until all but about one third of the ventral aspect is complete.
4. The symphysial rim is complete.

5. Ventral margin of dorsal demiface may break down so that gaps appear in the rim, or it may round off so that there is no longer a clear dividing line between the dorsal demiface and the ventral rampart.

To illustrate these stages (Figure 48) I have photographed

Figure 48. Gilbert's and McKern's five phases of each of three components of pubic metamorphosis in female whites. (Courtesy Smithsonian Instittuion.)

the casts which Gilbert selected and has offered in sets for sale (in the original publication these are shown in drawings). For the determination of age from this figure, Table XX repeats the pattern of Table XIX. Note, however, that there is both a greater range and a greater standard deviation for most mean ages.

TABLE XX

AGE RANGE, MEAN AGE AND STANDARD DEVIATION CALCULATED FOR EACH TOTAL SCORE OF THE SYMPHYSIAL FORMULA: FEMALES*

Total score	No.	Age range	Mean age	Standard Deviation†
0	2	14-18	16.00	2.82
1	12	13-24	19.80	2.62
2	13	16-25	20.15	2.19
3	4	18-25	21.50	3.10
4- 5	7	22-29	26.00	2.61
6	8	25-36	29.62	4.43
7- 8	14	23-39	32.00	4.55
9	5	22-40	33.00	7.75
10-11	11	30-47	36.90	4.94
12	12	32-52	39.00	6.09
13	8	44-54	47.75	3.59
14-15	7	52-59	55.71	3.24
Total	103			

*From Gilbert and McKern, A method for aging the female *os pubis*. *Am J Phys Anthropol*, *38*:31-38, Table 2, 1973. Courtesy of *Am J Phys Anthropol*.
†Corrected in accordance with personal communication from Gilbert to D. H. Ubelaker.

At this point a word of caution must be entered regarding the effect on the pubic articular surface of the trauma of pregnancy and childbirth. Gilbert and McKern had parity records for most of their specimens so they were able to take this effect into consideration. In their opinion (p. 37):

> The degree of traumatic change observed . . . indicated that only rarely is a pubis rendered impossible to age . . . Sometimes an individual in the mid-thirties will have experienced sufficient parity trauma that the dorsal plateau will become pitted to the extent that it appears to be in stage 5 of Component I . . . It is therefore cautioned that an unknown pubis with extensive parity damage may be much younger than it appears . . . Certainly, a large sample of nulliparous pubes would yield much smaller standard deviations than those in Table [XX].

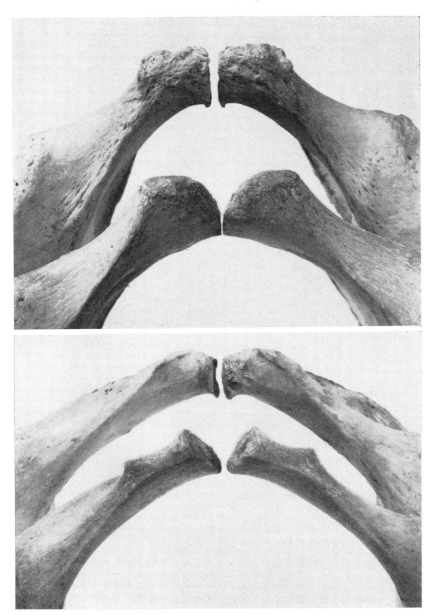

Figure 49. The pubic symphysis in the two sexes viewed from above to show metamorphic differences in youth and maturity. *Above*—male whites aged 24? and 64; Terry Collection Nos. 645 and 651, respectively; *below*—female blacks, aged 20 and 41; Terry Collection Nos. 929 and 1015, respectively. (Courtesy Smithsonian Institution.)

By way of summarizing the sex differences in the metamorphosis of the pubic symphysis, I show in Figure 49 the superior aspect of two pairs of male and two pairs of female articulated pubic bones. One pair of each sex is in the twenty-year-old period; the other pair is in the age period when the articular faces have reached the plateau stage (the actual age differences between the older pairs are not important in this connection).

This figure illustrates in a dramatic fashion the amount of build-up of bone required to complete the ventral sides of the articular faces and the different appearances of the end products in the two sexes. Note, too, that the dorsal margins are the only parts in close proximity at the beginning of adulthood, a fact that seems to explain why the first signs of lipping (a degenerative change) appear here and why eventually this is the site of the most pronounced lipping seen in the symphysis.

Gilbert and McKern do not include lipping among their criteria of pubic aging. Todd noted it, but did not emphasize it. Actually, Todd reported a distinct difference in the ages when the two sexes show beginning lipping along the dorsal margin of the articular face. In his description of the third phase for white females (Age 25-26?) he said, "Dorsal margin becoming more defined and *sharply lipped*" (1921, p. 29, italics added both here and below). A similar statement ("Dorsal margin clearly defined and *somewhat lipped*"—1921, p. 29) for Negro-hybrid females does not appear until the description of his fifth phase (Age ?-30), perhaps because of poor specimen representation. By contrast, Todd does not mention lipping for either white males or Negro-hybrid males until the descriptions of his eighth phase (Ages 39-44 and 39-45, respectively). The wording of the respective statements is as follows: "*no marked lipping* of either dorsal or ventral margin" (1920, p. 31) and "*some lipping* of dorsal but none of ventral border" (1921, p. 12). I suspect that the earlier onset of lipping at this point in females, if confirmed, is due to the extra mobility of the symphysis during pregnancy.

All of this suggests the following question: How well can the metamorphic stages of the female pubic articular surface be judged by different observers? This was the subject of a recent

(1977) study by Judy Suchey of California State University at Fullerton. In order to get an answer she sent eleven sets of female pubes obtained at autopsy to thirteen different observers and asked them to provide her with their age estimates by reference to a given set of Gilbert-McKern casts. Upon tabulating the estimates (Table XXI) she decided that "it is not easy for an observer to select the exact stage of development which is present in any of the three components using the Gilbert-McKern method" (p. 5); that "only 54 percent of the assessments yielded age ranges which would include the known age of the specimen in question" (p. 4) ; and that of four most problematic cases, "C and K were commonly scored to be in the older ranges and G and H were commonly scored in the younger ranges" (p. 5). In her opinion (p. 5),

TABLE XXI

PERCENTAGES OF THIRTEEN OBSERVERS USING GILBERT-MCKERN METHOD WHOSE ESTIMATED AGE RANGES INCLUDED A PARTICULAR SPECIMEN*

Specimen (Age)	Observer Success (%)
E (19)	76.9
B (23)	38.4
J (25)	92.3
F (29)	69.2
G (60)	0
D (31)	84.6
C (34)	69.2
K (44)	46.1
A (45)	61.5
I (47)	61.5
H (51)	0

*Modified from Suchey, Problems in the aging of females using the pubic symphysis. *Am Acad For Sci* (Ann. Meeting, San Diego, CA), Paper No. 81, Feb. 1977 Table 3. Courtesy of Dr. Suchey.

These mistakes appear to center on one of the focal problems of the Gilbert-McKern system. It is often difficult to tell when the ventral rampart is building up or breaking down. Assessing Component III (the symphysial rim) encompasses the same difficulty.

Suture Closure

The earliest well-founded studies on cranial suture closure are those by Pommerol (1869), Ribbe (1885), and Frédéric (1906) in Europe; and by Dwight (1890b) in the United States. The facial sutures have received far less attention. Dwight was not impressed by the utility of closure of the vault sutures for aging purposes. He opened his paper on this subject by saying (p. 389), "It is, I believe, pretty generally admitted among anatomists that the time and order of the closing of the cranial sutures are very uncertain, far too much so for them to be trustworthy guides to determine the age of the skull." And he concluded by saying (p. 392),

> It must not be forgotten that there are other guides to the age of the skull; and I am not prepared to assert that taken together with them, the sutures are absolutely worthless in the hands of an experienced anatomist. I am sure that to anyone else the rules in question are misleading and dangerous.

All this was changed by the extensive studies of Todd and Lyon which appeared in the *American Journal of Physical Anthropology* in four parts in 1924-25. By stressing the definite pattern of the closure, these authors led many physical anthropologists to believe that they could arrive at a satisfactory estimate of age by this means. As late as 1948 Charles Snow judged the ages of the Indian Knoll skulls from suture closure and as a result reported 75 percent of the females as being between twenty and twenty-four years of age, a figure that was reduced to 25 percent in a subsequent reassessment using other skeletal features (Johnston and Snow, 1961; Stewart, 1962b). This result of the reassessment confirms Dwight's opinion and supports the following statement by Todd and Lyon (1924, pp. 379-380) :

> . . . it cannot be denied that so far our work does not justify the uncontrolled use of suture closure in estimation of age . . . Our results are of distinct value however when taken in conjunction with indications given by other parts of the skeleton.

It is now generally agreed that suture closure by itself is too unreliable for aging purposes, especially from the forensic standpoint. Much support for this view has been assembled; for example, by Singer (1953) and McKern and Stewart (1957). For this reason, and because the inner surface of the skull is not readily visible in most forensic specimens, I shall give for reference purposes here (Table XXII) only Todd's and Lyon's ages of ecto-

TABLE XXII

AGES OF ECTOCRANIAL SUTURE CLOSURE*

Suture	White males			Black males		
	C†	T‡	Remarks	C	T	Remarks
1. Sagittal	20	29	3.9§ in obelica, 2.4 alone; 2.9 in gen. Slow to 26	20	32	Slowly to 24, 2.9-3.6 in gen., 4.0 in obelica alone
2. Sphenofrontal-orbital	28	46	2.3 at 31, 3.8 at 46	21	35	3.5 at 35, may reach 4.0 at 43
3. Sphenofrontal-temporal	28	38	2.1 at 38, may reach 4.0 in old age	25	46	1.9 at 35
4. Coronal 1 and 2	26	29	Bregmatica at 2.3, complicata at 0.9	23	32	Bregmatica at 2.4, complicata at 1.7
5. Coronal 3	28	50	3.8 at 50, spurious rise at 21	25	35	2.8 at 35, spurious rise at 21
6. Lambdoid 1 and 2	26	30	Spurious rise at 21. Lambdica 2.3, media 1.9	23	31	Lambdica 2.4, media 2.0
7. Lambdoid 3	26	?30	Not more than 1.0	22	?31	Not more than 1.0
8. Masto-occipital 3	26	33	1.4 at 33, may reach 4.0 in old age	26	31	Spurious rise at 21, sec. act. at 50
9. Sphenoparietal	28	38	2.0 at 38, 3.5 at 31, continues to old age	28	46	1.4 at 31
10. Sphenotemporal 2	36	?65	Probably never closes	?50	0	Probably never closes
11. Sphenotemporal 1	37	?65	Probably never closes	?50	0	Probably never closes
12. Masto-occipital 1 and 2	28	32	0.8-1.0 at 32, may reach 3.5 in old age	27	31	2.7 at 31, spurious rise ca. 18, sec. act. at 50
13. Parieto-mastoid	39	?64	Probably never closes	?50	0	Probably never closes
14. Squamous posterior	38	?65	Probably never closes	?50	0	Probably never closes
15. Squamous anterior	38	?65	Probably never closes	?50	0	Probably never closes

* Modified from Cobb, Skeleton. In Lansing, Albert I. (Ed.): *Cowdry's Problems of Ageing; Biological and Medical Aspects.* 3rd ed., Table 3, p. 806, 1952. Courtesy of Williams & Wilkins.

† C = Commencement.

‡ T = Termination.

§ Closure graded on a scale of 0 to 4.

cranial suture closure as conveniently summarized by Cobb (1952). As thus set forth the sagittal suture has four readily-recognizable subdivisions (pars bregmatica, pars verticis, pars obelica, pars lambdica) ; the coronal suture three (pars bregmatica-1, pars complicata-2, pars pterica-3) ; the lambdoid suture three (pars lambdica-1, pars intermedia or media-2, pars asterica-3) ; the masto-occipital suture three (superior-1, middle-2, inferior-3) ; the spheno-temporal suture two (superior -1, inferior-2); and the squamous suture two (anterior, posterior) .

For lack of space, Table XXII necessarily does not include any reference to the phenomenon of lapsed union. As Cobb explains (pp. 807-808) :

> That there is some general or constitutional influence which modifies progress in suture closure, commencing approximately at thirty years, is evident since all sutural elements, whatever their degree of union, show arrested activity at this age . . .
>
> While bone along a suture edge is still in a state of active change it possesses a granular texture difficult to describe but easy to recognize. After activity has ceased the granularity gives place to a waxy smoothness of texture. Heaped-up edges on an unclosed suture are characteristic evidence of quiescence which absolutely differentiates the suture from one still in a state of active closure. Todd called this condition lapsed union. It is very frequent in the sutures on the endocranial aspect of human skulls and is almost constant on the ectocranial surface where, however, it does not present the characteristic heaped-up feature.

The only attempt by Todd and Lyon to turn their findings around and use them for determining the ages of a series of skulls yielded the results shown in Table XXIII. Note that this test involves only endocranial closure, which is said to be more reliable than ectocranial closure; also that the authors' tendency was to overage the younger adults and to underage the older adults, but otherwise to come closer to the true age in the below-forty group.

Part of the impressiveness of this test may be due to the authors' great experience. In fact, two of the test skulls (Nos. 445 and 649) had been eliminated from the study series for reasons of abnormality and therefore must have been well known

TABLE XXIII
RELIABILITY OF AGING SKULLS FROM ENDOCRANIAL SUTURE
CLOSURE: WHITE MALES*

Under 40 Years		40 Years and Over	
Actual age	Deviation of estimate	Actual age	Deviation of estimate
22	+ 5	40	—
25	—	40	— 3
28	— 3	40	+ 3
30	—	40	— 5
32	+ 1	40	+ 5
32	+ 5	42	+23
32	+13	45	— 2
33	+ 2	45	— 5
33	— 3	47	— 4
34	+ 1	48	+17
36	— 1	49	—14
36	— 6	53	+ 2
37	— 2	55	—12
38	+ 2	60	—19
38	+17	68	—10
Average	{ +2.07† { 4.06‡		{ —1.60† { 8.02‡

*Modified from Todd and Lyon, Cranial suture closure; its progress and age relationship. *Am J Phys Anthropol,* 7:325-384, Table III, 1924. Courtesy of *Am J Phys Anthropol.*
†With regard to sign.
‡Without regard to sign.

to the authors. This makes one wonder how well they knew the other skulls also. Incidentally, the skulls eliminated from the study series of male whites amounted to forty (13%) and from that of male blacks forty-one (34.2%). Extreme forms of abnormal suture closure are easily detected, but how readily would most observers recognize precocity and retardation in suture closure?

BY AMOUNT OF DEGENERATIVE CHANGE
In the Joints

The most obvious skeletal changes of a degenerative nature are those that occur in and around joints subject to more motion and weight transmission than the pubic symphysis. Changes here include, on the one hand, the loss of bone from the articular surfaces through mechanical erosion and pathological destruction, and on the other, the formation of new bone around the joint margins through the development of exostoses (osteophytes). In so far as these changes result from the wear and tear of motion and weight transmission, and tend only in advanced age to become crippling, they are designated as osteoarthritis. Care must be taken to distinguish between osteoarthritis and less benign types of arthritis (especially rheumatoid arthritis) which are much more likely to lead to joint fusion and at an earlier age.

The diarthroidial (or synovial) joints, such as the shoulder and hip joints, tend gradually to develop sharp margins and then raised margins. Subsequent progressive changes include massive build-up of bone along the lines of attachment of the joint capsule and eburnation (polishing) of the articular surfaces.

Jurmain (1975) has provided detailed observations on the rate of such changes in the knee (femur, tibia, patella), hip (femur, innominate), shoulder (humerus, scapula), and elbow (humerus, ulna, radius) for fairly sizeable samples of whites and blacks (210 and 234, respectively) from the Terry Collection. He arrived at a 4+ grading system (none, slight, moderate, and severe) by first comparing individuals of known age (young vs. old) and eliminating the variables that proved impossible to judge consistently, and eventually ending up with a total of fifty characters per side (he explained these by means of drawings in an appendix). Figure 50 shows for whites (sexes combined) the average rate of change in the four joints by side. Comparable data for blacks show a slightly earlier onset and somewhat greater severity with advancing age.

The joints between the centra of the vertebral segments, which are classed as synarthrodial (or cartilaginous), tend also to accumulate degenerative changes in an age-related manner. We have just seen that this is the case in the pubic symphysis, another synarthroidal joint. I first got interested in this subject in the early 1940s because I thought that different racial patterns of vertebral osteoarthritis might exist, as indeed they do (Stewart,

1947, 1966). Not until 1958, however, did I put together my findings on white males derived from the Terry Collection and the dead of the Korean War to show the rate of development.

Figure 51 shows my findings in the latter regard for the lumbar region alone, based on a total of 306 white males. It is in this region of the vertebral column that the greatest arthritic changes occur. In explanation of the five categories or degrees of lipping charted, the first point to note is that the observations were recorded on a scale of 5 (0 to 4+). Next, that the observations for the opposing borders of the corpora were averaged (for example, readings of + on one side of a joint and ++ on the other side give an average of $1\frac{1}{2}+$). And then, by adding the averages for the individual joints in a region and dividing by the number

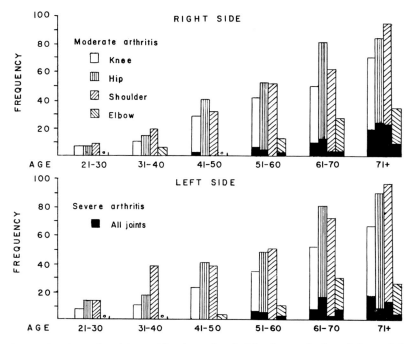

Figure 50. Age-related intensification of arthritic change in four joints of the extremities in 210 American whites (sexes combined). (From Jurmain, *Distribution of Degenerative Joint Disease in Skeletal Populations.* Thesis Harvard University, 1975, Elements of Figures 5, 11, 17, and 23 combined, Courtesy of Robert Douglas Jurmain.)

of joints in that region, figures were obtained that could be categorized.

The reason for giving Figures 50 and 51 here is not to enable an investigator to estimate with some degree of accuracy the age of a skeleton, but solely as a demonstration of the fact that a clear intensification of degenerative joint change sets in around the age of forty. Faced with a skeleton showing this degree of arthritic intensification, one is justified in saying only that the decedent *probably* was forty years of age or older at the time of death. The use of the word "probably" is necessary because some individuals show very little evidence of arthritis into the fifth decade. Although males are better documented in this regard than females, Jurmain's findings indicate that females follow much the same pattern.

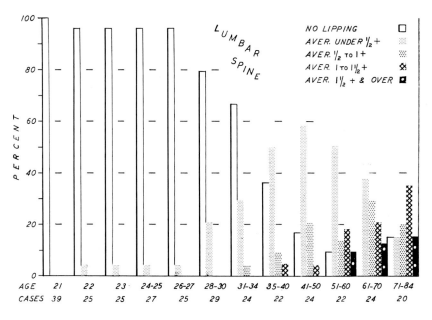

Figure 51. Rate of intensification of arthritic change in the lumbar centra of male American whites. (From Stewart, The rate of development of vertebral osteoarthritis in American whites and its significance in skeletal age identification. *The Leech (Johannesburg) 28:* (3-5) 144-151, Figure 1, 1958, Courtesy of *The Leech.*)

In the Teeth

In earlier times, and especially among peoples of simple culture, diets tended to be very coarse, with the result that the chewing process produced rapid wearing away of the occlusal surfaces of the teeth. A less obvious result was the abrasion of the buccal surfaces of the enamel crowns, producing more and more exposure of the enamel prisms which constitute the structural elements of the enamel. The latter type of wear has received attention so far from only a few dentists (see particularly Scott *et al.,* 1949) .

Physical anthropologists have been accustomed to using wear of the occlusal surfaces as a criterion of aging, but only in a general way since they have been aware of the great variability between peoples with different diets. Today, especially in the United States, diets tend in general to be far less abrasive than in earlies times and consequently to produce much less occlusal wear than in the past, even by old age. As yet, however, the rate of this type of wear has not been standardized for forensic use on American populations.

Occlusal wear is one of the age changes included in the Gustafson method of aging based on the teeth (Gustafson, 1950, 1966). This method is rather involved and requires facilities for tooth sectioning. So far as I am aware, therefore, the only forensic anthropologist who has attempted, not only to master the method, but to improve upon it, is W. R. Maples of the Florida State Museum in Gainesville, Florida (Burns and Maples, 1976) . Apparently the method yields estimates within three years of the actual age in from 23 to 28 percent of cases.

Incidentally, tooth sectioning, which is the basis of the Gustafson method, requires that the specimen be sacrificed. On the other hand, aging by means of the changes in the enamel prisms can be done from surface replicas which do not require that the tooth even be removed from the jaw. The latter method has yielded encouraging results in ten-year age groupings over the age of twenty and in five-year groupings under this age. In my opinion both of these methods of aging are best left in the hands of experienced people.

Another complicated method of determining age from the teeth, that based on the racemization of aspartic acid in dentine (Helfman and Bada, 1976), sounds promising but is still inadequately tested. As in the Gustafson method, the specimen must be sacrificed.

In Cancellous Tissue

A number of European investigators (Wachholz, 1894; Schrantz, 1933, 1959; Bruno, 1934; Berndt, 1947; Hansen, 1953-54; Nemeskéri *et al.,* 1960) have recorded the age changes in the cancellous tissue in the interior of the upper end of the humerus. Less attention has been given to that in the upper end of the femur (Hansen, 1953-54; Jacqueline and Veraguth, 1954; Nemeskéri *et al.,* 1960), seemingly because the changes with age here are said to be less than in the humerus.

The latest of these studies—that by Nemeskéri *et al.* (1960) on the humerus—provides the smallest number of stages of change, along with the best diagrams of these stages, and the best appraisal of the success in applying the method. For all these reasons I shall summarize only this latest version of the method.

Using 105 documented and macerated humeri (61 males and 44 females, 23 to 93 years of age), these authors sectioned each one of them longitudinally through the center of the head and greater tuberosity. Study of these sectioned bones enabled the authors to separate the six stages of degenerative change pictured in Figure 52 and defined (pp. 82-83, freely translated) as follows:

> I. (Mean age 41.1 ± 6.60 years) * The cone of the medullary cavity is located well below the surgical neck; the system of cancellous bone exhibits a radial structure.
>
> II. (52.3 ± 2.51 years.) The cone has reached the level of the surgical neck or somewhat above. The cancellous bone already is more sparse and exhibits a somewhat pointed-arch structure.
>
> III. (59.8 ± 3.59 years.) The cone can reach to the epiphysial line; above this the cancellous bone is pointed-

---

*Nemeskéri *et al.,* 1960, Table 13.

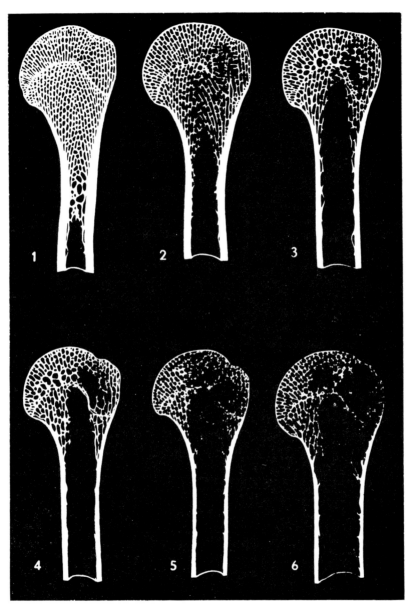

Figure 52. Six age-correlated stages in the decrease of cancellous tissue in the head of the humerus in whites, sexes combined. (Nemeskéri *et al.* Methoden zur diagnose des Lehensalters von Skelettfunden. *Anthrop Anz, 24:* 70-95, Tafel 1, 1960. Courtesy of *Anthrop Anz.)*

arch shaped, and along the cortex exhibits a columnar structure at the border of the diaphysis and of the epiphysis.

IV. (56.0 ± 1.84 years.) The cone has arrived at the epiphysial line or reaches beyond; in the greater tubercle the cancellous bone is disturbed, along both sides of the medullary cavity the cancellous bone shows columnar structure and here and there is torn.

V. (61.0 ± 2.05 years.) In the greater tubercle a lentilto pea-sized cavity has formed; the cone ranges above the epiphysial line and the remains of the columnar structure are visible on both sides of the medullary cavity.

VI. (61.1 ± 3.39 years.) The diameter of the cavity which has formed in the greater tubercle exceeds 5 mm and can reach to the cortex. The cancellous bone in the head of the humerus is completely disturbed, here and there is cobweb-thin and torn off. The cone has run into the cavity in the greater tubercle and forms with this a uniform cavity system. The cortex is thin and transparent. Also, general atrophy has become apparent on the outer surface of the bone.

The degree of success attained by Nemeskéri and his associates in estimating age from the cancellous tissue of the upper end of the humeri of their original sample is shown in Table XXIV. There it appears that the estimated age agreed with the true age in only 18 percent of cases. In another 21 percent the deviation of the estimate from the true age was between one and five years. In the remaining 61 percent the deviation of the estimate from the true age was more than six years, with those under fifty years of age more often being overaged and those over fifty being underaged. This is an unimpressive record. However, in fairness to the authors it should be said that they intended this feature to be observed along with three others—suture closure, pubic metamorphosis, and cancellous structure of the upper end of the femur—and thus not in isolation. With the full combination the authors claim to have gotten their estimates within ± 2.5 years in 80 per-

TABLE XXIV

DISTRIBUTION OF THE DEVIATIONS BETWEEN
TRUE AGE AND AGE ESTIMATED FROM THE STATE OF
THE CANCELLOUS TISSUE IN THE PROXIMAL END OF THE HUMERUS*

Columns 21–30 through 71–80 fall under the heading "Relation of estimate to true age in decades"; each decade column shows the pair "+ −".

Range of deviation in years	21–30 (+ −)	31–40 (+ −)	41–50 (+ −)	51–60 (+ −)	61–70 (+ −)	71–80 (+ −)	Plus Deviation No.	Plus Deviation %	Minus Deviation No.	Minus Deviation %	Total No.	Total %
0	− 2 −	− 6 −	− 3 −	− 6 −	− 2 −	− − −	−	−	−	−	19	18
1-5	2 − −	1 − −	− − 2	5 − 2	1 − 7	− − 2	9	31	13	23	22	21
6-10	1 − −	− − −	1 − 2	1 − 4	·1 − 1	− − 2	4	14	9	16	13	12
11-20	− − −	1 − −	8 − 4	− − 4	− − 3	− − 7	9	31	18	31	27	26
21-30	− − −	3 − −	2 − −	− − 2	− − 7	− − 3	5	17	12	21	17	16
> 31	2 − −	− − −	− − −	− − −	− − 2	− − 3	2	7	5	9	7	7
Total	5 − −	5 − −	11 − 8	6 −12	2 −20	− −17	29	100	57	100	105	100

* From Nemeskéri, et al., Methoden zur Diagnose des Lebensalters von Skelettfunden.
Anthrop Anz 24:70-95, Table 7, 1960. Courtesy of *Anthrop Anz.*

cent of cases. But even this result may not justify the bone sectioning.

The alternative is to use tomography. Judging from the single trial with this approach thus far (Bergot and Bocquet, 1976) the coefficient of correlation between stage of change in the cancellous tissue and age is only around .5 and lower than this in males.

In the Microstructure

Other parts of the bones besides the joints are subject to degenerative change, but in an inconspicuous manner, because the change involves mainly the microstructure. Loss of bone substance in the condition known as osteoporosis is a fairly common finding among the elderly, and one that sets in earlier in females than in males, presumably because of the withdrawal of estrogen at menopause. Forensic anthropologists will need to decide from any evidence of reduced bone weight in a skeleton under investigation whether or not it represents abnormal osteoporosis or is within the range of normal bone loss with age. Pathological bone loss probably can lead to quite erroneous age estimates.

The socalled atrophic spots in the body of the scapula, and the surface distortions that accompany them, are about the only evidence of internal bone loss that lends itself to visual appraisal. W. W. Graves (1865-1949), a pioneer radiologist from St. Louis, seems to have been the only one to analyze this phenomenon (1922). He used the Todd Collection for the purpose. Although the details of his work have been included in subsequent forensic texts (Stewart, 1954a, 1968; Krogman, 1962), they appear now much less important on account of the introduction of a tested quantitative method by Ellis Kerley to be described next. Furthermore, Graves himself said (p. 21) that "[the value of the scapula] as a 'time-marker' should only be evaluated in connection with other bones and when possible with other tissues." I would recommend, therefore, that forensic anthropologists spend time learning from documented skeletal collections how the translucence of the scapular body under transillumination varies with age.

More recently, in seeking to understand the nature of osteoporotic change, investigators have had to work out the changing microscopic patterns of cortical bone remodeling and mineralization from youth to old age. The first to do this in a manner applicable to the estimation of age in forensic cases was Kerley (1965, 1969, 1970), who was mentioned in Chapter 1 in connection with the identification of the American dead of the Korean War. Using thick cross-sections removed from the mid-diaphysis of the femur, tibia, and fibula of 126 whites and blacks of known sex in the age range from birth to ninety-five years, Kerley made thin ground sections and mounted them as histological slides.

Using a microscope with 10x ocular wide-field lenses and a 10x objective lens, he then viewed circular-field areas* located on the anterior, posterior, medial, and lateral sides of the sections and as near as possible to their outer edge. At each of these four points he recorded (1) osteon number, (2) osteon fragment number, (3) non-Haversian canal number, and (4) the percentage of circumferential lamellar bone. The record for each individual thus con-

---

*This lens combination yields varying sizes of viewing field in different makes of microscopes. According to Bouvier and Ubelaker (1977, p. 392), the diameter of the field viewed by Kerley likely was larger than the reported 1.25 mm. Since then Ubelaker and Kerley have calculated that it was 1.62 mm. (personal communication.)

sisted of the total number of each of the first three components in the four viewing fields and the average percentage of the fourth component in these fields.

Rather than quote here Kerley's lengthy descriptions of the four observed microstructural components, I suggest that anyone desirous of learning how to recognize and quantify these components apply directly to Kerley or one of his students for instructions.* Unless one assembles the basic data correctly, there is no use in attempting to work out an age estimate.

The figures for the four components of each bone obtained in the manner outlined can be used to obtain an age estimate either by inserting them into regression equations or by entering them on a specially-designed age-profile chart (Figure 53). For those who prefer to use the equations it is important to know that a re-study of Kerley's original data by Ubelaker (1977) has led to revisions of the figures. In the following listing of the equations as thus revised the names of the components are abbreviated so that O.n. = osteon number, F.n. = fragment number, L.p. = lamellar bone percentage, and C.n. = non-Haversian canal number:

Femur

$$2.278 + 0.187(O.n.) + 0.00226(O.n.)^2 \qquad \pm\ 9.19$$
$$5.241 + 0.509(F.n.) + 0.017\ (F.n.)^2 - 0.00015(F.n.)^3 \quad \pm\ 6.98$$
$$75.017 - 1.790(L.p.) + 0.0114\ (L.p.)^2 \qquad \pm 12.52$$
$$58.390 - 3.184(C.n.) + 0.0628\ (C.n.)^2 - 0.00036(C.n.)^3 \quad \pm 12.12$$

Tibia

$$-13.422 + 0.660(O.n.) \qquad \pm 10.53$$
$$-26.997 + 2.501(F.n.) - 0.014\ (F.n.)^2 \qquad \pm\ 8.42$$
$$80.934 - 2.281(L.p.) + 0.019\ (L.p.)^2 \qquad \pm 14.28$$
$$67.872 - 9.070(C.n.) + 0.440\ (C.n.)^2 - 0.0062\ (C.n.)^3 \quad \pm 10.19$$

Fibula

$$-23.59 + 0.745(O.n.) \qquad \pm\ 8.33$$
$$-9.89 + 1.064(F.n.) \qquad \pm\ 3.66$$
$$124.09 - 10.92\ (L.p.) + 0.3723\ (L.p.)^2 - 0.00412(L.p.)^3 \quad \pm 10.74$$
$$62.33 - 9.776(C.n.) + 0.5502\ (C.n.)^2 - 0.00704(C.n.)^3 \quad \pm 14.62$$

Use of the age-profile chart probably improves the accuracy of

---

*Ubelaker, who has received instruction from Kerley, offers helpful information on the technique in his new book (1978).

estimate somewhat because it offers one the opportunity of combining the indications of the cortical components of all three leg bones. Kerley seems to have come to this opinion because he reported (1970, Table XXV) only the results of using the chart: ages within ± five years in twelve cases.

As shown in Figure 53 the chart illustrates a case lacking a femur and therefore providing information on the cortical com-

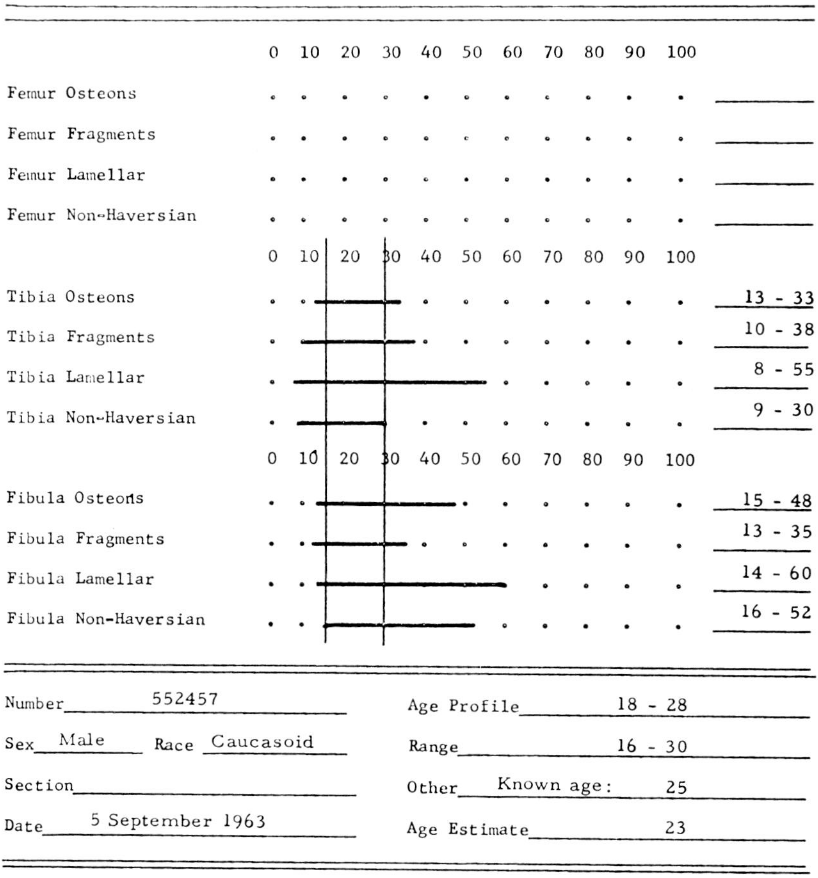

	0	10	20	30	40	50	60	70	80	90	100	
Femur Osteons												
Femur Fragments												
Femur Lamellar												
Femur Non-Haversian												
	0	10	20	30	40	50	60	70	80	90	100	
Tibia Osteons												13 - 33
Tibia Fragments												10 - 38
Tibia Lamellar												8 - 55
Tibia Non-Haversian												9 - 30
	0	10	20	30	40	50	60	70	80	90	100	
Fibula Osteons												15 - 48
Fibula Fragments												13 - 35
Fibula Lamellar												14 - 60
Fibula Non-Haversian												16 - 52

Number _____ 552457 _____   Age Profile _____ 18 - 28

Sex__Male__ Race Caucasoid __   Range _____ 16 - 30

Section _____   Other__ Known age: __ 25

Date ____ 5 September 1963 ____   Age Estimate _____ 23

Figure 53. Age-profile chart showing method of estimating age from cortical components of two leg bones. (From Kerley, Estimation of skeletal age after about 30. In Stewart, T.A. (Ed.): *Personal Identification in Mass Disasters*, pp. 57-70, Figure 19, 1970, citing Kerley, 1965. Courtesy of the National Museum of Natural History, Washington.)

ponents of only the tibia and fibula. The tibial osteon count will
serve to show how the findings on these two bones are translated
into age ranges and entered on the chart. First, the osteon count
is located on the left side of the respective age-range curve in
Figure 54B. At this level the two points where a horizontal
intersects the two sides of the age-range curve are noted. Then, in
Kerley's own words (1970, p. 65) —

> By dropping verticals from these intersection points to the base line,
> the absolute age range for that number of osteons in the original
> sample is obtained; namely, thirteen to thirty-three years. These
> figures are entered on the age-profile chart at the indicated place, and
> also in the form of a horizontal line that conforms with the given age
> scale. The same procedure is then repeated for each of the other

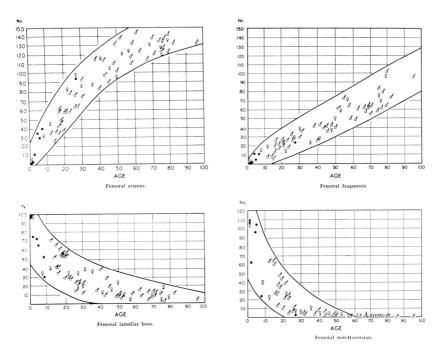

Figure 54A. Age-range curves for the four cortical components of the femur.
(From Kerley, Estimating skeletal age after about age 30. In Stewart T.D.
(Ed.): *Personal Identification in Mass Disasters,* pp. 57-70, Figure 16, 1970,
citing Kerley, 1965. Courtesy of the National Museum of Natural History,
Washington.)

three tibial components and for all four fibular components. There-upon all eight horizontal lines are connected by two vertical lines at a distance apart that is indicated by the highest *minimum* age and the lowest *maximum* age for all eight ranges (respectively, sixteen for fibular non-Haversian canals, and thirty for tibial non-Haversian canals). The distance between these vertical lines then represents the age range for which all cortical components of all available bones are in agreement. Estimated age in this case is the midpoint in the six-teen to thirty year range, namely, twenty-three years.

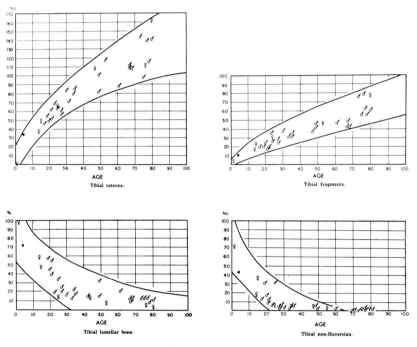

Figure 54B.   Age-range curves for the four cortical components of the tibia. (From Kerley, Estimating skeletal age after about age 30. In Stewart, T.D. *Personal Identification in Mass Disasters*, pp. 57-70, Figure 17, 1970, citing Kerley, 1965.   Courtesy of the National Museum of Natural History, Wash-ington.)

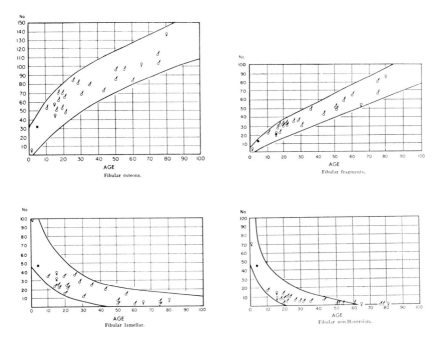

Figure 54C. Age-range curves for the four cortical components of the fibula. (From Kerley, Estimating skeletal age after about 30. In Stewart, T.S. (Ed.): *Personal Identification in Mass Disasters,* pp. 57-70, Figure 18, 1970, citing Kerley, 1965. Courtesy of the National Museum of Natural History, Washington.)

Chapter 9

ESTIMATION OF STATURE

N o other identification procedure used by forensic anthropologists has undergone such a complicated course of development involving so many identifiable contributors as that concerned with the estimation of stature from more or less detached parts of the skeleton. This being the case, the rationale governing the current use of particular methodologies needs to be preceded by an historical accounting of how it came to be accepted. In order to simplify the story as much as possible, I shall distinguish two different methods to which Dwight (1894a) gave the names "mathematical" and "anatomical." In his words,

> The mathematical method rests on the proportion of certain bones to the height . . . . There are persons with short legs and persons with long legs, and therefore no single rule of proportion can be true for both. This method, therefore, is to be used when we can do no better. (P. 7.)
> The [anatomical method] consists simply in putting the bones together, in reproducing the curves of the spine, in making due allowance for the soft parts, and in measuring the height. (P. 1.)

As we shall see, Dwight did not foresee the improvement in the mathematical method that Karl Pearson of the British biometric school would introduce in a matter of only five years. Nevertheless, there is some truth in what Dwight said, for if it is a matter of finding the closest possible estimate in a particular case, the anatomical method should yield it. On the other hand, for most purposes, application of the mathematical method will suffice.

One gets the feeling from Dwight's publications on stature estimation that he opposed the use of the mathematical method. Yet maybe he felt that it was being handled ably by European investigators and that, rather than follow in their footsteps as regards the use of the long limb bones for stature estimation, he should give his attention to the skeletal parts the Europeans were ignoring. In any event, he directed his studies along this line to the sternum and vertebrae. Being isolated in this way, geographically no less than methodologically, Dwight cannot be fitted easily into the history of the subject.

The only way I can think of to solve the problem of Dwight's exception to historical continuity is to comment here on his contributions to the mathematical method, minor though they are, and to postpone consideration of the rest of his contributions until I take up the anatomical method.

Briefly, then, the ratio of the length of the sternum (excluding the xiphoid) to body length (living stature?) was dealt with by Dwight in two publications (1890a, 1894a). In a final sample of seventy-nine males and thirty-one females he found the average ratio to be 9.59 percent and 9.07 percent, respectively. He concluded (1894a, p. 294), however, that "While I believe that a typical sternum has a fairly constant ratio to the height in each sex, [sternal] variations are so numerous that this method must be discarded."

In connection with his study of the vertebrae Dwight (1894a) obtained from cadavers the straight-line length of the whole spine (atlas to promontory of sacrum) and by relating this to body length (living stature?) derived the following coefficients (p. 295):

Male*		Female†	
Length of spine	Coefficient	Length of spine	Coefficient
cm		*cm*	
Under 57	2.93	Under 54	2.94
57 to 60	2.84	54 to 57	2.82
60 to 63	2.78	57 to 60	2.79
63 to 66	2.79	Over 60	2.76
Over 66	2.65	—	—

*Based on fifty-six subjects, mostly in the three intermediate categories of spinal length.
†Based on twenty-one subjects.

These figures would seem to have great utility for determining the stature of burned remains in which only the spinal column has survived intact. When one has determined the length of the spine in such a case, one locates in the above table the coefficient for the category into which this length falls and multiplies the two. The accuracy of this method of estimating stature is suspect on two counts: (1) A high percentage of Dwight's sample was sixty years of age or over; and (2) his method of measuring body length is not explained; he may have used cadaver length without correcting for living stature.

MATHEMATICAL METHOD

History

SUE TO TOPINARD. The earliest nineteenth century medico-legal textbooks that I have consulted cite only the data of Sue and Orfila of France for the purpose of stature estimation from skeletal and body parts. Jean Joseph Sue (1710-1792), an anatomy professor at the Louvre (see Figure 55), published in 1755 four body measurements and the maximum length of many of the bones of fourteen cadavers ranging in age from a six-week-old fetus to an adult of twenty-five years. The body measurements—stature, trunk length, upper-extremity length, and lower-extremity length —provided perhaps the first clear documentation of two important facts concerning changes in body proportions during growth, namely, (1) that the length of the trunk exceeds that of the lower extremities until about fourteen years of age, after which both lengths are equal (in other words, after fourteen the pubic symphysis is usually the center of body length) ; and (2) that the length of the upper extremities exceeds that of the lower extremities until about birth, after which the lower extremities are the longer. Sue said little about how the measurements were taken, but clearly indicated that the units of measure were the *pied* (foot), *pouce* (thumb or inch), and *ligne* (line, 12 to the inch). His purpose in publishing the measurements was to provide artists with a means of rendering the human body in correct proportions.

Matthieu Joseph Bonaventure Orfila (1787-1853), a professor of legal medicine in Paris (see Figure 56), brought Sue's measurements to wider attention in two medicolegal textbooks (1821-23, 1831). Also, in these books he followed Sue's example and reported the same selection of measurements for his own series of fifty-one cadavers and twenty skeletons. He departed from Sue's example only in using the metric units of measure. In order to determine the stature of a skeleton from the measurements of Sue and Orfila one needed to measure the length of one or more bones, say a femur and/or a humerus, then find in the tables comparable bone lengths and note the corresponding cadaver statures. Not until some years later did anyone question the equivalence of cadaver stature and living stature.

Soon the authors of other medicolegal textbooks picked up the Sue-Orfila measurements. In the United States one of the earliest to do so was T. R. Beck (1823). Unfortunately, Beck and some of the other English-speaking authors simply interpreted Sue's units of measure as equivalent to the Anglo-American foot, inch and line, which they are not; they are shorter (in the latter system also there are sixteen lines to the inch instead of twelve). This mistake was perpetuated through the middle of the nineteenth century (see, for instance, any of the twelve editions of Beck's work and the 1882 American edition of Tidy). As a result of the mistake, Sue's adult male was reported as having a stature in our present measuring system of only 5′ 4″ instead of 5′ 8″.

In Britain early in the nineteenth century much effort was being expended on determining the statures of the ancient races of that country. Consequently the British anthropologists appear to have taken as much interest in the Sue-Orfila measurements as did the British medicolegal experts. John Thurnam (1810-1873), Sir George Humphry (1820-1896), and John Beddoe (1826-1911) in particular combined the Sue-Orfila measurements with their own to investigate the relationship of long-bone lengths to stature. While differing from the French methods of stature estimation, the British methods had in common an adjustment of femur length and the multiplication of this length by a given number. Beddoe's description of his own method (1888, p. 205) provides a good example: "I take away from the length of the femur one-quarter of the excess over 13 inches up to 19, and thereafter only one-eighth; and then multiply by four."

While this was going on in Britain, the French anthropologists were still active. Paul Broca (1824-1880), a medical anthropologist (see Figure 57), founded the *Société d'Anthropologie de Paris* in 1859 and, among many other things, introduced the osteometric board for measuring long-bone length more accurately. Then between 1885 and 1888 Paul Topinard (1830-1911), Broca's successor as head of the *Société* (see Figure 58), published papers (1885a, b, c; 1888) discrediting the procedures being used in Britain, giving a method of his own, and appealing for skeletal data collected according to recommendations he set forth.

By combining his own data with those of Orfila and Humphry, Topinard by 1888 had measurements on a series of 141 skeletons with which he showed (p. 471) that for the combined sexes the following average long bone/stature (= 100) ratios held:

Maximum length of humerus	*Maximum length of radius*	*Maximum length of femur*	*Maximum length of tibia*
20.0	14.3	27.3	22.1

Using these ratios, he offered the following formula for stature estimation:

> R : 100 :: L : x; where R = the relationship of the particular long-bone length to stature (= 100), L = the length of the bone measured, and x = the stature sought. The latter is the stature of the skeleton. Add 35 mm and you have the true stature, that of the living.

ROLLET TO PEARSON. An answer to Topinard's appeal for better-documented skeletal data was not long in coming. Soon after 1885, Alexander Lacassagne (1843-1924), the professor of legal medicine in the medical school at Lyon and an active member in the local anthropological society (see Figure 59), set one of his students to work measuring the stature and long bones of cadavers from the dissecting room there. Ètienne Rollet (1862-1937) was the student (see Figure 60); the project was for his doctoral thesis. The latter was published in either 1888 or 1889 (the first date appears on the title page, the second on the cover). Although Rollet had set out to follow Topinard's recommendations about methods of measurement, size of series, age limitations, etc., he succeeded in completing only fifty male and fifty female cadavers instead of the desired 100 of each sex, and fifty-one of those studied were over sixty years of age, the recommended upper age limit. Nevertheless, he offered his data in a variety of ways, including tables which enable one to see readily the bone length corresponding to a particular stature and *vice versa*.

Rather tragically, the general acclaim that Rollet had a right to expect did not ensue. Almost immediately (1893) Léonce Manouvrier (1850-1927), Topinard's successor as the leader of anthropology in Paris (see Figure 61), having taken exception to the way in which Rollet had developed and organized his tables, published his own version which thereafter, owing to Manouvrier's prestige, alone was widely used. The following comparison of samples from both men's tables show the nature of the differences, namely, in Rollet's case, the average lengths of long bones from cadavers of the same length, and in Manouvrier's case, the average lengths of cadavers with the same long-bone length:

Rollet, 1889, p. 30:

Male	Lower extremity			Upper extremity		
stature	Femur	Tibia	Fibula	Humerus	Radius	Ulna
cm	*mm*	*mm*	*mm*	*mm*	*mm*	*mm*
152	415	334	329	298	223	233
154	421	338	333	302	. . .	. . .
156	426	343	. . .	. . .	. . .	. . .

Manouvrier, 1893, Table 2:

Lower extremity			Male	Upper extremity		
Fibula	Tibia	Femur	stature	Humerus	Radius	Ulna
mm	*mm*	*mm*	*cm*	*mm*	*mm*	*mm*
318	319	392	153.0	295	213	227
323	324	398	155.2	298	. . .	. . .
328	330	404	157.1	. . .	. . .	. . .

Manouvrier also took into account the fact that Rollet had measured the bones while fresh. He included with his tables

Figure 55. Jean Joseph Sue.

Figure 56. Matthieu Joseph
Bonaventure Orfila.

Figure 57. Paul Broca.

Figure 58. Paul Topinard.

Figure 59. Alexander Lacassagne.

Figure 60. Étienne Rollet.

Figure 61. Léonce Manouvrier.

Figure 62. Karl Pearson.

therefore the recommendation that in using them to determine stature from dried bones, 2 mm be added to the dried-bone length for cartilage loss and that 2 cm be added to the corresponding statures in the tables to convert cadaver stature to living stature.

Manouvrier's tables in turn were superseded, although not as quickly, by a new statistical procedure of the biometric school in England. It is a tribute to Rollet, nevertheless, that his detailed skeletal data made possible this further advance. Karl Pearson (1857-1936), who was mainly responsible for this advance (see Figure 62) said at the time (1899, p. 178) that "The only data available for the calculation of the correlation between stature and long bones occur in the measurements made by Dr. Rollet on 100 corpses in the dissecting room at Lyons [sic]."*

Pearson's approach to stature estimation was based on the regression theory, which involves the calculation of standard deviations for the series of long bones and of coefficients of correlation between the different bones and stature. He regarded this theory as

> . . . better than any which has so far existed—it might not be too much to say that nothing which can be called a theory has hitherto existed [and] that it determines the constants of the formulae given by that theory as well as the existing data allow of. (P. 240.)

This evaluation still holds true.

It is to be noted in this connection that Pearson not only changed completely the prevailing approach to stature estimation, giving us a more truly "'mathematical method," but he departed in other ways from previous practices. Whereas Topinard, like his predecessors, had preferred maximum femur length (Rollet took both maximum and oblique femur lengths) and Manouvrier had preferred oblique length, Pearson went back to maximum length. And whereas both Topinard and Manouvrier had objected to the inclusion in the cadaver series of individuals over

---

*Most physical anthropologists today are aware of Rollet's contribution to stature estimation, but probably few know that, although he kept up his interest in anthropology for some time (he was President of the *Société d' Anthropologie de Lyon* in 1902), he rapidly became better known in Europe as an opthalmologist. One of his obituary notices (Bussy, 1937) fails even to mention his single foray into the forensic field.

sixty years of age, Pearson saw no reason to omit any of Rollet's aged subjects. Moreover, since Pearson's main reason for entering this field was to continue the traditional British investigation of the statures of ancient races, he produced separate series of regression equations for both fresh and dried bones.

In the latter pursuit he had to estimate what Rollet's bone lengths would have been if taken after the bones had dried. This led him to deduct from Rollet's fresh-bone lengths (1) the thicknesses of the joint cartilages given in Heinrich Werner's Inaugural Dissertation (1897), and (2) the amount of lengthening found to occur in ancient long bones when immersed in water for 120 hours. Whatever the validity of these actions, Pearson's tests of his equations led him to believe that they had general applicability, regardless of race and time period.

STEVENSON TO TROTTER. Paul Stevenson (1890-1971) was the first to test the general applicability of Pearson's equations. An American trained at Washington University School of Medicine in St. Louis (see Figure 3), he served from 1917 to 1937 as Associate Professor of Anatomy at Peking Union Medical College in China. During that time he followed Rollet's procedure of measuring the statures and long-bone lengths of the cadavers in the dissecting room, eventually ending up with data on forty-eight male Chinese. Like Pearson, he used these data to derive regression equations for estimating stature (Stevenson, 1929). Surprisingly, his equations did not work successfully with European data, and neither did Pearson's equations work successfully with Chinese data. Because Stevenson's subjects were North Chinese and most of the Chinese migrants to the United States have been the shorter South Chinese, his equations have received infrequent usage here.

Leaving aside Breitinger's (1937) contribution to this field because of its very different methodological approach, Manouvrier's tables and Pearson's equations were regarded throughout the early decades of the twentieth century as the only acceptable means of stature estimation. Also, each had its advocates. In the United States Hrdlička, who had studied with Manouvrier in 1896 and who had no taste for anything statistical, included Manouvrier's tables, but not Pearson's equations, in his *Anthro-*

pometry (1920, 1939). On the other hand, Martin's *Lehrbuch der Anthropologie* (1928), a widely used reference work on this side of the Atlantic, offered both the tables and the equations; whereas Krogman offered in his *Guide* (1939) only the equations.

The next turning point came as a result of the symposium on applied physical anthropology in 1948 mentioned in Chapter 1. In my paper at that symposium (Stewart, 1948) I commented (p. 319) on the deficiencies of the Rollet data upon which both Manouvrier's tables and Pearson's equations are based, and then said:

> Someone should work up the extensive records of cadaver stature and bone lengths assembled at Western Reserve University and Washington University [St. Louis]. We need not only better correlation data for whites, but special data for other races and a better idea of the probable error involved in individual determinations.

As it happened, Wesley Dupertuis of Case Western Reserve University and Mildred Trotter of Washington University were present at that meeting and acted upon the suggestion within the next few years (Dupertuis and Hadden, 1951; Trotter and Gleser, 1952).*

Although Dupertuis and Hadden were the first to publish, usage of their equations was almost immediately superseded by that of Trotter's and Gleser's equations. Three circumstances mainly were responsible for this: (1) Trotter and Gleser had supplemented their cadaver data with the extensive data obtained by Trotter on the young American dead of World War II (Pacific Theater) for which statures measured in life were available; (2) they had extended their racial coverage to the Mongoloid war dead; and (3) they had introduced with their equations a correction for age (Trotter and Gleser, 1951).

It is noteworthy, too, that besides producing specific equations for American whites and blacks, Dupertuis and Hadden, ignoring Stevenson's experience, had produced general equations for use on any group. They did this "by averaging the slopes and origins of the three [equations, i.e. those of Pearson's whites and their whites and blacks] for the same long bone from each racial group, weighting each according to the number in the respective population"

---

*For confirmation of this sequence of events see Trotter and Gleser, 1952, p. 467.

(p. 43). In a test, which was in no way rigorous, of one of these general equations against the corresponding Trotter and Gleser specific equation (Stewart, 1973, p. 196) I found the differences in the results to be only minimal but favorable to Trotter and Gleser. As Trotter (1970, p. 82) says,

> There is abundant evidence to indicate that, in general, the most accurate estimates of stature are obtained when the equation applied to the unknown has been derived from a representative sample of the population of the same sex, race, age, geographical area, and time period to which the unknown is believed to belong.

Recommended Procedures

WITH ADULT LIMB BONES. The foregoing explains why I am omitting here the equations of Pearson and of Dupertuis and Hadden (and of course Manouvrier's tables) and concentrating on the results of Trotter's and Gleser's studies as the best now available for use on the long limb bones of specific elements of the American population. In the event that someone should want some of the older regression equations not given here, he or she likely will find them in Krogman's book (1962). For more recent ones on East Africans see Allbrook (1961), on western Europeans (mainly French) see Lorke *et al.* (1953), and on Japanese see Fujii (1958).

A further reason for concentrating .here on the results of the Trotter and Gleser studies is the fact that these results were put to a test in connection with the Korean War (see Chapter 1). This test led Trotter and Gleser to conclude (1958) that the original findings needed no change. At the same time the data studied enabled them to develop new equations for American Mongoloid and Mexican males, and to show that the original equations for blacks are appropriate for Puerto Ricans. Since these investigators were the first Americans in this century to deal with samples of more than 100 of each sex, their work gains in impressiveness when considered in relation to the size of the samples used in the combined studies (Table XXV).

The most useful of the Trotter and Gleser equations are given in Table XXVI. For each equation read: Estimated stature (cm) = Factor × bone length (cm) + factor ± standard error of estimate (cm). To be on the safe side double the standard

TABLE XXV

SOURCES AND NUMBERS OF THE INDIVIDUALS STUDIED BY
TROTTER AND GLESER*

Racial Groups	World War II Males	Korean War Males	Terry Collection Males	Terry Collection Females	Total
Whites	710	2817	255	63	3845
Blacks	80	385	360	177	1002
Mongoloids	—	68	—	—	68
Mexicans	—	63	—	—	63
Puerto Ricans	—	49	—	—	49
Total	790	3382	615	240	5027

*As summarized by Trotter, Estimation of stature from intact long limb bones. In Stewart, T. D. (Ed.): *Personal Identification in Mass Disasters,* p. 72, 1970. Courtesy of the National Museum of Natural History, Washington.

error. For convenience Table XXVII gives the maximum stature expected from a wide range of lengths of long bones for each sex of both whites and blacks.

In using the equations Trotter and Gleser recommend (1952, p. 474) that when both bones of a pair are present their maximum lengths be averaged. "It seems impractical and unnecessary," they say (p. 476), "to make an adjustment when only one bone of a pair is available for stature estimation." For all the long bones except the tibia, maximum length is just what the term has always implied as regards bones which are dry and without cartilage. In the exceptional case, the tibia is placed on the osteometric board dorsal side down, with the end of the maleolus touching the fixed vertical end, and with the long axis of the bone parallel with the long axis of the board. The movable block or upright is then applied to the most prominent part of the lateral half of the lateral condyle.

Given a skeleton with some or all of the long bones present, it is not necessary to measure every one of them in order to estimate stature by the mathematical method of Trotter and Gleser. In the first place, since the lengths of the lower-limb long bones are more highly correlated with stature than are the lengths of the upper-limb long bones (r is approximately 0.86 vs. 0.76), "it can be stated as a general rule that in no case should lengths of upper

TABLE XXVI

TROTTER'S AND GLESER'S BEST EQUATIONS FOR ESTIMATING
LIVING STATURE (CM) FROM THE LONG BONES, ARRANGED
IN ORDER OF INCREASING STANDARD ERROR*

White Males			Black Males		
1.30 (Fem + Tib)	+ 63.29	± 2.99	1.15 (Fem + Tib)	+ 71.04	± 3.53
2.38 Fem	+ 61.41	± 3.27	2.19 Tib	+ 86.02	± 3.78
2.68 Fib	+ 71.78	± 3.29	2.11 Fem	+ 70.35	± 3.94
2.52 Tib	+ 78.62	± 3.37	2.19 Fib	+ 85.65	± 4.08
3.08 Hum	+ 70.45	± 4.05	3.42 Rad	+ 81.56	± 4.30
3.78 Rad	+ 79.01	± 4.32	3.26 Ulna	+ 79.29	± 4.42
3.70 Ulna	+ 74.05	± 4.32	3.26 Hum	+ 62.10	± 4.43
White Females			Black Females		
1.39 (Fem + Tib)	+ 53.20	± 3.55	1.26 (Fem + Tib)	+ 59.72	± 3.28
2.93 Fib	+ 59.61	± 3.57	2.28 Fem	+ 59.76	± 3.41
2.90 Tib	+ 61.53	± 3.66	2.45 Tib	+ 72.65	± 3.70
2.47 Fem	+ 54.10	± 3.72	2.49 Fib	+ 70.90	± 3.80
4.74 Rad	+ 54.93	± 4.24	3.08 Hum	+ 64.67	± 4.25
4.27 Ulna	+ 57.76	± 4.30	†3.67 Rad	+ 71.79	± 4.59
3.36 Hum	+ 57.97	± 4.45	3.31 Ulna	+ 75.38	± 4.83
Mongoloid Males			Mexican Males		
1.22 (Fem + Tib)	+ 70.37	± 3.24	******		
2.40 Fib	+ 80.56	± 3.24	2.44 Fem	+ 58.67	± 2.99
2.39 Tib	+ 81.45	± 3.27	2.50 Fib	+ 75.44	± 3.52
2.15 Fem	+ 72.57	± 3.80	2.36 Tib	+ 80.62	± 3.73
2.68 Hum	+ 83.19	± 4.25	3.55 Rad	+ 80.71	± 4.04
3.54 Rad	+ 82.00	± 4.60	3.56 Ulna	+ 74.56	± 4.05
3.48 Ulna	+ 77.45	± 4.66	2.92 Hum	+ 73.94	± 4.24

*From Trotter, Estimation of stature from intact long limb bones. In Stewart,
T.D. (Ed.): *Personal Identification in Mass Disasters*, pp. 71-83, Table XXVIII,
1970. Courtesy of the National Museum of Natural History, Washington.
These equations apply to individuals between the ages of eighteen and thirty.
To estimate stature of older individuals subtract 0.06 (age in years —30) cm;
to estimate cadaver stature add 2.5 cm.
†Corrected in accordance with Trotter and Gleser (1977).

limb bones be used in the estimation of stature unless no lower
limb bone is available" (Trotter and Gleser, 1958, p. 120). Be
guided in the choice of equation to use by the smallness of the
error of estimate. "Do not estimate stature by determining the
average of estimates obtained from several equations, each of
which is based on a different bone or a combination of bones"
(Trotter and Gleser, 1958, p. 119).

Essentials of Forensic Anthropology

TABLE XXVII
EXPECTED MAXIMUM STATURE FROM LONG BONE LENGTHS
(MAXIMUM)AS DETERMINED WITH THE APPROPRIATE EQUATION
IN TABLE XXVI: AMERICAN WHITE MALES*

Hum	Rad	Ulna	Stature†		Fem	Tib	Fib	Fem + Tib
mm	*mm*	*mm*	*cm*	*in‡*	*mm*	*mm*	*mm*	*mm*
265	193	211	152	59^7	381	291	299	685
268	196	213	153	60^2	385	295	303	693
271	198	216	154	60^5	389	299	307	701
275	201	219	155	61	393	303	311	708
278	204	222	156	61^3	398	307	314	716
281	206	224	157	61^6	402	311	318	723
284	209	227	158	62^2	406	315	322	731
288	212	230	159	62^5	410	319	326	738
291	214	232	160	63	414	323	329	746
294	217	235	161	63^3	419	327	333	753
297	220	238	162	63^6	423	331	337	761
301	222	240	163	64^1	427	335	340	769
304	225	243	164	64^5	431	339	344	776
307	228	246	165	65	435	343	348	784
310	230	249	166	65^3	440	347	352	791
314	233	251	167	65^6	444	351	355	799
317	235	254	168	66^1	448	355	359	806
320	238	257	169	66^4	452	359	363	814
323	241	259	170	66^7	456	363	367	821
327	243	262	171	67^3	461	367	370	829
330	246	265	172	67^6	465	371	374	837
333	249	267	173	68^1	469	375	378	844
336	251	270	174	68^4	473	379	381	852
339	254	273	175	68^7	477	383	385	859
343	257	276	176	69^2	482	386	389	867
346	259	278	177	69^5	486	390	393	874
349	262	281	178	70^1	490	394	396	882
352	265	284	179	70^4	494	398	400	889
356	267	286	180	70^7	498	402	404	897
359	270	289	181	71^2	503	406	408	905
362	272	292	182	71^5	507	410	411	912
365	275	294	183	72	511	414	415	920
369	278	297	184	72^4	515	418	419	927
372	280	300	185	72^7	519	422	422	935
375	283	303	186	73^2	524	426	426	942
378	286	305	187	73^5	528	430	430	950
382	288	308	188	74	532	434	434	957
385	291	311	189	74^3	536	438	437	965
388	294	313	190	74^6	540	442	441	973
391	296	316	191	75^2	545	446	445	980

TABLE XXVII — CONTINUED (1)

395	299	319	192	75^5	549	450	449	988
398	302	321	193	76	553	454	452	995
401	304	324	194	76^3	557	458	456	1003
404	307	327	195	76^6	561	462	460	1010
408	309	330	196	77^1	566	466	463	1018
411	312	332	197	77^4	570	470	467	1026
414	315	335	198	78	574	474	471	1033

AMERICAN BLACK MALES

Hum	Rad	Ulna	Stature		Fem	Tib	Fib	Fem + Tib
mm	*mm*	*mm*	*cm*	*in*	*mm*	*mm*	*mm*	*mm*
276	206	223	152	59^7	387	301	303	704
279	209	226	153	60^2	391	306	308	713
282	212	229	154	60^5	396	310	312	721
285	215	232	155	61	401	315	317	730
288	218	235	156	61^3	406	320	321	739
291	221	238	157	61^6	410	324	326	747
294	224	242	158	62^2	415	329	330	756
297	226	245	159	62^5	420	333	335	765
300	229	248	160	63	425	338	339	774
303	232	251	161	63^3	430	342	344	782
306	235	254	162	63^6	434	347	349	791
310	238	257	163	64^1	439	352	353	800
313	241	260	164	64^5	444	356	358	808
316	244	263	165	65	449	361	362	817
319	247	266	166	65^3	453	365	367	826
322	250	269	167	65^6	458	370	371	834
325	253	272	168	66^1	463	374	376	843
328	256	275	169	66^4	468	379	381	852
331	259	278	170	66^7	472	383	385	861
334	262	281	171	67^3	477	388	390	869
337	264	284	172	67^6	482	393	394	878
340	267	287	173	68^1	487	397	399	887
343	270	291	174	68^4	491	402	403	895
346	273	294	175	68^7	496	406	408	904
349	276	297	176	69^3	501	411	413	913
352	279	300	177	69^5	506	415	417	921
356	282	303	178	70	510	420	422	930
359	285	306	179	70^4	515	425	426	939
362	288	309	180	70^7	520	429	431	947
365	291	312	181	71^2	525	434	435	956
368	294	315	182	71^5	529	438	440	965
371	297	318	183	72	534	443	445	974
374	300	321	184	72^4	539	447	449	982

TABLE XXVII — CONTINUED (2)

377	302	324	185	72^7	544	452	454	991
380	305	327	186	73^2	548	456	458	1000
383	308	330	187	73^5	553	461	463	1008
386	311	333	188	74	558	466	467	1017
389	314	336	189	74^3	563	470	472	1026
392	317	340	190	74^6	567	475	476	1034
395	320	343	191	75^2	572	479	481	1043
398	323	346	192	75^5	577	484	486	1052
401	326	349	193	76	582	488	490	1061
405	329	352	194	76^3	586	493	495	1069
408	332	355	195	76^6	591	498	499	1078
411	335	358	196	77^1	596	502	504	1087
414	337	361	197	77^4	601	507	508	1095
417	340	364	198	78	605	511	513	1104

AMERICAN WHITE FEMALES

Hum	Rad	Ulna	Stature		Fem	Tib	Fib	Fem + Tib
mm	mm	mm	cm	in	mm	mm	mm	mm
244	179	193	140	55^1	348	271	274	624
247	182	195	141	55^4	352	274	278	632
250	184	197	142	55^7	356	277	281	639
253	186	200	143	56^2	360	281	285	646
256	188	202	144	56^6	364	284	288	653
259	190	204	145	57^1	368	288	291	660
262	192	207	146	57^4	372	291	295	668
265	194	209	147	57^7	376	295	298	675
268	196	211	148	58^2	380	298	302	682
271	198	214	149	58^5	384	302	305	689
274	201	216	150	59	388	305	309	696
277	203	218	151	59^4	392	309	312	704
280	205	221	152	59^7	396	312	315	711
283	207	223	153	60^2	400	315	319	718
286	209	225	154	60^5	404	319	322	725
289	211	228	155	61	409	322	326	732
292	213	230	156	61^3	413	326	329	740
295	215	232	157	61^6	417	329	332	747
298	217	235	158	62^2	421	333	336	754
301	220	237	159	62^5	425	336	340	761
304	222	239	160	63	429	340	343	768
307	224	242	161	63^3	433	343	346	776
310	226	244	162	63^6	437	346	349	783
313	228	246	163	64^1	441	350	353	790
316	230	249	164	64^5	445	353	356	797
319	232	251	165	65	449	357	360	804

TABLE XXVII — CONTINUED (3)

322	234	253	166	65^3	453	360	363	812
324	236	256	167	65^6	457	364	366	819
327	239	258	168	66^1	461	367	370	826
330	241	261	169	66^4	465	371	373	833
333	243	263	170	66^7	469	374	377	840
336	245	265	171	67^3	473	377	380	847
339	247	268	172	67^6	477	381	384	855
342	249	270	173	68^1	481	384	387	862
345	251	272	174	68^4	485	388	390	869
348	253	275	175	68^7	489	391	394	876
351	255	277	176	69^2	494	395	397	883
354	258	279	177	69^5	498	398	401	891
357	260	282	178	70^1	502	402	404	898
360	262	284	179	70^4	506	405	407	905
363	264	286	180	70^7	510	409	411	912
366	266	289	181	71^2	514	412	414	919
369	268	291	182	71^5	518	415	418	927
372	270	293	183	72	522	419	421	934
375	272	296	184	72^4	526	422	425	941

AMERICAN BLACK FEMALES

Hum	Rad§	Ulna	Stature		Fem	Tib	Fib	Fem + Tib
mm	*mm*	*mm*	*cm*	*in*	*mm*	*mm*	*mm*	*mm*
245	186	195	140	55^1	352	275	278	637
248	189	198	141	55^4	356	279	282	645
251	191	201	142	55^7	361	283	286	653
254	194	204	143	56^2	365	287	290	661
258	197	207	144	56^6	369	291	294	669
261	199	210	145	57^1	374	295	298	677
264	202	213	146	57^4	378	299	302	685
267	205	216	147	57^7	383	303	306	693
271	208	219	148	58^2	387	308	310	701
274	210	222	149	58^5	391	312	314	709
277	213	225	150	59	396	316	318	717
280	216	228	151	59^4	400	320	322	724
284	218	231	152	59^7	405	324	326	732
287	221	235	153	60^2	409	328	330	740
290	224	238	154	60^5	413	332	334	748
293	227	241	155	61	418	336	338	756
297	229	244	156	61^3	422	340	342	764
300	232	247	157	61^6	426	344	346	772
303	235	250	158	62^2	431	348	350	780
306	238	253	159	62^5	435	352	354	788
310	240	256	160	63	440	357	358	796

Essentials of Forensic Anthropology

TABLE XXVII — CONTINUED (4)
AMERICAN BLACK FEMALES

Hum	Rad§	Ulna	Stature		Fem	Tib	Fib	Fem + Tib
313	243	259	161	63³	444	361	362	804
316	246	262	162	63⁶	448	365	366	812
319	249	265	163	64¹	453	369	370	820
322	251	268	164	64⁵	457	373	374	828
326	254	271	165	65	462	377	378	836
329	257	274	166	65³	466	381	382	843
332	259	277	167	65⁶	470	385	386	851
335	262	280	168	66¹	475	389	390	859
339	265	283	169	66⁴	479	393	394	867
342	268	286	170	66⁷	484	397	398	875
345	270	289	171	67³	488	401	402	883
348	273	292	172	67⁶	492	406	406	891
352	276	295	173	68¹	497	410	410	899
355	279	298	174	68⁴	501	414	414	907
358	281	301	175	68⁷	505	418	418	915
361	284	304	176	69²	510	422	422	923
365	287	307	177	69⁵	514	426	426	931
368	289	310	178	70¹	519	430	430	939
371	292	313	179	70⁴	523	434	434	947
374	295	316	180	70⁷	527	438	438	955
378	298	319	181	71²	532	442	442	963
381	300	322	182	71⁵	536	446	446	970
384	303	325	183	72	541	450	450	978
387	306	328	184	72⁴	545	454	454	986

*From Trotter, Estimation of stature from intact long limb bones. In Stewart, T.D. (Ed.): *Personal Identification in Mass Disasters,* pp. 71-83, Appendices 1-4 to Table XXVIII, 1970. Courtesy of the National Museum of Natural History, Washington.

†The expected maximum stature should be reduced by the amount of .06 (age in years —30) cm to obtain expected stature of individuals over thirty years of age. "Do not infer any relationship between bone lengths given on the same line. Differences in standard errors and regression coefficients preclude the possibility of using one bone length in this table to obtain the best estimate of another bone length or to estimate a bone length from a given stature." (Personal communication from Trotter, March 16, 1977.)

‡The raised number indicates the numerator of a fraction of an inch expressed in eighths, thus 59⁷ should read 59⅞ inches.

§Figures in this column corrected (Trotter and Gleser, 1977).

With Adult Limb Bones Plus Vertebrae. In 1960 Fully and Pineau of France introduced an important variation of the prevailing mathematical method of stature estimation.* They took into consideration the fact that the combined lengths of the femur and tibia represent less than half of the combined lengths of all the skeletal parts contributing to stature and that of all the other parts the longest and most variable is the vertebral column. Recognizing that in a disarticulated skeleton quantification of the total length of the vertebral column in its natural position is a time-consuming operation, these authors interpreted vertebral column length as the summation of the maximum heights of the individual vertebral bodies of C2 to L5 inclusive. They simplified the procedure further by searching for the most representative parts of the column and found that, for example, the coefficient of correlation (r) for the vertical heights of D5-7 + L1-3 vs. total length of the column is 0.952 and thus higher than that of the femur or tibia.†

Next, Fully and Pineau examined the correlation between stature and a combination of representative parts from the trunk and lower extremities. The combinations most favored were (1) femur length with length (height) of the five lumbar vertebrae (correlation with stature 0.926), and (2) tibia length with length (height) of the five lumbar vertebrae (correlation with stature 0.908). For these two combinations they developed the following regression equations for use in estimating male stature:

---

*Fully had already published (1956) an important simplification of the anatomical method (see concluding subsection of this chapter.)

†Fully and Pineau do not indicate whether or not they were aware that Pearson had advocated this course of action in an editorial note to Stevenson's (1929) publication (pp. 320-321):

> If we consider the parts of the skeleton not taken into consideration [in stature-prediction formulae] . . . we naturally turn to the vertebral column as the most important. Of course the pelvic and cranial heights might present appreciable correlations, but the first subject for study seems to me the vertebral column. At present nobody knows the correlation between individual vertebrae, nor the correlation between any individual vertebra and the total length of the column. It is quite possible that it might not be needful to use all the vertebrae, but that the correlation of stature with the height of one or two vertebrae might be nearly as efficient as measuring the whole series.

$$2.09 \text{ (Fem + 5 lumbars)} + 12.67 \pm 2.35 \text{ cm}$$
$$2.32 \text{ (Tib + 5 lumbars)} + 48.63 \pm 2.54 \text{ cm}$$

Considering their low standard errors, these equations may prove to yield more reliable stature estimates for some European populations than any of the Trotter and Gleser equations. Keep in mind, however, that they have not yet been tested on the generally taller American population. Actually, the Fully and Pineau equations have a substantial basis in that for their calculation these authors drew upon their measurements on 164 skeletons of males (15% French, 27% Italians; 58% other European nationalities) who had died in a World War II concentration camp (their statures recorded in life).*

In using the equations of Fully and Pineau it is important to measure the long bones in the same ways as in the original study, i.e. to take the oblique length of the femur and the maximum length of the tibia (spine excluded). These measurements are different from those used in the Trotter and Gleser equations (see final subsection of this chapter). For convenience, Fully and Pineau supplement the equation involving the femur with Table XXVIII.

WITH PARTIAL ADULT LIMB BONES. Up to this point the long bones used in the estimation of stature have been assumed to be complete. What about skeletons with long limb bones fragmented and none entire? Gertrude Müller of Vienna attempted to answer this question in 1935. Limiting her attention to the tibia, humerus and radius, she divided them into readily defined segments and calculated the percentage of whole bone length represented by each.

More recently (1970) Gentry Steele used the least squares method of regression correlation in an attempt to improve the answer. Replacing the radius with the femur (Figure 63), he defined (pp. 87-88) the following bony landmarks:

---

*Tibbetts (1977) obtained a maximum corpus height/total spinal length ratio for each vertebra in 100 male blacks from the Terry Collection that in the mean was virtually identical with each of those given by Fully and Pineau.

TABLE XXVIII

EXPECTED STATURE FROM COMBINATIONS OF OBLIQUE FEMUR
LENGTH AND LUMBAR SPINE LENGTH: WHITE MALES*

Femur plus lumbar spine	Stature	Femur plus lumbar spine	Stature
cm	*cm*	*cm*	*cm*
49	145.08	60	168.07
50	147.17	61	170.16
51	149.26	62	172.25
52	151.35	63	174.34
53	153.44	64	176.43
54	155.53	65	178.52
55	157.62	66	180.61
56	159.71	67	182.70
57	161.80	68	184.79
58	163.89	69	186.88
59	165.98	70	188.97

*From Fully and Pineau, Détermination de la stature au moyen du squelette. *Ann Méd Lég*, *40*:145-154, Table II, 1960. Courtesy of *Ann Méd Lég*.

Femur:

1. The most proximal point on the head.
2. The midpoint of the lesser trochanter.
3. The most proximal extension of the popliteal surface at the point where the medial and lateral supracondylar lines become parallel below the linea aspera.
4. The most proximal point of the intercondylar fossa.
5. The most distal point of the medial condyle.

Tibia:

1. The most prominent point on the lateral half of the lateral condyle.
2. The most proximal point of the tibial tuberosity.
3. The point of confluence for the lines extending from the lower end of the tuberosity.
4. The point where the anterior crest crosses over to the medial border of the shaft above the medial malleolus.
5. The proximal margin of the inferior articular surface at a point opposite the tip of the medial malleolus.

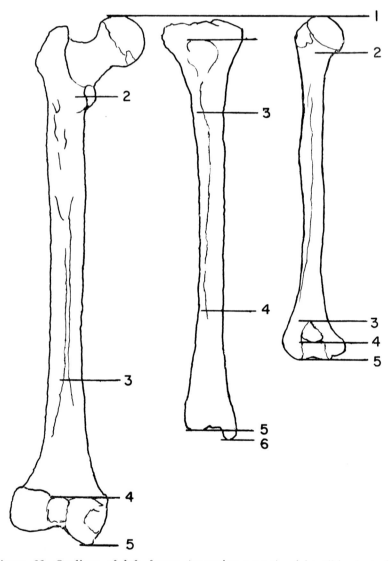

Figure 63. Outlines of left femur (posterior aspect), right tibia (anterior aspect), and left humerus (posterior aspect) shown in the positions used to measure their maximum lengths and the lengths of segments thereof between numbered landmarks (segment 1 is between landmarks 1 and 2; segment 2 is between landmarks 2 and 3, etc.). The line leading from Number 1 does not touch the proximal end of the tibia due to the fact that the landmark there is on the lateral side of the lateral condyle. (From Steele, Estimation of stature from fragments of long limb bones. In Stewart, T.D. (Ed.): *Personal Identification in Mass Disasters*, pp. 85-97, Figure 23, 1970b. (Courtesy of the National Museum of Natural History, Washington.)

6. The most distal point on the medial malleolus.

Humerus:

1. The most proximal point on the head.
2. The most distal point of the circumference of the head.
3. The proximal margin of the olecranon fossa.
4. The distal margin of the olecranon fossa.
5. The most distal point on the trochlea.

Applying the segments thus defined to documented bones from the Terry Collection (113 whites, 99 blacks) Steele produced large series of equations involving various combinations of the segments. To reproduce all of these equations here would be too space consuming. Therefore, I have selected the equations (Tables XXIX-XXXI) that are useful when the incomplete bones under study lack

TABLE XXIX

REGRESSION EQUATIONS FOR CALCULATING LIVING STATURE
AND STANDARD ERROR (IN CM) FROM AN INCOMPLETE FEMUR*

White Males (mean age = 52.97)

2.71 (Fem 2) + 3.06 (Fem 3) + 73.00 ± 4.41
2.89 (Fem 1) + 2.31 (Fem 2) + 2.62 (Fem 3) + 63.88 ± 3.93
2.35 (Fem 2) + 2.65 (Fem 3) + 7.92 (Fem 4) + 54.97 ± 3.95

Black Males (mean age = 43.25)

2.59 (Fem 2) + 2.91 (Fem 3) + 75.74 ± 3.72
1.20 (Fem 1) + 2.48 (Fem 2) + 2.78 (Fem 3) + 69.94 ± 3.71
2.53 (Fem 2) + 2.84 (Fem 3) + 2.40 (Fem 4) + 68.32 ± 3.72

White Females (mean age = 63.35)

2.80 (Fem 2) + 1.46 (Fem 3) + 76.67 ± 4.91
2.16 (Fem 1) + 2.50 (Fem 2) + 1.45 (Fem 3) + 68.86 ± 4.81
2.57 (Fem 2) + 1.21 (Fem 3) + 5.03 (Fem 4) + 66.05 ± 4.77

Black Females (mean age = 39.58)

2.12 (Fem 2) + 1.68 (Fem 3) + 93.29 ± 6.17
3.63 (Fem 1) + 1.86 (Fem 2) + 1.27 (Fem 3) + 77.15 ± 5.80
2.00 (Fem 2) + 1.08 (Fem 3) + 6.32 (Fem 4) + 77.71 ± 6.01

*From Steele, Estimation of stature from fragments of long limb bones. In Stewart, T.D. (Ed.): *Personal Identification in Mass Disasters*, pp. 85-97, Table XLVIII, 1970b. Courtesy of the National Musems of Natural History, Washington. See text for age correction.

TABLE XXX

REGRESSION EQUATIONS FOR CALCULATING LIVING STATURE
AND STANDARD ERROR (IN CM) FROM AN INCOMPLETE TIBIA*

White Males (mean age = 52.97)

3.52 (Tib 2) + 2.89 (Tib 3) + 2.23 (Tib 4) + 74.55 ± 4.56
2.87 (Tib 3) + 2.96 (Tib 4) − 0.96 (Tib 5) + 92.36 ± 5.45
4.19 (Tib 1) + 3.63 (Tib 2) + 2.69 (Tib 3) + 2.10 (Tib 4) + 64.95 ± 4.22
3.54 (Tib 2) + 2.96 (Tib 3) + 2.8 (Tib 4) − 1.56 (Tib 5) + 75.98 ± 4.60

Black Males (mean age = 43.25)

2.26 (Tib 2) + 2.22 (Tib 3) + 3.17 (Tib 4) + 5.86 ± 3.88
2.23 (Tib 3) + 3.51 (Tib 4) + 0.51 (Tib 5) + 91.70 ± 4.49
1.79 (Tib 1) + 2.18 (Tib 2) + 2.25 (Tib 3) + 3.10 (Tib 4) + 75.87 ± 3.88
2.32 (Tib 2) + 2.23 (Tib 3) + 3.19 (Tib 4) − 1.60 (Tib 5) + 82.50 ± 3.92

White Females (mean age = 63.35)

4.17 (Tib 2) + 2.96 (Tib 3) + 2.16 (Tib 4) + 66.09 ± 4.69
2.75 (Tib 3) + 3.65 (Tib 4) + 1.17 (Tib 5) + 79.92 ± 5.69
1.51 (Tib 1) + 4.03 (Tib 2) + 2.97 (Tib 3) + 2.12 (Tib 4) + 62.89 ± 4.71
4.31 (Tib 2) + 3.05 (Tib 3) + 2.20 (Tib 4) − 2.34 (Tib 5) + 66.60 ± 4.72

Black Females (mean age = 39.58)

2.56 (Tib 2) + 2.21 (Tib 3) + 1.56 (Tib 4) + 91.91 ± 4.59
2.11 (Tib 3) + 2.61 (Tib 4) + 3.58 (Tib 5) + 94.57 ± 5.69
3.60 (Tib 1) + 2.15 (Tib 3) + 2.26 (Tib 3) + 1.84 (Tib 4) + 81.11 ± 4.46
2.58 (Tib 2) + 2.17 (Tib 3) + 1.63 (Tib 4) + 3.80 (Tib 5) + 86.64 ± 4.59

*From Steele, Estimation of stature from fragments of long limb bones. In Stewart, T.D. (Ed.): *Personal Identification in Mass Disasters,* pp. 85-97, Table XLIX, 1970b. Courtesy of the National Museum of Natural History, Washington. See text for age correction.

no more than one or both extremities and that enable one to go directly to the stature estimate, employing at the same time a modification of the Trotter and Gleser correction for age. In the latter connection note that in Tables XXIX-XXXI a mean age is given for each sex of each racial group. This figure is to be used in the age-correction formula referred to: 0.06 [(mean age of sample−30) − (assumed age of individual) −30/cm)].

The following example shows how to use the equations and the age correction. If a fragment of femur from a black male with an estimated age of thirty-five years includes segments 2 and 3 measuring 28.34 and 7.51, respectively, then the pertinent equa-

TABLE XXXI
REGRESSION EQUATIONS FOR CALCULATING LIVING STATURE
AND STANDARD ERROR (IN CM) FROM AN INCOMPLETE HUMERUS*

White Males (mean age = 52.97)

3.42 (Hum 2) + 80.94 ± 5.31
7.17 (Hum 1) + 3.04 (Hum 2) + 63.94 ± 5.05
3.19 (Hum 2) + 5.97 (Hum 3) + 74.82 ± 5.15
7.84 (Hum 1) + 2.73 (Hum 2) + 6.74 (Hum 3) + 55.45 ± 4.80
2.94 (Hum 2) + 6.34 (Hum 3) + 4.60 (Hum 4) + 72.54 ± 5.14

Black Males (mean age = 43.25)

3.80 (Hum 2) + 70.68 ± 4.94
8.13 (Hum 1) + 3.34 (Hum 2) + 51.98 ± 4.56
3.79 (Hum 2) + 0.69 (Hum 3) + 69.53 ± 5.00
8.12 (Hum 1) + 3.33 (Hum 2) + 0.56 (Hum 3) + 51.08 ± 4.62
3.76 (Hum 2) + 1.19 (Hum 3) + 4.54 (Hum 4) + 61.58 ± 5.00

White Females (mean age = 63.35)

3.87 (Hum 2) + 66.14 ± 5.40
8.84 (Hum 1) + 3.65 (Hum 2) + 42.43 ± 5.14
3.77 (Hum 2) + 3.35 (Hum 3) + 62.59 ± 5.42
8.55 (Hum 1) + 3.60 (Hum 2) + 1.93 (Hum 3) + 41.16 ± 5.18
3.44 (Hum 2) + 2.92 (Hum 3) + 10.84 (Hum 4) + 54.91 ± 5.16

Black Females (mean age = 39.58)

2.95 (Hum 2) + 89.15 ± 4.88
5.05 (Hum 1) + 2.64 (Hum 2) + 80.13 ± 4.83
2.75 (Hum 2) + 3.76 (Hum 3) + 87.08 ± 4.85
4.54 (Hum 1) + 2.50 (Hum 2) + 3.19 (Hum 3) + 79.29 ± 4.82
2.66 (Hum 2) + 4.03 (Hum 3) + 2.83 (Hum 4) + 84.25 ± 4.87

*From Steele, Estimation of stature from fragments of long limb bones. In Stewart, T.D. (Ed.): *Personal Identification in Mass Disasters*, pp. 85-97, Table L, 1970b. Courtesy of the National Museum of Natural History, Washington. See text for age correction.

tion in Table XXIX is:

2.59 (Fem 2) + 2.91 (Fem. 3) + 75.74 ± 3.72 cm

The mean age of the sample from which this equation was developed is 43.25 years. Substituting and calculating:

2.59 (28.34) + 2.91 (7.51) + 75.74 = 170.99 ± 3.72 cm

Age correction:

0.06 [(43.25 − 30) − (35 − 30)], or 0.06 (13.25 − 5) = 0.4950 cm.

Therefore, the estimated stature is 170.99 + 0.4950, or 171.48 ±

3.72 cm.*

WITH SUBADULT LIMB BONES. Investigations of stature estimation from skeletal parts have been confined until recently to adults. This is due both to the lack of documented subadult skeletons for study and to the failure usually of parents to keep up-to-date and accurate records of their rapidly-growing children's statures for purposes of comparison in forensic situations.

In Finland Telkkä *et al.* (1962) sought to remedy this deficiency by measuring on radiographs the diaphysial lengths of the long limb bones of 3848 children under fifteen years of age. The authors were well aware that the application of their resulting regression equations to the skeletonized remains of children other than those of the Finnish and related peoples might produce misleading results. Therefore, their main objective was to show the way in this line of research. Since I agree with this attitude, I shall simply bring this matter to attention here without giving further details.

ANATOMICAL METHOD

As pointed out at the beginning of this chapter, in 1894 Dwight felt that his anatomical method (which he had been perfecting since 1875) yielded a more accurate estimate of stature than any form of the mathematical method developed up to that time. Yet he seems not to have given much thought to such practical considerations as the great amount of time and expertise required to apply the anatomical method and the great dependence of this method on skeletal completeness. Putting such drawbacks in the form of a question: In view of the fact that for most unknowns records of stature made in life are unavailable for comparison, are efforts to achieve highly accurate estimates by the anatomical method warranted? In seeking an answer to this question the main thrust of this subsection will be to show the progress made in simplifying the anatomical method while at the same time maintaining the claimed accuracy.

Since Dwight appears to have been the first to provide a sound

---

*Note: If the assumed age is greater than the mean age of the sample, the correction is subtracted.

base of observations for the anatomical method, the procedure by which he estimated stature is the standard, naturally, against which progress toward greater practicality must be judged. Acceptance of this point requires a summary of the Dwight method.

As Practiced by Dwight

Essentially the Dwight method comprises nine steps for the execution of which a stout laboratory table long enough for laying out a supine skeleton is required, along with enough modeling clay to support the individual bones in proper articulation. Presumably Dwight had the table graduated metrically to facilitate measuring the total length of the skeleton. The steps are as follow:

1. Making due allowance at the top end of the table for the eventual addition of the skull (step 8), embed the atlas and each succeeding vertebra down to the sacrum in a bed of clay with careful attention to the articulation of the posterior facets and thereby the reconstruction of the original curves.*

2. Add the pelvis, articulating the posterior sacral facets with those of L5 in the same way as for the other vertebrae and taking care that the anterior superior spines of the ilia are on the same horizontal plane as the spines of the pubes.

---

*As a check on the accuracy of the result Dwight provided (1894a, p. 293) the following average lengths (following the curvatures) of the three regions of the spine, along with their percentages of the whole spinal length (disk at the junction of two regions reckoned with the upper one):

	Male		Female	
	cm	%	cm	%
Cervical	13.3	21.5	12.1	21.2
Thoracic	28.7	46.3	26.5	46.1
Lumbar	19.9	32.2	18.7	32.7
Total	61.9	100.0	57.3	100.0

This system of proportions is especially valuable in cases where a few vertebrae are missing. However, Dwight advised (1894a, pp. 293-294) that in so far as anomalies of number in the spine concern the putting together the bone "it obliges the expert to disregard the arbitrary rules of proportions and to arrange the vertebrae as best he can."

3. Place the head of one of the femora in its acetabulum, making sure that the femoral head does not touch the rim of the acetabulum and that the plane of the inferior surfaces of both condyles is at a right angle to the long axis of the table.
4. Add the tibia, leaving a space of 6 mm between it and the femur.
5. Add the talus, leaving a space of 3 mm between it and the tibia.
6. Add the calcaneus, leaving a space of 3 mm between it and the talus.
7. Allow 12 mm for the soft parts of the sole of the foot.
8. Add the skull to the atlas, leaving a space of 3 mm between their condyles.
9. Allow 6 mm for the thickness of the scalp.

The sum of the allowances for cartilage and external tissues in the foregoing procedure amounts to 32 mm. This figure seems to have satisfied Dwight because of its closeness to the figure recommended by Topinard—35 mm—to be added to skeletal length for the soft parts.

As Practiced by Fully

Fully's interest in using the vertebral column in connection with the estimation of stature has already been mentioned. It is helpful to know how he came by this interest. In 1955 the French *Ministère des Anciens Combattants et Victimes de la Guerre* charged him with the medicolegal examination and identification of the French deportees who, before the date of liberation, had died in, and been buried near, the concentration camp at Mauthausen, Austria. Of 3165 skeletonized remains examined there only 102 retained identification tags that led to records of stature made in life. In each case in this documented sample Fully estimated stature by both mathematical and anatomical methods, i.e. the Rollet-Manouvrier mathematical method vs. an anatomical method of his own devising to be described next. As compared with the recorded statures, the results by his anatomical method proved to be better than those by the Rollet-Manouvrier method, with the error of estimation for the former not exceeding 2 to 3 cm (62% under 1 cm). The error by the Rollet-Manouvrier method extended to 8 to 9 cm (with only 25% under 1 cm).

In 1956 when Fully described his anatomical method in print he called it a "new method," because he was not aware of Dwight's effort along this line. In 1960 when he mentioned this matter again in connection with his (and Pineau's) variation of the mathematical method described above, he gave proper credit to Dwight and reserved credit to himself only for some important simplifications of the procedure.

The essence of Fully's simplifications are (1) the putting together of the bone measurements instead of the bones themselves, and (2) the substitution of a single correction factor for all the spaces between the bones plus scalp and sole thicknesses. The measurements utilized (pp. 268-269) are as follow:

SKULL. Basion-bregma height taken with spreading caliper.

C2 TO L5 INCLUSIVE. Maximum height of the corpus of each taken with spreading caliper.*

S1. Anterior height taken with sliding caliper.

FEMUR. Oblique length taken on standard osteometric board.

TIBIA. Length without spine (the bicondylar length of Hrdlička (Stewart, Ed., 1947, p. 170)) taken on Broca's osteometric board.

TALUS AND CALCANEUS ARTICULATED. Distance between the superior part of the tibiotalar articular surface and the most inferior part of the bearing surface of the calcaneus taken on standard osteometric board.

The correction factor is as follows:

For skeletal statures of 153.5 cm or less add 10.0 cm
For skeletal statures of 153.6 — 165.4 cm add 10.5 cm
For skeletal statures of 165.5 cm or more add 11.5 cm

An example of how the stature calculation is carried out is

---

*The height of the dens is included in the height of C2 and thus takes care of the height of the atlas. Adjustments must be made for pathological conditions affecting the length of the spine. Scoliosis is best represented by the mean of the heights of the two sides of the involved segments.

given in Table XXXII. A word of caution is in order: Having been constructed on the basis of European skeletons, Fully's anatomical method needs to be tested on the taller population of the United States to see if the correction factor needs any adjustment

TABLE XXXII

EXAMPLE OF STATURE CALCULATION

BY FULLY'S ANATOMICAL METHOD*

	mm			mm
Basion-bregma height	140		C2	41
			C3	13
Combined heights C2-L5	517	←	C4	13
			C5	15
Height of S1	30		C6	15
			C7	15
Length of femur	465		T1	18
			T2	19
Length of tibia	366		T3	20
			T4	21·
Talocalcaneal height	60		T5	20
	———		T6	22
Skeletal height	1578 (157.8 cm)		T7	22
			T8	23
Correction	+ 10.5 "		T9	23
	———		T10	24
Estimated stature	168.3 "		T11	25
			T12	27
			L1	28
			L2	28
			L3	29
			L4	27
			L5	29
				517

* From Fully, Une nouvelle méthode de détermination de la taille. *Ann Méd Lég, 35:*272,1956. Courtesy of *Ann Méd Lég.*

before being used in forensic cases in this country. In general, however, I favor this method over all the others for use in cases where the skeleton is sufficiently complete (see Fully and Pineau, 1960, for a way to cope with missing vertebrae).

Chapter 10

ESTIMATION OF BODY WEIGHT

STANDING IN MARKED CONTRAST to the foregoing long and involved record of attempts to achieve the best estimate of the length of the living body (stature) from the length of the skeleton or its parts is the lone record of a single attempt to find a good method of estimating body weight in life from the weight of the skeleton or its parts. This lone record is that of Baker and Newman (1957) referred to in Chapter 1.

In searching for an explanation for the lack of attention to the estimation of body weight from the skeleton I decided that if Thomas Dwight were still around to query, probably he would paraphrase the statement he made in 1905 regarding the attribution of sex from the length of the humerus (see under humerus in Chapter 7) and say, "As a practical anatomist I know that no one would think of determining the weight of the body in life by its skeletal weight."

As we have seen, this practical attitude did not deter Thieme and Schull (1957) from looking into the matter of the sexing ability of the length of the humerus. Nor did it deter Baker and Newman from looking into the matter of weight; but in their case the step required more courage on account of the widely held belief (implied above) in the impracticality of the undertaking. Some historical notes will help make this clear.

The body being made up mainly of bone, muscle, and fat, anatomists and physical anthropologists have shown considerable interest in the relative amount of each present in the two sexes and at different times during life. One way of establishing the relative amount of bone is by weighing macerated whole skeletons and by relating the resulting figures to the records of body weight made in life or following death. The Todd Collection offered N. W. Ingalls this opportunity and he responded with a detailed study in 1931. Using 100 white males, he compared, among many

222

other things, dry bone weight and body weight. The conclusion
he drew from this was not surprising (p. 50) : "Body weight is
extremely variable, much more so than dry bone weight. It fluctu-
ates readily and rapidly and undue significance should not be
attached to it."

In 1954 Trotter took note of Ingalls' findings and, with her
access to the Terry Collection, decided that, rather than follow
along the same route, she would check on the formula evolved by
Matiegka (1921) for estimating the weight of the skeleton in the
living from data which can be gathered from the living. The fact
that, after having been deeply involved in the estimation of living
stature from the lengths of the long bones, Trotter turned away
from the opportunity to estimate living weight from skeletal
weight suggests that she, too, regarded the latter as impracticable.
In any event, her interest lingered for a while with the estimation
of skeletal weight in the living and then turned to bone density.

From the forensic standpoint Trotter's correlations are the
most interesting part of her 1954 paper. Using twenty-four white
male skeletons (defleshed but not really dry) she found that
stature had a correlation with skeletal weight of .6909, whereas the
average bi-epicondylar diameter of the humeri and the average bi-
epicondylar diameter of the femora (both measures obtainable
from the living) had correlations with skeletal weight of .4319
and .5344, respectively. On the other hand, she found that femur
weight had a correlation with skeletal weight of .9591. Taking
her clue from the latter finding, she decided (p. 550) that the
estimate of skeletal weight in life with the least standard error of
estimate would be one obtained "from stature and the sum of the
areas of compact bone in the middle half of the femurs (as shown
in an Xray, posteroanterior view) ."

Trotter's correlations, especially as they involve the femur, an-
ticipate the findings of Baker and Newman and the way in which
the latter used their findings to identify commingled skeletal remains. First, however, a brief description of the procedures developed by Baker and Newman are in order. These procedures
were determined in some measure by the nature of the study
material, the American dead from the Korean War. As explained

in Chapter 6, the state of preservation of the skeletons of the soldiers missing in action (MIA) and those taken prisoners of war (POW) was quite different, the latter being rather like archeological specimens. The reduction of organic matter in the POW skeletons accounts for the fact that Baker and Newman restricted their final analysis to this group (80 whites and 19 blacks).

To get the bones as dry as possible they heated them in a thermostatically-controlled electric oven at a temperature of 150°F until weight loss was less than 10 gm per hour. This usually took ten to fifteen hours. Weighing of the skeleton as a whole, and of certain selected bones separately, was carried out as rapidly as possible at the end of the period of drying so as to keep reabsorbed atmospheric moisture to a minimum.

In general agreement with the earlier studies, Baker and Newman reported (p. 607) that "the correlation coefficients of dry femur weight to living weight for whites [.535] and Negroes [.449] are equivalent to those obtained by using the [weight of] the total skeleton [by race respectively .544 and .392]." However, when they plotted the regression of living weight, first on dry skeletal weight (their Figures 1 and 2) and then on femur weight (their Figures 3 and 4), the scatter of the subjects on either side of the regression lines was so great that the relative utility of the two weights as predictors remained in doubt. Nevertheless, the authors recommended the use of femur weight over skeletal weight because of the greater procedural simplicity.

In this connection the pertinent regression equations for use in estimating weight in life (in pounds) are as follows:

> WHITE MALES
> .024 (Dry skeletal weight)*   + 50.593 ± 20.1
> .233 (Dry femur weight)   + 57.385 ± 22.2
>
> BLACK MALES
> .013 (Dry skeletal weight)   + 85.406 ± 13.7
> .163 (Dry femur weight)   + 76.962 ± 13.3

Summing up this part of the study, "It appears," the authors said (pp. 605-606),

---

*Dry skeletal (or femur) weight in grams.

that whatever relationship exists between total [or living] weight and skeletal weight is a function of the correspondence between the bone and the rest of the fat free tissue. Therefore, very obese individuals have the same weights that would be found for men who weighed as much as a hundred pounds less.

Certainly the equations given above reflect a selected, youthful, physically-fit population. This in itself makes it likely that the standard errors of estimate, even when doubled, will not cover the range of the general population.

A serendipidous result of this study was a method of using dry-bone weights for sorting commingled fat-free skeletal remains. It is based on the finding that the dry weight of the femur is highly correlated with that of each of the other major bones. As an aid in sorting, therefore, Baker and Newman developed the regression equations given in Table XXXIII. To apply these equations in a case of commingling the stated procedure (p. 615-616) is as follows:

All of the long bones should first be measured for length. Then they should be dried, as described . . . , and the individual bones weighed. [The right femur] is a logical initial choice. The left femur will be easy to determine as it has an almost identical weight and length. From the right femur the weight of almost any bone belonging to the same individual can be predicted using the formulae presented in [Table XXXIII]. For example, if the femur weighs 409 gm, then the associated right humerus should weigh about 152 gm. It is not probable that any of the right humeri found will have exactly the predicted value, but one should fall within plus or minus 40 gm of this value. If more than one or none of the humeri are between these values, then using Trotter's regression equations [1952, Table 12], length measurement may be applied to determine the associated bone.

The same basic procedure applies to the association of the other long bones [not all included in Table XXXIII] . . .

The use of bone weights and lengths in this manner will accurately segregate the major bones into individuals, but it does not solve the difficult problem of segregating the small bones such as ribs, vertebrae, and phalanges. However, the positive segregation of the major bones will provide the worker with a more accurate basis for applying subjective techniques to the rest of the skeleton.

Given the limitation of the method to fat-free bones, I feel compelled to express doubt that the separation of commingled

TABLE XXXIII

REGRESSION EQUATIONS FOR ESTIMATING BONE ASSOCIATION FROM
DRY WEIGHT (IN GM) OF THE BONE(S) FROM THE RIGHT SIDE*

WHITE MALES			BLACK MALES		
Femur weight =			*Femur weight =*		
.089 Total skeleton	+	27.593 ± 28	.076 Total skeleton	+	70.915 ± 23
1.121 (Tibia + fibula)	+	72.505 ± 26	1.023 (Tibia + fibula)	+	89.930 ± 21
1.965 Humerus	+	109.678 ± 41	1.407 Humerus	+	188.383 ± 28
3.022 (Radius + ulna)	+	88.023 ± 39	1.988 (Radius + ulna)	+	183.385 ± 32
9.120 Clavicle	+	204.009 ± 48	No significant correlation to clavicle		
1.470 Innominate	+	139.354 ± 34	1.123 Innominate	+	218.453 ± 27
.240 Skull	+	246.713 ± 54	No significant correlation to skull		
Tibia + fibula weight =			*Tibia + fibula weight =*		
.071 Total skeleton	+	5.292 ± 23	.058 Total skeleton	+	56.488 ± 23
.733 Femur	+	.572 ± 21	.726 Femur	+	17.745 ± 18
1.650 Humerus	+	49.532 ± 32	1.118 Humerus	+	138.634 ± 25
2.512 (Radius + ulna)	+	33.443 ± 30	1.824 (Radius + ulna)	+	105.431 ± 25
7.415 Clavicle	+	133.187 ± 39	No significant correlation to clavicle		
1.100 Innominate	+	98.584 ± 31	.785 Innominate	+	181.783 ± 27
.201 Skull	+	164.481 ± 43	No significant correlation to skull		
Humerus weight =			*Humerus weight =*		
.932 Total skeleton	+	16.634 ± 12	.029 Total skeleton	+	29.575 ± 17
.278 Femur	+	38.482 ± 15	.392 Femur	+	.078 ± 15
.352 (Tibia + fibula)	+	46.336 ± 15	.439 (Tibia + fibula)	+	23.091 ± 16
1.250 (Radius + ulna)	+	19.021 ± 12	1.237 (Radius + ulna)	+	17.367 ± 14
3.765 Clavicle	+	67.482 ± 17	No significant correlation to clavicle		
.515 Innominate	+	57.576 ± 14	.508 Innominate	+	73.608 ± 17
.089 Skull	+	92.025 ± 20	No significant correlation to skull		

*From Baker and Newman, The use of bone weight for human identification, *Am J Ph Anthropol*, *15*:601-618, Appendix B, 1957. Courtesy of *Am J Phys Anthropol.*

remains by this untested metrical means can be done any better than, if as well as, by eye. Also, most certainly the eye can do the job faster.

Chapter 11

ATTRIBUTION OF RACE

T HE TERM "race" means different things to different people. In
the original zoological sense it means a sub-division of a species
based on appearance (phenotype), mankind today being one
species. Many laymen find the ramifications of this zoological
concept difficult to understand and as a result often confuse race
with national, religious, and sociological groupings. Actually, in
spite of the likelihood that mankind in the past exhibited clear-
cut subdivisions by appearance, today such a state of panmixia
exists that subdivisions by appearance can be defined only very
broadly. Adding to the confusion is the recent introduction of a
genetical concept of race based on the unseen genes (genotype),
the units of inheritance. Appearance, of course, simply reflects
inheritance, and so phenotype and genotype are really different
aspects of the same thing. In any event, from the standpoint of
forensic anthropology it is necessary to categorize the skeletal
remains of unknowns in terms that reflect racial reality as locally
understood.

Since most of the long-held zoological concepts arose from
observations on living populations, and not all of these observations involve the hidden bony structures, the concept of phenotypic race can be applied only to a limited extent to human
skeletal remains. And unless racially specific genes are still detectable in the organic matter remaining in the bones, the geno-
typic concept of race is entirely inapplicable to human skeletal
remains. All of this means that the attribution of race to skeletons
of unknowns often cannot be made with any degree of certainty.

Among the phenotypic racial traits observed in the living that
are identifiable still in the disarticulated skeleton are head shape,
nose shape, face shape, stature, and the relative proportions of the
extremities. These traits are not very useful for identifying the
race of unknowns because none of them is unique to a particular

racial group and all of them occur in a wide range of variation in every racial group. It serves little purpose, therefore, to take up space here with tables of measurements and indices for different populations. I have not found the tables of this sort assembled by Krogman (1962) helpful in skeletal identification, and I have suspected that they have tended to foster the idea that forensic anthropology is an exact science, which it is not.

In the United States most of the skeletons of unknowns are likely to be either black or white. With few exceptions the remainder are some form of Mongoloid, either pure or admixed (American or Mexican Indian, Chinese, Japanese, Filipino, Southeast Asiatic). As pointed out in Chapter 3, it is not safe in the case of a skeleton to be swayed in the judgment of race by knowledge of the predominant race in the region where the skeleton was found; a skeleton could just as well represent an itinerant from afar or have been a member of a local minority racial group.

Interbreeding between blacks and whites began making notable headway in the United States in the eighteenth century and since then has accelerated markedly. Today the resulting hybrids range in appearance from nearly black to nearly white. Yet the grades of intermixture rarely are given separate names, as in some parts of Latin America, and anyone with apparent black admixture is classified as black. Obviously this classification is sociological rather than biological, but a "fact of life" that every forensic anthropologist must recognize; in other words, unless a skeleton of an unknown is judged by a forensic anthropologist to be entirely free from black traits, he or she should not attribute it to the white race, for such a racial attribution could well be misleading to the investigators.

In general, the attribution of race in skeletal remains, just as the attribution of sex, is accomplished in two ways: (1) by evaluating anatomical details, and (2) by utilizing certain measurements in special regression equations. However, skeletal characters indicative of race are much less obvious than those indicative of sex; hence the evaluation of the former, as compared with the latter, requires much more experience on the part of the examiner. I would go even further and urge those dealing with forensic cases to search carefully for head hairs during the recovery and study of the skeletal remains. Microscopic analysis of head hairs seems likely to supply a sure racial diagnosis or at least confirm the attribution suggested by the skeletal features.

I have no personal experience in the microscopic examination of hairs. I attribute this deficiency mainly to the fact that in the forensic cases I have handled I have been able to "pass the buck," so to speak, i.e. to refer hair samples to experts on the staff of the laboratory in the FBI headquarters. A check of the literature suggests that I am not unusual among American physical anthropologists in not studying hair. The only ones to my knowledge who have given serious attention to the subject during the last twenty-five years are Mildred Trotter (1964, with O. H. Duggins), Stanley Garn (1951), and Ellis Kerley (1971, 1973, with S. I. Rosen).

As for the reliability of racial attributions based on hair, I have not found a satisfactory statement in the literature. Although details of the hair of many racial groups have been described, along with the techniques involved in their study, applications of the knowledge in the forensic setting, particularly as regards American populations, seems to have received little, if any, attention. Thus, for example, Gradwohl's *Legal Medicine* (1954) includes a twenty-one-page chapter by Evans on "The Examination of Hairs and Fibers," but this contains no mention of racial differences. Although I am reasonably sure, nevertheless, that most stereotypic American blacks, whites, and mongoloids can be distinguished by their hair, I have no way of knowing to what extent this holds true of the hybrids between these groups. This is an area where forensic anthropologists would do well to develop their own expertise.

BY ANATOMICAL MEANS
Blacks vs. Whites

It should be obvious to anyone who has observed American blacks closely that they have inherited the highly variable combinations of physical traits that characterize their parental racial stocks. Also, this inheritance seems to involve some dissociation of external and internal traits; in other words, such external traits as dark pigmentation, tightly curled hair, and thickened lips, tend to persist to a recognizable degree when the underlying bony traits of the face have become almost indistinguishable from those of whites. Therefore, individuals in whom this dissociation has occurred present clear evidence of their sociological race in life but obscure or conflicting evidence of this in their skeletons after death.

Figures 64 to 67 contrast male and female skulls of typical American blacks selected for their close resemblance to the stereotype of African blacks with male and female skulls of typical

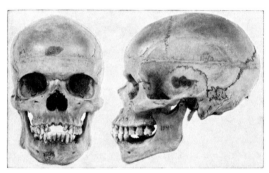

Figure 64

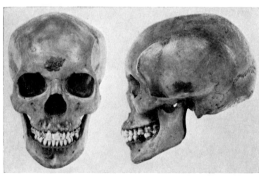

Figure 65

Figure 64. Front and left lateral views of the skull of a male American black aged 46 years (Terry Collection No. 1140). (Courtesy Smithsonian Institution.)

Figure 65. Front and left lateral views of the skull of a female American black aged 35 years (Terry Collection No. 766). (Courtesy Smithsonian Institution.)

American whites. Note particularly that in this type of black skull in contrast to the white skull, the orbits are lower, the inter-orbital distance is wider, the nasal bones are less salient, the nasal aperture is broader and less sharply defined inferiorly, and alveolar prognathism is pronounced. Most American blacks today do not show such extreme African traits as here pictured; indeed, they are uncommon in the Terry Collection. Instead, most American black skulls tend to look more or less like the white stereotype. It is because of this situation that the forensic anthro-pologist must rely on his experience in deciding for a particular skeleton which racial attribution to make. Sometimes this experi-ence is likely to tell one only that there is an indefinable "some-thing" about the skeleton that suggests black.

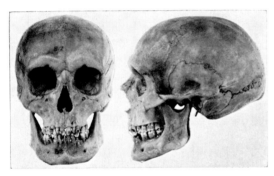

Figure 66

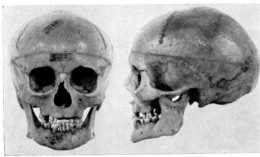

Figure 67

Figure 66. Front and left lateral views of the skull of a male American white aged 56 years (Terry Collection No. 812). (Courtesy Smithsonian Institution.)

Figure 67. Front and left lateral views of the skull of a female American white aged 67 years (Terry Collection No. 722R). (Courtesy Smithsonian Institu-tion.)

As an example of an indefinable "something" of a racial nature in skulls, I call attention to the preliminary report by Finnegan and Schulter (1975) on a feature said to have no sexual dimorphism, but to be almost completely different in blacks and whites. The feature in question is the shape of the anterior border of the external auditory meatus as seen in an X ray taken in *norma verticalis*. This border was found to be straight in fifty whites, but distinctly curved in forty-seven of fifty blacks. Since this finding is based on skulls in the Terry Collection, which in the case of blacks generally do not show the pronounced traits that distinguish the African stereotype, and since I have not looked for the feature in question in X rays (a racial difference is not apparent to me in the actual skulls), I feel that I should defer judgment for the present as regards the utility of the feature for racial attributions. Certainly few investigators will want to go to the trouble of taking the required X ray without further assurances that it is worthwhile.

As a rule the postcranial bones have less to say about race than do those of the skull. In 1962 I called attention to the possibility of femoral shape helping to distinguish blacks from whites. In this connection I presented evidence that American blacks, at least in so far as some of the less admixed individuals are concerned, have femora which in comparison with those of American whites are less curved anteroposteriorly, more flattened anteroposteriorly in midshaft, and have less anterior twist (torsion) at the upper end (Figure 68). All this amounts to is that a pair of straight, flat femora which have only slight torsion are more likely to be those of an American black than an American white; but, on the other hand, the reverse traits do not necessarily indicate an American white; they could indicate an American Indian.

Figure 68. Two right femora showing racial differences in anterior curvature. *Left*—male white, Terry Collection No. 1026; *right*—male black, U.S.N.M. No. 255,591. (Courtesy Smithsonian Institution.)

Mongoloids

Figure 69 shows the skull of a Chinaman who worked in the Alaskan fish canneries and is reported to have come from Canton in mainland China. Here the features pointed out above as distinguishing American blacks and whites—particularly nasal shape and alveolar prognathism—are intermediate in grade. Three features which are fairly indicative of the Mongoloid racial stock are: (1) Extreme narrowing of the nasal bones at the nasal bridge, (2) prominent cheekbones giving rise to a face breadth exceeding head breadth, and (3) shovel-shaped incisors (Figure 70). Obviously, the expression of these features in any particular individual is highly variable and considerable experience on the part of the forensic anthropologist is needed to reach a racial assessment by these means.

BY METRICAL MEANS

Blacks vs. Whites

A quarter of a century ago W. W. Howells (1951) began to look into the "need for further analytical techniques, especially statistical ones, in anthropometry" (p. 190). Starting with factor analysis, by 1957 he was able to show (p. 190) that "10 measurements account for virtually all of the correlation in the cranial vault proper." Thereafter he turned to multivariate analysis and embarked on a long-range program of assembling and analyzing selected measurements on carefully controlled cranial populations. The results appeared in book form in 1973. Although Howells mainly had taxonomy in mind, two of his associates, Eugene Giles and Orville Elliot, saw possibilities in the methodology for forensic applications and in 1962 produced the first discriminant functions for the attribution of race. (For their methods of sexing by metrical means see Chapter 7.) Howells published his first discriminant functions for the attribution of race in 1970.

The main difference between the Giles-Elliot and Howells methods resides in the sets of cranial measurements employed. Besides employing more measurements than Giles-Elliot (15 vs. 8), and a quite different set for each sex, Howells includes among

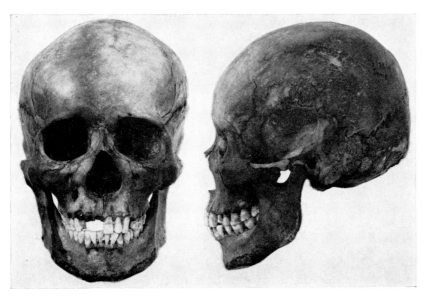

Figure 69. Front and left lateral views of the skull of an adult male Chinese (U.S.N.M. No. 374,818). (Courtesy Smithsonian Institution.)

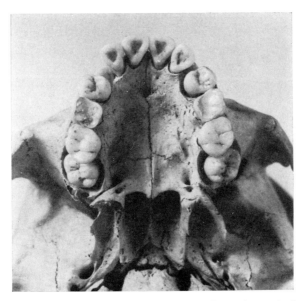

Figure 70. Shovel-shaped incisors in the upper jaw of an Archaic Indian from Kentucky around 10 years of age (U.S.N.M. No. 290,076). (Courtesy Smithsonian Institution.)

his measurements many that are untraditional and must be secured by means of four special types of coordinate calipers. On the other hand, all of the smaller number of measurements used by Giles-Elliot are traditional and can be secured by the two instruments (sliding and spreading calipers) available to every physical anthropologist. Because of the large amount of space required to do justice to the Howells method (there are twenty measurements and six angles to be defined, to say nothing of the instruments needing description), I have decided reluctantly from the standpoint of practicality to limit attention here to the Giles-Elliot method. However, because the Howells method appears to have a 90 percent accuracy, I urge readers to become familiar with it.

The essential data for applying the Giles-Elliot method in the case of an unknown are given in Table XXXIV. The first thing to do is to take the measurements listed in that table, being careful that glabella-occipital length is maximum in the midline and that the landmark prosthion is on the part of the alveolar border between the central incisors most distant from the other landmark used in the measurement. Then simply multiply each measurement by the corresponding discriminant-function weight for the assumed sex and sum the products. If the unknown has

TABLE XXXIV

DISCRIMINANT FUNCTION WEIGHTS FOR DISTINGUISHING BETWEEN THE SKULLS OF BLACKS AND WHITES*

Measurement	Weight	
	Male	Female
Basion-prosthion	+ 3.06	+ 1.74
Glabella-occipital length	+ 1.60	+ 1.28
Maximum width	− 1.90	− 1.18
Basion-bregma height	− 1.79	− 0.14
Basion-nasion	− 4.41	− 2.34
Maximum bizygomatic diameter	− 0.10	+ 0.38
Prosthion-nasion	+ 2.59	− 0.01
Nasal breadth	+ 10.56	+ 2.45

*Frim Giles and Elliot. Race identification from cranial measurements. *J For Sci,* 7:152, 1962. Courtesy of *J For Sci.*

been judged to be male and the sum of the products or score exceeds 89.27, the race likely is black; a score less than 89.27 likely indicates that the race is white. In the case of a female, on the other hand, if the score exceeds 9.22 the race most likely is black, and if less than 9.22, probably white.

In tests on the original specimens Giles and Elliot found those correctly attributed as to race to range between 80 and 88 percent, the higher percentage occurring in females. New test specimens (fewer in number) gave somewhat better results.

American Indians vs. Whites

Giles and Elliot (1962) are the only ones who have developed discriminant functions for race applicable to the American Indians. They freely admit, however, that their Indian sample was less than satisfactory for the purpose, because it is prehistoric in age (Indian Knoll, Kentucky) and had to be sexed by eye. Probably for this reason they make no claim for the method yielding reliable results for other Mongoloid elements of the present American population.

The American Indians, being much more generalized Mongoloids than the recent immigrants from Asia, have cranial features often rather like those of American whites. For this reason the main utility of the part of the Giles-Elliot method involving Indians is likely to be that in which comparison is made with whites. Accordingly, this is the only part included here.

Given an unknown that could be either Indian or white, a score is derived, as explained above, from the data in Table XXXV according to sex, and the likely race determined by the relationship of the score to the sectioning point. If the unknown is judged to be male, a score above 22.28 indicates Indian, whereas one below 22.28 indicates white. Similarly, for an unknown female a score above 13.01 indicates Indian and one below 13.01 indicates white.

In tests on the original specimens Giles and Elliot found those correctly identified as to race to range between 93 and 95 percent. Different test specimens (more in number) gave less satisfactory results.

TABLE XXXV

DISCRIMINANT FUNCTION WEIGHTS FOR DISTINGUISHING BETWEEN
THE SKULLS OF INDIANS AND WHITES*

Measurement	Weight	
	Male	Female
Basion-prosthion	+ 0.10	+ 3.05
Glabella-occipital length	− 0.25	− 1.04
Maximum width	− 1.56	− 5.41
Basion-bregma height	+ 0.73	+ 4.29
Basion-nasion	− 0.29	− 4.02
Maximum bizygomatic diameter	+ 1.75	+ 5.62
Prosthion-nasion	− 0.16	− 1.00
Nasal breadth	− 0.84	− 2.19

*From Giles and Elliot, Race identification from cranial measurements. *J For Sci,* 7:152, 1962. Courtesy of *J For Sci.*

Chapter 12

INDICATIONS OF HANDEDNESS

I^T IS CUSTOMARY to classify individuals as right-handed, left-handed, or ambidextrous. This order of the categories reflects, at least for the first two, their relative frequencies in the population. Although figures vary, in the United States probably eighteen to twenty-four individuals become right-handed for every one who persists in left-handed tendencies. The use here of the word "persists" suggests the difficulty in accounting for the proportion of the population that becomes ambidextrous.

No one is sure what causes an individual to favor one hand over the other. Some maintain that there are a number of factors, among which training and/or imitation during infancy may rank higher than inheritance. In this connection it is noteworthy that the dominant hand is not always on the side of the dominant foot. Also, a higher proportion of right-handed than of left-handed people (75% vs. 33%) use the right eye in sighting.

Anthropologists long have been aware that asymmetries in length exist between the long limb bones of the two sides, the longer ones most often being on the right side in the upper extremities and on the left side in the lower extremities (Schultz, 1937). However, F. Wood Jones (1910) noted an exception to this rule in a skeleton (Case 34:16:B) recovered by the Archaeological Survey of Nubia in the area to be flooded by the first Aswan Dam. Of this case, he said (p. 226):

> The right side of the occipital region was markedly more prominent than the left side, and with the preponderance of the right side of the posterior part of the skull, there was associated a marked change in the usual ratio of the length of the arms.
>
> Instead of the bones of the right arm being longer and more muscular than those of the left side, the conditions were exactly reversed: the left arm (oblique length of humerus + axial length of radius) measured 292 + 215 = 507 millimetres, while the right arm measured only 281 + 211 = 492 millimetres, [a difference of 15 mm].

My first encounter with such a specimen happened in the first case about which I testified in court as an expert witness, namely, the one in Virginia mentioned in Chapter 2. In my testimony I was careful to point out the unusual nature of the finding and to say only that it might have predisposed to left-handedness. Since other testimony at the trial established the fact that the decedent had indeed been left-handed, this may be the only court case on record where a left-handed individual has been shown convincingly to have had longer arm bones on the left than on the right.

Indications of handedness in a skeleton are not of much help in leading investigators to the initial identification of a decedent, because the records of missing persons almost never include information on this subject. Once a tentative identification has been made, however, acquaintances of this person can be asked to recall his or her hand preference and in this way the identification possibly can be checked out.

The disregard of handedness in personnel, hospital, military, and other records has retarded the study of this subject in skeletons. For example, when I was examining the American dead from the Korean War for changes in the joints with age, I noticed that often in older individuals I could distinguish the right scapula from the left simply because the right one had very evident beveling of the dorsal margin of the glenoid cavity (Figure 71). I did not see any cases in which the beveling was more evident on the left side. Although these observations, including the ratio of side involvement, are suggestive of the actual nature of the handedness in the particular cases where they were noted, there was nothing in the military records to confirm this and naturally the military authorities were unwilling to forward inquiries to the next of kin.

During recent years I have followed up on this matter by examining skeletons in the Terry Collection (Stewart, 1976a). Among these I found not only the same pattern of differential beveling of the dorsal border of the glenoid cavity, but also a tendency for the plane of the right cavity as a whole to be more dorsally inclined, and for the proximal end of the right humerus to show more torsion. Moreover, occasionally I found this combination of traits on the right side occurring together with longer upper-extremity bones, and with pronounced arthritic changes in one or more of the joints to which these bones contribute.

Figure 72 is an example of marked dorsal beveling of the right glenoid cavity accompanied by arthritic lipping of the elbow joints that is more pronounced on the right. Figure 73 shows that the right glenoid cavity in this same individual has in addition more dorsal inclination than the left. Although there is no difference in the lengths of the long bones of the two arms in this case, the right humerus shows more torsion than the left (76° vs. 48°).

Two other extreme cases among those I studied in the Terry

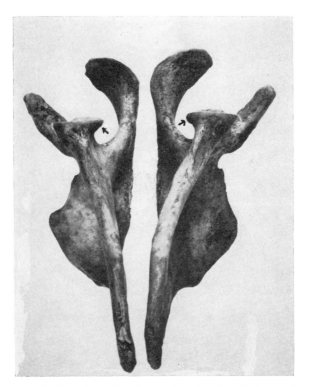

Figure 71. Lateral view of a pair of scapulae showing different shapes of the dorsal margins (arrows) of the glenoid cavities (Korean war-dead series No. 450, a male white aged 30 years). (Courtesy National Anthropological Archives.)

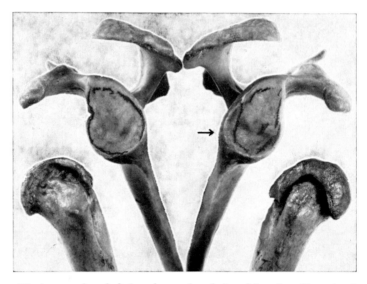

Figure 72. A more beveled dorsal margin of the right glenoid cavity (arrow) associated with more arthritic lipping of the trochlea of the right humerus (Terry Collection No. 763, male white aged 46 years). To emphasize the glenoid beveling a pencil was shaved down to expose some 2 inches of lead and the latter, placed across the top of the cavity, was moved downward so as to mark the high points on the margins. (Courtesy Smithsonian Institution.)

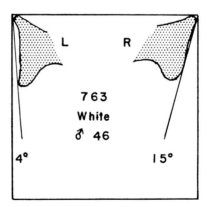

Figure 73. Cross-sections of the glenoid cavities shown in Figure 72 viewed from above. The angle of dorsal inclination, here greater on the right side than on the left, was measured from the ventral infraspinous plane. (For method of determining angle see Stewart, 1964, Figures 6-8.)

Collection, but suggestive of left-handedness rather than right-handedness, should be mentioned also. In one of these (No. 556, a black male, age sixty) the long arm bones on the left are 25 mm longer than those on the right. Beveling of the dorsal margins of the glenoid cavities, while not marked, is more evident on the left. The left glenoid cavity is inclined dorsally 11.5°, whereas the one on the right is inclined 6.0°. And finally, not only does the left humerus show more torsion than the right (not measured), but the tuberosity for the insertion of the tendon of the biceps on the left radius, unlike that on the right, is massively lipped.

In the other case (No. 614, a white male, age fifty) the difference in the lengths of the long arm bones of the two sides is 13 mm in favor of the left. The left glenoid cavity, besides showing more beveling of the dorsal margin than the right, is inclined dorsally 21.8° as compared with 16.5° on the right. As for the humeri, although torsion is more evident on the right (not measured), the lateral epicondyle on the left, unlike that on the right, exhibits large exostoses.

Left-sided cases as extreme as the last two appear to be rare. Of 128 male skeletons from the Terry Collection examined for evidence of handedness, only twenty-one (19.4%) had combined arm/forearm bones longer on the left than on the right, and in only the two described above did the length differential exceed 10 mm. None of the forty females examined had longer left arm bones.

Now that many people are willing their bodies to anatomy departments for dissection, an effort should be made while these people are still alive to learn about their hand preferences so that the differences in lateral morphology found at dissection can be better understood. Only from such studies will it be possible with assurance to interpret evidence of laterality in skeletons of unknowns.

At present the best I can do by way of explaining the beveling of the dorsal margin of the glenoid cavity is to quote Terry's (1942) descriptions of the shoulder joint and of the relative motions of the humerus and scapula during flexion and extension of the former:

The inequality in size of the two articular surfaces, the shallowness of the glenoid cavity and the looseness of the articular capsule combine to make the shoulder joint most free in the range of movements . . . . Flexion is the swinging forward, extension, the swinging backwards of the humerus: . . . In extreme flexion the scapula follows the head of the humerus, keeping the articular surfaces in apposition. In extension the scapula moves much less, if at all. (P. 311.)

If I interpret correctly the last sentence of this quotation as meaning that the limited motion, or lack of motion, on the part of the scapula during extension of the humerus brings the head of the humerus into forceful contact with the dorsal margin of the glenoid cavity, then the resulting pressure at this point would seem to be the cause of the beveling. In this sense the beveling can be considered an extension facet comparable perhaps to a squatting, or flexion, facet in the ankle.

Returning to Figure 72, it is clear that the changes in the elbow joint due to stress are apt to be far more conspicuous than those on the scapular side of the shoulder joint. For a more detailed study of the different manifestations of these changes in the elbow joint see Ortner (1968). On the other hand, the reader should not be led by a few illustrations into believing that joint asymmetries are very common. In this connection the following figures on osteoarthritis of the elbow joint from Jurmain's findings (1974, p. 339) should be taken into consideration:

	Asymmetric %	Right dominant %
White males (107)	17.6	55.6
White females (104	8.9	77.8
Black males (116)	16.7	78.9
Black females (118)	22.1	64.0

Section III

SPECIFIC SKELETAL TRAITS

As explained at the beginning of Section II, the rationale for separating specific from general traits is that the former, unlike the latter, are unique to the individual; in other words, a general trait merely places an unknown skeleton into a large class, such as males, Europeans, the elderly, etc., whereas a specific trait offers the possibility for making a match-up with a very personal record made in life and thereby gaining a sure identification.

In addition to particular bony details, both cranial and post-cranial, normal and abnormal, I shall include in this section the combinations of features in the facial part of the skull which by various forms of artistic treatment yield likenesses that in turn sometimes lead to identifications. As we shall see, a likeness may be developed from a skull or a skull may be fitted to a pre-existing likeness. Either way, a successful result is one of the more dramatic accomplishments of forensic anthropology.

Chapter 13

TRAITS PECULIAR TO THE INDIVIDUAL

CRANIAL

MOST OF THE records on the head made in life that relate to the skull are those of surgeons and dentists. In both cases the records are likely to include radiographs that reveal details of bony structures. Also, the radiographs usually are supplemented by written notes made at the time by the surgeon or dentist. In the case of the dentist the notes detail the nature and location of fillings, the sequence of extractions, etc. Thus from the standpoint of identification the surgical and dental records often can be considered the equivalent of a set of fingerprints. Yet unlike fingerprints, the surgical and dental records are neither coded nor assembled in a central repository. In order to use them for identification purposes, therefore, it is necessary first to locate the surgeon or dentist who has a particular record. Sometimes an observation made in the course of the examination of the skeletal remains will suggest a lead in this direction.

A case in point is the one mentioned in Chapter 6 in which a fully-clothed male skeleton was found in the Potomac River valley near Washington. The teeth of this skeleton exhibited such extensive dental restorations that everyone who saw them immediately concluded that the decedent could be identified if only his dentist could be located. In fact, the dentist was located and did make the identification.

The identification came about in this way: A reporter on the *Washington Post* became interested in the case and arranged for an artist to make a pen-and-ink portrait from the skull, using my estimate of age, race, and body-build (the belt still in place when the skeleton was found indicated a slender build). Publication of this likeness as part of the story in the *Post* led a reader to report that it reminded him of his roommate who had been missing for a year. When the latter had been reported missing a year earlier the police had failed to locate him, but now, having a skeleton fitting his general description and his name to follow up on, they went to the missing man's dentist and asked the latter to compare the dental record under the missing man's name with the teeth in the skull. The two matched. The record does not show whether the portrait made from the skull was a good likeness or whether it was the newspaper story that served as the memory jogger.

Another case in which identification was made on the basis of the teeth—that of the twelve and one half-year-old girl in Mississippi mentioned in Chapter 2 and again in Chapter 6—did not need the assistance of a dentist. In my examination of her skull I noted a small white spot (aplasia) on the labial surface of the upper left central incisor. Since the labial surfaces of the front teeth become visible when an individual smiles broadly, and defects therein are likely to be remembered, I suggested to the FBI agent who brought the skeleton to me that the right missing girl might be identified by means of this spot. However, I advised against making the rounds of the dentists because three of the decedent's first molars were extremely carious and no restorations were present. This suggested that she had not received any dental attention.

The advice paid off in an unexpected way: The authorities produced a school photograph in color showing the girl smiling and the spot clearly evident. Moreover, a malpositioned upper left lateral incisor evident in the picture matched that present in the actual dentition. On the witness stand I stated that the chances of any other twelve and one half-year-old white girl with these same two dental anomalies having been killed in that community at the indicated time of year were extremely slim.

In this connection it is worth noting that one well-known anomaly of the upper front teeth, namely, a wide space or diastema between the central incisors, is too common to be of much help by itself in making an identification. However, in the case from Kentucky mentioned in Chapter 2 and again in Chapter 6 involving two black women of about the same age, this anomaly served to distinguish one from the other.

Perhaps the earliest case of identification involving both surgery and radiology was reported by Culbert and Law in 1927. These New York physicians were called upon in 1925 to help identify skeletonized remains believed to be those of a male patient of theirs who had had a simple left-sided mastoid operation five years previously. This man had disappeared mysteriously while camping along the Indus River in India. Seventeen days later not one, but two, unrecognizable male bodies were recovered seventy miles down river. Both had had mastoid operations, one radical and the other simple. Upon being appealed to for help in identifying their former patient, Culbert and Law rejected the remains with the radical operation. Arrangements were then made to send the other remains to New York for further examination. There Culbert and Law made anteroposterior and lateral X rays of the skull for comparison with ones they had made in 1918, i.e. prior to the operation.

Prints made from the two sets of X rays, taken eight years apart, appear in the cited publication and reveal six points of identity in the nasal accessory sinuses and six points of identity in the area of the normal mastoid. This extensive agreement in bony details between X rays taken before and after death leaves no doubt as to the certainty of identification. Note, however, that identification was possible only because there was a decedent's name to go on. Without the name it would have been impossible to locate the X rays taken in life.

Positive identification by means of bone pathology of the temporal bone, but in a part thereof different from that of the preceding case and not involving X rays, was reported by William R. Maples of the University of Florida at the twenty-eighth annual meeting (1976) of the American Academy of Forensic Sciences in Washington. In the course of examining the skeletonized remains of an elderly and presumably indigent man recovered in Florida, Maples noted bone destruction around, and enlargement of, the lumen of the external auditory meatus on one side. The most likely diagnosis of this lesion, according to the medical authority consulted, was cholesteatoma in the draining stage. Since the effluent from such a lesion is likely to be offensive and because of this is likely to require frequent attention, inquiries were made at outpatient clinics of local hospitals with the result that the personnel at one of them remembered the case and produced the man's name.

Surgery for bone infections around the head is no longer common, of course, because infections of this sort usually respond to treatment by antibiotics. On the other hand, skull trauma is more common than ever before, owing especially to the high frequency of automobile accidents. Trauma produced in this way is likely to leave evidence of fractures of such delicate bony facial structures as the nose and zygomata, along with signs of ablated teeth.

A case involving facial trauma which was not detected in the initial handling of the corpse and should have been evident had the remains been skeletonized, was reported by Prinsloo (1953). The investigators, having obtained an indistinct photograph of the supposed victim, a young adult male, decided to make an enlargement of the facial part and to superimpose thereon a comparable-sized view of the skull taken in the same position. Upon doing this, according to Prinsloo (p. 15) —

> ... the impression was gained [from the photograph taken in life] that the nose was slightly deviated to his right side. An attempt was made to prove that this observation was correct. A line drawn down from the nasion to the point midway between the two external nasal apertures and extended downward was seen to lie to the right side of the philtrum of the upper lip ... In a person with a nose that is not deviated, a line such as this should fall to the left side of the philtrum when the head is turned to the [right].

To find out whether this was indeed so, the investigators took a closer look at the skull and found, according to Prinsloo (p. 16) —

> ... an incompletely ossified vertical fissured fracture of the wing of the left maxillary bone with deviation of the fractured part of the bone to the right side. In addition, there was an old fracture of the right nasal bone.

In Sydney Smith's (1939a) strangulation case mentioned in Chapter 6 the skull of the young female victim showed asymmetries typical of congenital torticollis, namely, the right side of the face, the right occipital condyle, and the right mastoid process all much enlarged as compared to their counterparts on the left. With such distinctive information to go on, the police had no difficulty, of course, in identifying the victim.

Not all cranial features that have the potential of yielding identifications are necessarily abnormal. In the Culbert and Law case outlined above the identification rested not only on the signs of previous mastoid surgery, but on the pattern of the paranasal sinuses and on the pattern of the air cells in the normal mastoid.

Evidence of this sort was sufficient to establish positive identification in a case brought to my attention by Dan Morse of Florida State University (Personal communication, 20 May, 1977). In December, 1976, the completely defleshed remains of a sixty-four-year-old black male were found scattered in a field in North Florida and with them a broken hospital ID bracelet. The latter led investigators to a hospital record that mostly agreed only in general, but indicated that the patient had disappeared in February, 1976. While a patient in the hospital this individual had had an X ray taken for nose fracture. Since this head X ray showed a very large frontal sinus with a distinctive pattern of compartmentation, an X ray was taken of the defleshed skull for comparison, with the impressive result shown in Figure 74.

POSTCRANIAL

For the parts of the skeleton other than the skull mainly surgical records relating to bone fractures and/or bone surgery, and particularly X rays taken in these connections, are likely to lead to positive identification, again provided that these records can be located. The truth of this generalization is well illustrated by the following case which I heard about while I was in Japan in 1954 studying the remains of the American soldiers killed in north Korea.

A rule of the U.S. Army pertaining to its war dead is that before the remains of a soldier are declared identified, the details of the skeletal examination must agree with those of the assembled records made in life. In the case I am referring to, one skeletal detail—an old healed fracture of one arm bone—was not included

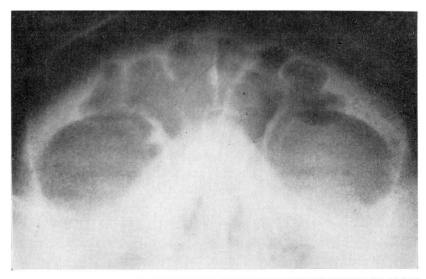

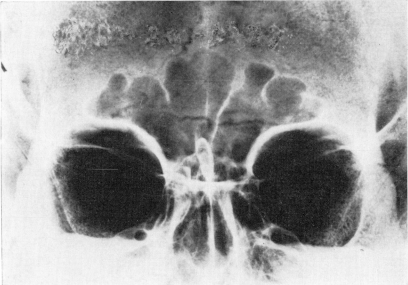

Figure 74. Identical frontal-sinus patterns in antemortem (above) and post-mortem (below) X rays. (Courtesy Florida Department of Criminal Law Enforcement.)

in the life record. Inquiries addressed to members of the family yielded firm denials of the injury. The matter was cleared up only when the decedent's college roommate was located. The latter explained that the decedent had tried out for football one spring and had received an arm fracture in the process. Not wishing the family to learn about the accident, the decedent had stayed at college through the summer session. Confirmation of this story came from the college infirmary, which was able also to produce an X ray for comparison with one taken on the arm bone in Japan. The two matched.

In other mass disasters besides war, the investigators have been able to accumulate for each victim whatever record of specific peculiarities had been made in life. This was true, for example, in the case of the fire that destroyed the ship *Noronic* at Toronto in 1949 (Singleton, 1951) and the flood that followed the collapse of the Teton dam in the Big Thompson Canyon in Idaho in 1976 (Charney, 1977). Perhaps no longer surprising under such circumstances, all of the victims of the two disasters mentioned were identified and in relatively short order.

It is important to note, however, that, because in the *Noronic* disaster the soft parts were so badly destroyed by fire, much dependence had to be placed on X rays in making the identifications. And the most useful traits for this purpose often had little to do with previous surgery, infection and/or fracture of bones, but instead were variations of normal bony structures. In other words, the victims of the fire mainly were affluent, older people who had received periodic medical examinations. Their X rays tended, therefore, to show normal bone structures. All of this constitutes a different set of circumstances from that encountered routinely by forensic anthropologists.

In Prinsloo's case cited above scars on the face of the skull were not discovered until a photograph of the suspected victim suggested their presence. A somewhat similar situation involving trauma of one of the postcranial bones is represented in the case of the burned-out automobile in Boston described by Dutra (1944, p. 346). Because the police found a set of house keys with the charred body in the remains of the automobile,

they jumped to the conclusion that the keys pertained to the presumed car-owner's home. When the keys failed to fit any doors
there, the police searched for persons missing from rooming
houses. In the case of one such missing person the keys did fit
doors in the rooming house. The police then learned that this
roomer had been in a hospital recently with a fractured femur.
From the hospital they obtained an X ray of the healed fracture
and with this in hand returned to the corpse to see if the same
femur there had been fractured in the same place. Dutra reproduced the hospital X ray alongside the one taken on the corpse to
show that, although some remodeling may have taken place, the
identity is evident.

Although the cases set forth here demonstrate ways in which
the recognition of various sorts of specific traits have led to
identifications, the additional lesson therein for the forensic
anthropologist relates to the cases that are still partly flesh covered
when received. Especial care must be taken in such cases not to
miss a significant specific trait through failure to get a clear look
at the bones.

Chapter 14

RECONSTRUCTION OF FACIAL SOFT PARTS

I N THE PRECEDING CHAPTER I described a case in which a skeletal identification resulted from the publication in a newspaper of a pen-and-ink portrait made from a skull by a newspaper artist. Another example of the successful use of this identification method, this time through the collaboration of a forensic anthropologist and a police artist, recently was described in the *FBI Law Enforcement Bulletin* (Cherry and Angel, 1977). After Dr. Angel's study showed that the skeletal remains in question were those of a young white woman, Cherry, the artist, made a portrait from the skull for publication in the newspapers. Soon after the picture appeared three readers reported to the police that it closely resembled a young woman who had disappeared some six months earlier. As it happened, the police had photographed the young woman six months before her death. This photograph does indeed closely resemble the artist's picture (see Figure 75). Other skeletal data supported the identification.

By contrast with these two cases, Prinsloo in the one mentioned in the previous chapter approached the problem in a related but different way. He attempted to show that the skull in question fitted an existing photograph of the supposed victim. However, the identification came about less through the goodness of fit of one outline on the other than through the discovery thereby that an observed facial asymmetry was due to facial injuries. As I pointed out, if the skull had been examined more closely in the beginning, there would have been no need to resort to the method of picture superimposition.

Nevertheless, these three cases typify two main approaches to skeletal identification through reference to the soft parts of the face: (1) the reconstruction of these soft parts on the skull of an unknown as they are supposed to have looked in life either in-

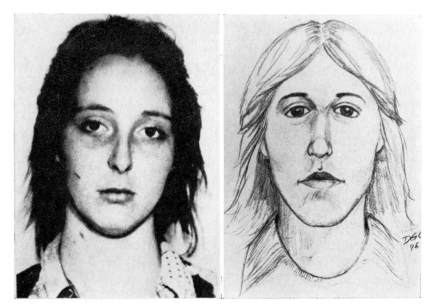

Figure 75. Two portraits of a girl, one made in life and the other some 6 months later from her skull. (From Cherry and Angel, Personality reconstruction from unidentified remains. *FBI Law Enf Bull, 46 (8):* 12-15, Figures 1 and 3, 1977. Courtesy of The Federal Bureau of Investigation.)

directly by means of a two-dimensional portrait made from the skull, or directly by means of clay (plasteline, plastilina) applied to the skull to form a three-dimensional portrait; and (2) the comparison of the skull of an unknown with a picture of a suspect made in life by superimposition of an outline of the skull, suitably scaled and oriented, on an outline of the picture. These methods can be considered as starting from directly opposite points: The first starts with a skull and arranges the soft parts on it in an attempt to achieve a recognizable likeness, whereas the second starts with the soft parts in the form of a purported likeness and arranges an overlay of the skull in an attempt to appraise the goodness of fit and hence the likelihood of a true association.

In the considerable literature on these methods there is clear evidence that both involve subjectivity to a high degree. Also, when the effort by one means or the other has led to an identification, too little attention has been focused on whether or not the likeness *per se* had anything to do with it. Therefore both methods are surrounded by an aura of glamour that may not always be warranted. In general, the first method requires the skills of an artist more than those of an anthropologist, whereas the reverse is true of the second method.

CREATING A LIKENESS FROM THE SKULL

With Pen or Pencil

When an artist sits down in front of a skull and attempts to make a picture of what that individual looked like in life, the only additional information that he or she usually has to go on is that which the anthropologist has discovered, namely, the sex, age, and race of the unknown individual. Without knowledge of the unknown individual's clothing sizes, the degree of fleshiness is a matter of guess. Everything else—face proportions, details of the features, and the amount and arrangement of the hair—must be developed subjectively by the artist with minimal help from the bones.

Few artists have been trained or have learned to develop a portrait in this way. It is difficult to discover the correct method of placing the eye in an orbit, or the proper arrangement of the alae of the nose relative to the nasal aperture, or the true relationship of the mouth to the dentition. But even with all the features correctly placed the chances that they will include the details that in subtle ways convert a standard set of features into a particular likeness are slim. Judging from my own experience in doing portraits of living people (I have been doing this as a hobby for some forty years), getting a recognizable likeness must be largely accidental when there is nothing to go on but the skull. Many artists have a hard enough time getting a sitter's eyes and mouth right when they are simply copying what is before them.

Reinforcement of these views is to be found in the report of David Waterston (1934) on his examination of the skeleton of Bishop James Kennedy (1408? - 1465). No likeness of the Bishop has survived, so, in Waterston's words (p. 81):

With a view of having a drawing of the Bishop's appearance during life made from the skull I consulted (the late) Mr. J. T. Murray, R.S.W., a skilled and well-known artist whose anatomical drawings have gained worldwide recognition for their accuracy and artistic qualities, and whose training had given him special knowledge of the relation between the form of the skull and the contour of the face and head. Mr. Murray studied the skull itself, and also photographs and orthogonal tracings made from it, and after several preliminary sketches produced . . . two drawings, one in profile, the other in three-quarter view [(see the profile view reproduced here as Figure 76)] . . .

The limitations in this direction are distinct, for facial contour and expression depend largely upon the amount and condition of the soft structures: the facial muscles, the amount of the subcutaneous tissues, and the development of the salivary glands . . .

As data upon which to work, we had the form of the cranium as a whole . . . We knew also that the Bishop had suffered for years from a chronic illness which must have affected all parts of the body and probably caused some impairment of nutrition.

The form of the mouth and the lips is hypothetical, but the form of the head and the general form of the face and jaw are strictly accurate.

As can be seen from Figure 76, Murray got around the troublesome problem of the eyes by showing them as closed. Obviously, too, he gave the Bishop a benign countenance in keeping with his role in life. All this is admirable and confirms Murray's artistic ability. However, the way in which the portrait was related to the skull was not made explicit. I have been unable to superimpose satisfactorily a suitably reduced profile of the skull on the portrait. For example, when I placed the nasal-bridge portion of the skull in position the chin of the mandible was further forward than that of the portrait and the eye was too low in the orbit. Be this as it may, from the forensic standpoint the procedure has the merit of being simple and on occasion, as I have shown, has led to an identification. For both of these reasons the procedure would seem to be worth trying when circumstances warrant.

With Clay

Anthropologists have been more inclined to use the three-dimensional approach than the two-dimensional one, because of the greater control over tissue thickness that the former provides.

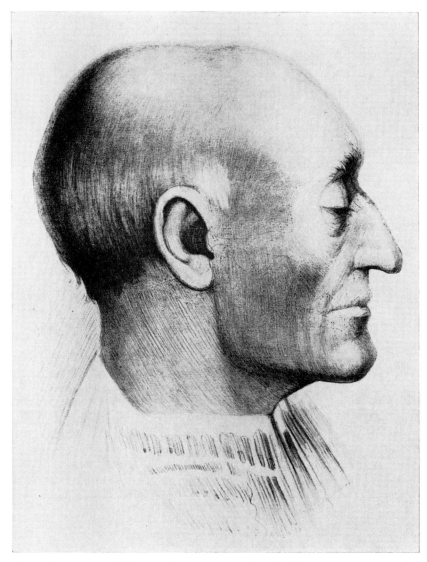

Figure 76. Presumed likeness of James Kennedy, the fifteenth century Scottish bishop, created from his skull. (From Waterston, Bishop James Kennedy: An anthropological study of his remains. *Trans Roy Soc Edinburgh, 58* (1 and 2): 75-111, Plate IX, 1934. Courtesy of *Trans Roy Soc Edinburgh.*)

Welcker (1883), His (1895), and Kollmann (1898) are generally credited with being the first to put the three-dimensional method on a scientific basis by establishing average tissue thicknesses at certain identifiable points over the face.

Welcker obtained his tissue thicknesses by inserting a thin blade vertically through the skin at selected points until the tip encountered the underlying bone and then by withdrawing it in such a way (perhaps with the thumb nail marking the extreme point of penetration) that the part below the skin surface could be measured. His, on the other hand, discarded the blade and substituted an ordinary sewing needle fitted with a small disk of rubber and set in a handle. When the oiled needle was thrust through the skin the disk remained in contact with the skin surface and thus marked the extent of penetration when the needle was withdrawn.

Kollmann simplified the needle technique by leaving off the rubber disk and blackening the needle with soot from a candle flame before insertion and afterwards noting how much of the soot was removed by the tissues. As Table XXXVI and Figure 77 indicate, the points on the face where tissue thickness has been measured have not varied much. Some of these, and their proportional thickness of overlying tissues, were illustrated by Büchly as shown in Figure 78.

Büchly was the sculptor who worked with Kollmann. The sculptor who worked with His was named Seffner. Probably nothing brought the sculptural approach so much to attention as when Seffner reconstructed a face upon Bach's supposed skull, thereby proving the identity of the skull in question beyond all doubt. The combined efforts of these paired experts added a new dimension to the descriptions of the remains of famous personages which had begun appearing rather frequently some thirty years earlier when the identity of Dante's skull came into question (Welcker, 1867).

Most of those who in this way have reconstructed a face on a skull have covered the entire facial part of the skull with clay. Vichow (1905, 1914), on the other hand, recommended reconstructing only one side of the face in order to give the viewer a

TABLE XXXVI

AVERAGE TISSUE DEPTH (IN MM) AT DIFFERENT POINTS ON THE FACE IN WHITE SUBJECTS,
BOTH MALE AND FEMALE, ACCORDING TO DIFFERENT AUTHORS

Location of point (symbol)[†]		Author (number of subjects)*						
		W (13)	H (24)	K (21)	H & K (45)	H (4)	K (4)	H & K (8)
		Male				*Female*		
Forehead; trichion	(A)	-	4.08	3.07	3.56	4.16	3.02	3.59
Forehead; middle	(B)	4.3	-	-	-	-	-	-
Forehead; glabella	(C)	-	5.17	4.29	4.69	4.75	3.9	4.32
Root of nose; nasion	(D)	5.9	5.45	4.31	4.93	5.0	4.1	4.55
Bridge of nose; middle of internasal suture	(E)	3.3	3.29	3.13	3.25	3.0	2.51	2.78
Bridge of nose; rhinion	(F)	2.2	-	2.12	2.12	-	2.07	2.07
Base of nasal septum; subnasale	(G)	-	11.25	11.65	11.59	9.75	10.1	9.92
Lower end of philtrum; prosthion	(I)	11.0	9.37	9.46	9.48	8.26	8.1	8.18
Mentolabial furrow	(J)	10.6	10.0	9.84	10.05	9.75	10.95	10.35
Chin; from in front	(L)	8.5	11.05	9.02	10.22	10.75	9.37	10.06
Chin; from below	(M)	-	6.16	5.98	6.08	6.5	5.85	6.18
Eyebrow; middle border	(N)	-	5.8	5.41	5.65	5.5	5.15	5.32
Lower border of orbit; middle	(O)	-	4.9	3.51	4.29	5.25	3.65	4.45
Cheekbone; prominence	(P)	-	-	6.62	6.62	-	7.73	7.73
Zygomatic arch; middle	(Q)	-	-	4.33	4.33	-	5.32	5.32
Zygomatic arch; near ear	(R)	-	6.05	7.42	6.74	6.75	7.1	6.92
Ascending ramus of mandible; middle	(S)	-	8.37	7.76	8.20	8.1	6.16	7.13
Horizontal ramus of mandible; in front of masseter	(T)	-	17.55	17.01	17.53	17.0	14.83	15.91

W = Welcker, 1883; H = His, 1895; K = Kollmann, 1898; H & K = His, 1895, and Kollmann, 1898, combined.
See Figures 77 and 78.

better idea of the relationship of the finished face to the underlying bony structures (Figure 79). J. H. McGregor of Columbia
University, a student of human paleontology, probably was the
first of the few workers in the United States to use this variant
technique. However, he seems to have used it mainly as a first
step in getting the facial features correctly modeled. From
around 1915 onwards for many years his busts of prehistoric men
modeled on skull casts were a feature of the Hall of the Age of
Man in the American Museum of Natural History in New York.

H. H. Wilder of Smith College, one of the pioneers in forensic
anthropology mentioned in Chapter 1, also figured prominently
during the second decade of this century in bringing to the atten-

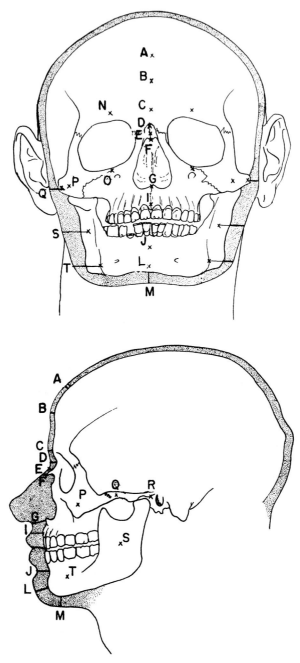

Figure 77. Diagrams of a flesh-enclosed skull to show the locations of 18 points where tissue thickness has been measured. (Modified from Kollmann and Büchly, 1898, Plates VII and VIII.)

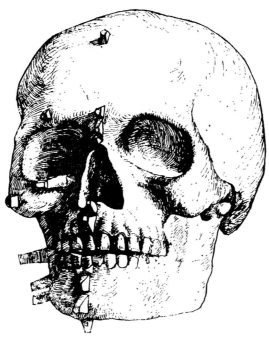

Figure 78. Skull with clay "cones" representing tissue thickness in place at some of the points shown in Figure 77. (From Kollmann and Büchly, 1898, Figure 2.)

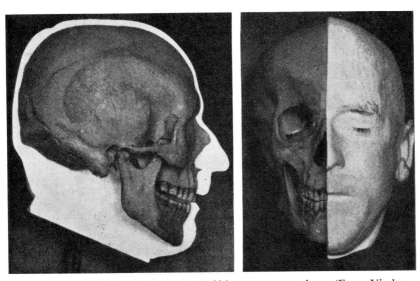

Figure 79. Side and front views of a half-face reconstruction. (From Virchow, Halb Schadel-halb Maske. *Z Ethnol, 46:* 180-186, Figures 1 and 2, 1914. Courtesy of *Z Ethnol.*)

tion of Americans the European techniques of facial reconstruction on the skull. He had learned about them while studying in Germany. Upon his return to the United States he began around 1912 to build up faces on American Indian skulls. And then later (1918), with Bert Wentworth as coauthor, he recommended the procedure for forensic purposes in a book entitled *Personal Identification.* Unlike McGregor, Wilder seems not to have made use of Virchow's "half face, half skull."

As a result of their extensive experience along these lines, McGregor and Wilder developed opinions about how to handle the details of facial reconstructions, and, unlike most of their followers, included valuable opinions and guidelines in their publications. I have selected from these publications a number of their most useful statements for inclusion here.

Writing in 1926 about his bust of La Chapelle-aux-Saints in the New York exhibition, McGregor said that "'On seeing these heads, the visitor, if he be of an inquiring turn of mind, is likely to wonder how authentic such effigies can be.' The form of the question that he preferred to reply to was, Is it possible to model a portrait head on a skull without other data?" To this his answer (p. 289) was—

> . . . a decided negative, if by a 'portrait' is meant a *personal likeness,* and if 'without other data' is to be taken literally. In a collection of modern skulls the anthropologist can distinguish race, approximate age, and usually sex, without difficulty, but even if, for example, he knows a certain skull to be that of a middle-aged man of northern Europe, he cannot say how fat or how thin that man was, whether he was bald or whether he wore a beard, yet obviously these are matters of importance in portraiture. Even when these details are known, they afford no index to certain subtleties of facial expression which are essential in a personal portrait.

The following guidelines are also included in the publication on the bust of La Chapelle-aux-Saints (1926, p. 292) :

> As published researches indicate a surprisingly slight correlation between the width of the nasal aperture and the external nose, the exact width of this organ is uncertain . . . In order to attain as great accuracy as possible in this feature, the nasal cartilages were modeled in 'moldolith,' a commercial plastic material which becomes hard when

dry. These were further constructed so that the two halves could be removed and replaced separately. Modeling the eyes required great care. It is known that the centers of the pupils, when the eyes are at rest, are slightly nearer the outer than the inner orbital border, and slightly nearer the upper than the lower border. The size of the adult human eyeball varies but little as compared with variation of the size of the orbits, . . . Eyeballs of the proper size were modeled, cast in plaster, and inserted in the orbits with due regard to their relations to the orbital rim. This is not so simple as might be supposed. There is a normal variation of some 12 millimeters in the prominence of the eyeball in its socket, but in the usual position, which was adopted in this restoration, the front of the cornea is about in the plane inter-secting the upper and lower borders of the orbit. The lacrymal sac and tarsal plates of the eyelids were modeled to serve as guides in constructing the soft tissues . . . In modeling the ear the point of greatest importance was to observe the normal relation to the bony meatus . . .

It seems likely that McGregor may have gotten the inspiration for modeling the nasal cartilages from one of Virchow's publica-tions (1912, pp. 329-337) where these cartilages are shown dis-sected out. As for the eyes, presumably he followed the figures on the dimensions of the eyeball given in the current anatomical text-books: 24.5 mm for the sagittal axis, 23.5 mm for the vertical equatorial axis, and about 23.9 for the transverse equatorial axis. Although McGregor's "half and half" models show the opening of the mouth coinciding with the line of occlusion of the front teeth, he gave no guidelines for the limits of mouth width. He was silent, too, on ear placement.

Wilder seems to have proceeded quite independently of Mc-Gregor in developing guidelines for modeling the features on the skull face. In determining the breadth of the nose, for example, he depended on the relationship between the nasal index in the skull and that in the living face. In his opinion (1912, p. 429), " . . . the points generally accepted in each case as the boundaries between the classes of nasal indices may be taken as equivalent." In the skull the lowest number of the mesorrhine class of nasal index is 47, whereas in the living head the corresponding number is 70. Similarly, the lowest numbers of the platyrrhine, or chamaerrhine, class of noses are 58 and 100 for the skull and living head respectively. Starting with these fixed points, it appeared to Wilder (p. 430) that " . . . every single point in skull indices corresponds to three on the living, or beginning with 48 = 70, we have 49 = 73, 50 = 76, and so on."

Accepting this relationship, Wilder pointed out that, since nasal length is measured in the same way in the skull and living head, one can easily convert the nasal index in the skull to that in the living head with a high expectation that the position of the reconstructed alae established on the basis of this calculation will be approximately correct.

Although seemingly ingenious, Wilder's solution of the nose problem may not be the best. The conventional categories of nasal indices were established arbitrarily and those for the skull independently of those for the living. Therefore, such a close relationship between nose shape in the skull and in the living as Wilder claimed is open to doubt. This opinion is supported by McGregor's statement quoted above regarding the surprisingly small correlation between the width of the nasal aperture and the external nose.

As regards the mouth, Wilder had formed the opinion (p. 430) from a few observations on the living that "the oral slit, when the mouth is in repose, seems to coincide with the line formed by the edges of the upper teeth, and to extend upon each side to about the middle of the second premolar (bicuspid) tooth."

With this in mind, his procedure was to fix the lateral limits of the fleshy mouth on the skull by inserting pins or small toothpicks at the indicated points, applying clay ("plastilina") to hold them in proper position. He could then reconstruct the tissues around the oral slit to the desired shape and thickness without losing sight of the markers. When the modeling was complete, of course, he withdrew the markers and obliterated the holes in the clay.

Mouth width gives no indication of the conformation of the lips. However, Wilder was convinced (p. 430) that the thickness of the lips could be inferred with reasonable assurance from the locations of two median points, one above and the other below the

lips, namely, prosthion in the skull and the bottom of the con-
cavity on the front of the mandible below the lower incisors.
Prosthion, he claimed, is located under the center of the hollow of
the upper lip (philtrum). "These points, with the slope of the
alvoli and teeth, together with the exact position of the mouth
slit," he said, "hedge the problem around with so many conditions
that there is slight opportunity for the manipulator to vary his
work, or to construct more than one type of mouth upon a given
skull."

I do not share Wilder's optimism about being able to accurately determine the type of fleshy mouth that goes with the bony
structures in the area. Lips in particular seem to me to vary much
more than the underlying bony structures. For this reason all one
can hope to achieve is a mouth that is consistent with the indicated
sex, age, and race.

Wilder's guidelines for the eye add nothing new to McGregor's;
those for the ear (p. 432), on the other hand, are worth noting.
They relate solely to the position of the opening of the fleshy ear,
which as Welcker (1883, p. 61) had pointed out, does not cor-
respond with that in the skull. Wilder recommended modeling
the fleshy ear so that its opening is 5.3 mm farther back, and the
same distance higher than the opening in the skull.

Wilder also gave (p. 424) a useful tip for controlling the
thickness of the clay at the points listed in Table XXXVI. Instead of using the little clay "cones" shown in Figure 78, he used
heavy writing paper, cut into strips about a millimeter wide. For
each landmark on the skull he would cut off a piece of the strip a
little longer than the indicated tissue thickness and bend it at a
right angle at the latter point. The extra part of the strip was
then fastened to the surface of the bone with a bit of plastilina.
This left the main part of the strip projecting perpendicularly.
Wilder added that he found it "advantageous to build up the surface as fast as the measures [were] located, rather than first to cover
the skull with these structures."

In the latter connection I would recommend following the
example of the American sculptor Leo Steppat (see Figure 124 in
Stewart, 1954a). When he restored the facial features of the

Tepexpan skull from Mexico, he connected the tissue-thickness markers in all directions with narrow strips of clay and only then began filling in the intermediate areas. This procedure gives additional control over tissue thickness.

When Krogman revived forensic anthropology with his FBI *Guide* in 1939 he included a mere mention of face reconstruction. This consisted of a list of tissue thickness at thirteen identified points over the face (whether they were his own or from some other source I have been unable to determine) and an illustration of one of McGregor's "half and half" heads (Cro-Magnon). In 1943 he replaced the earlier tissue-thickness list with another (fifteen of Kollmann's points) and gave two new illustrations, one of a skull with tissue-thickness markers of proper size attached at the fifteen points, the other with a pen-and-ink face restoration on the right side (reproduced also as Figures 79 and 80 in Krogman, 1962).

Not until 1946 did Krogman take a more serious look at the possibility of getting a good likeness by this method. At that time he reported in the *FBI Law Enforcement Bulletin* on his efforts, aided by a "sculptress" (McCue), to record the details of a cadaver head (black male), and then after reducing it to a skull, the process of restoring the face in clay for comparison with the original face. The result, which did not require the opening of the eyes, was reasonably satisfactory in Krogman's opinion, but showed the following large dimensional differences:

Forehead breadth	+ 4.0 mm	Nose breadth	− 4.0 mm
Bigonial breadth	+10.5 mm	Mouth breadth	− 3.0 mm
Nose length	− 4.5 mm	Ear height	+ 9.0 mm

Krogman's last effort, aided by another artist (Frost), came in 1948 when he applied the method for the first time in a forensic case. Although a realistic-appearing, whole head was created and photographs of it were widely circulated, no identification had been made at the time the report was published by the FBI nearly a year later.

The most recent appraisal of the method, and the first to test likenesses objectively, is that by Snow *et al.* (1970). The artist of this group (Gatliff) reconstructed faces on the skulls of several individuals by Krogman's (1943, 1962) method. For two of them, a female aged sixty-seven and a male aged thirty-six, both known whites, the authors next made up posters in which each reconstruction appeared with a row of seven portraits of individuals of the same sex and general age made contemporaneously in life, one of them (No. 2) being of the reconstructed individual (see Figure 80). Then (p. 224)—

The posters were set up in a central location along with a supply of blank forms. On the latter were printed instructions for selecting the

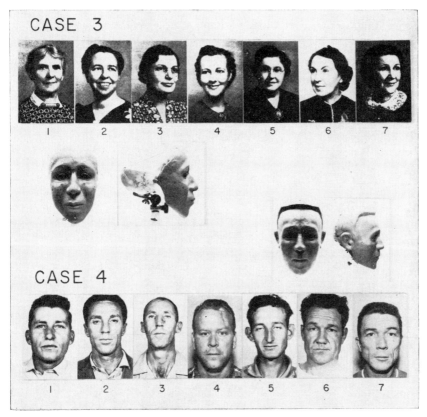

Figure 80. Poster used in a test of likeness in two cases of a face reconstructed on a skull. (From Snow, C. C. *et al*, Reconstruction of facial features from the skull: An evaluation of its usefulness in forensic anthropology. *Am J Phys Anthropol, 33:* 222-227, Figure 2, 1970. Courtesy of *Am J Phys Anthropol.)*

photograph that the identifier thought most resembled the reconstruction. Identifiers were also asked to give their sex, age, and if police officers, their number of years of experience. A sealed box was placed beside the poster for deposition of the completed forms.

Table XXXVII shows the results of this ingenious test. The poorer showing of the female subject probably is due to the fact that all of the female portraits from life used for comparison had been made some twenty-five years earlier. The method of reconstruction also may have affected the scoring, because, since only one side of the face actually was reconstructed, each of the full-faced reconstructions shown in the posters had to be made by combining the photograph of the reconstructed half with its reversed image. This process yields an unnaturally symmetrical face and an unnatural lighting effect.

TABLE XXXVII
TEST OF LIKENESS IN TWO CASES OF A FACE RECONSTRUCTED
ON A SKULL*

Type of observer	No. of observers	No. making correct identification
Case 3 (female age 67)		
Policeman	36	10
Civilian male	34	7
Civilian female	34	10
Total	104	27†
Case 4 (male age 36)		
Policeman	91	73‡
Civilian male	76	39‡
Civilian female	33	23‡
Total	200	135‡

*From Snow, C.C. *et al.*, Reconstruction of facial features from the skull: an evaluation of its usefulness in forensic anthropology. *Am J Phy Anthropol, 33:* 221-227, table 1, 1970. Courtesy of *Am J Phys Anthropol.*
†p < 0.05
‡p < 0.005
(Probabilites are based on 2×2 chi-square analyses using N/7 for the number of chance-expected correct identifications.)

Considering that previous criticisms of facial reconstructions of this sort, especially those of Suk (1935), Montagu (1947), Stewart (1954a), and Brues (1958), had no test as objective as this one available as a basis of judgment, I am inclined now to believe that the method has more potential than heretofore granted.

MATCHING SKULL AND PORTRAIT

Most of the literature on the alternate approach to identification through likenesses deals with the authentication of the skeletal remains of historic personages by means of one or more existing portraits and/or the evaluation of the likeness achieved in the portrait(s) as judged from the skull. In most respects this is the simplest of the two methods under discussion in this chapter because the main requirements are to photograph the skull as nearly as possible in the same position as, and to somewhat smaller size than, the head in the portrait(s), and to superimpose the two for comparison.

Unfortunately, the features in some portraits are so vague that a great deal of subjectivity is involved in locating the underlying bony landmarks so as to orient the skull overlay properly. So much is this the case in some of the classical reports on the subject that one wonders about the reliability of the conclusions reached (see, for example, Welcker, 1883a and b, 1888; Pearson, 1924, 1926, 1928; and Pearson and Morant, 1934). In the case of Sir Thomas Browne, Tildesley (1923) did not even offer an overlay of skull on portrait because the skull indicated an unusually low forehead and such was not the case in any of the putative portraits.

On the other hand, J. Capitan and G. Papillault, who in 1905 were called in to help identify the preserved remains of John Paul Jones following their exhumation in Paris, showed convincingly that when photographs of the mummified head and of Houdon's sculptured head were superimposed, the features coincided nicely (Stewart, C. W., 1907).

From the forensic standpoint, the most instructive examples of the application of this approach are provided by the head of a criminal executed in Egypt (Derry, 1934), the head of an embalmed cadaver from a medical institution in England (Glaister and Brash, 1937), and the two skulls from the Ruxton murder case in England (Glaister and Brash, 1937). Subsequent to getting a clear photograph of the Egyptian's head following execution, Derry was able to photograph the macerated skull in the same position and show that the skull fitted the face convincingly when the two views were superimposed (Figure 81).

Brash followed the same procedure with his cadaver head, and

Figure 81. Superimposed facial tracings from Derry's photographs of an executed Egyptian criminal and his skull. (From Pearson and Morant, The Wilkinson head of Oliver Cromwell and its relationship to busts, masks, and painted portraits. *Biometrika, 26:* 269-378, Plate II, 1934. Courtesy of *Biometrika.)*

with equally good results (see Figures 72-74 in Krogman, 1962). However, when Brash used this approach in the Ruxton case he had to carry out elaborate calculations to determine the perspective in one photographic portrait made in life. His reason for using this approach in the Ruxton case was that proof was required as to which of two recovered skulls belonged to each of two victims, Mrs. Ruxton, and her maid, Mary Rogerson. During the investigation the skulls were known only as No. 1 and No. 2. When Brash carried out the matching of skulls and portraits, it seemed clear to him that No. 1 gave the better fit with portraits of Miss Rogerson and No. 2 gave the better fit with portraits of Mrs. Ruxton (see Figures 68-71 in Krogman, 1962) .

In view of this, it is interesting to note in Brash's court testimony that he was careful to express his conclusions about the comparisons of the skull and portraits in terms primarily of what they ruled out. Thus, speaking of the comparisons in Mrs. Ruxton's case, he said (p. 165) that

> . . . Skull No. 1 could not possibly be the skull of Mrs. Ruxton. His Lordship said that that was clear, but did they demonstrate more than this? The witness then stated his opinion that the comparisons also demonstrated that Skull No. 2 might be the skull of Mrs. Ruxton . . .

Asked next about the comparisons in Miss Rogerson's case, he said (p. 165) that

> . . . Skull No. 2 could not possibly be the skull of Miss Rogerson, but that Skull No. 1 might be.

Following this testimony, upon which Brash was not cross-examined, "His Lordship" addressed the Judge as follows (p. 170) :

> . . . there is always or may be a liability to error, and you might get a false value from a photograph at any time, and you might get a doubly false value if one photograph is superimposed on another. On the other hand it might be of use in some way.

From all this it seems evident that, when one has the skull and a portrait known to be of one and the same individual and knows that these have been photographed in the same manner, one is easily led to assume that identity is established when superimposi-

tion of the photographs looks good. Such assurance is not justified, however, when the skull is that of an unknown and when the
suspect's photograph does not indicate the perspective. How
often an erroneous skull/portrait fit can occur is not known.
Knowledge of the possibility of such an error may have led to
Brash's laudable caution in giving evidence on his experiments.

BIBLIOGRAPHY

Adelson, Lester: *The Pathology of Homicide:* a *Vade Mecum Counsel; with a Foreword by Samuel Gerber.* Springfield, Thomas, 1974.

Allbrook, David: The estimation of stature in British and East African males. Based on tibial and ulnar bone lengths. *J For Med., 8:* 15-28, 1961.

Amprino, Rodolfo, and Godina, Giovanni: La struttura delle ossa nei vertebrati. Ricerche comparative negli anfibi e negli amnioti. *Commentat Pontif Accad Scient, 11*(9): 329-464, 1947.

Angel, J. Lawrence: Bones can fool people. *FBI Law Enf Bull, 43(1):* 17-20, 30, 1974.

Anonymous: FDI approves two-digit system of tooth designation. *Dent Abs,* pp. 65-66, Feb., 1971.

Baby, Raymond S.: Hopewell cremation practices. *Ohio Hist Soc Papers Archaeol, 1:* 1-7, 1954.

Baker, Paul T., and Newman, Russell W.: The use of bone weights for human identification. *Am J Phys Anthropol, 15:* 601-618, 1957.

Bass, William M.: *Human Osteology: A Laboratory and Field Manual of the Human Skeleton.* Columbia, Missouri Archaeological Society, 1971.

Beck, Theodoric Romeyn: *Elements of Medical Jurisprudence.* 2 vol. Albany, 1823. (12th ed., 1863, by John B. Beck.)

Beddoe, John: On the stature of the older races of England as estimated from the long bones. *J Anthropol Inst Gr Brit & Ire, 17:* 202-209, 1888.

Bemis, George: *Report of the Case of John Webster, Indited for the Murder of George Parkman,* etc. Boston, 1850.

Bergot, Catherine, and Bocquet, Jean-Pierre: Étude systématique en fonction de l'âge de l'os spongieux et de l'os cortical de l'humérus et du fémur. *Bull Mém Soc Anthropol Paris,* xiiie sér., *3:* 215-242, 1976.

Berndt, H.: Entwicklung eines röntgenologischen Altersbestimmung am proximalen Humerusende aus den bisherigen Methoden. *Z Ges Inn Med, 2:* 122-148, 1947.

Binford, Lewis R.: *An Archaeological Perspective.* New York, Seminar, 1972.

Borovanský, L., and Hněvkovský, O.: The growth of the body and the process of ossification in Prague boys from 4 years to 19 years. *Anthropologie (Prague), 7:* 169-208, 1929.

Boucher, Barbara J.: Sex differences in the foetal sciatic notch. *J Forensic Med, 2:* 51-54, 1955.

Boucher, Barbara J.: Sex differences in the foetal pelvis. *Am J Phys Anthro-*

pol, 15: 581-600, 1957.

Bouvier, Marianne, and Ubelaker, Douglas H.: A comparison of two methods for the microscopic determination of age at death. *Am J Phys Anthropol, 46:* 391-394, 1977.

Boyd, J. D., and Trevor, J. C.: Problems in reconstruction— I: Race, sex, age and stature from skeletal material. In Simpson, Keith (Ed.): *Modern Trends in Forensic Medicine,* pp. 133-152. London, Butterworths, 1953.

Breitinger, E.: Zur Berechnung der Körperhöhe aus den langen Gleid-massenknochen. *Anthrop Anz, 14:* 249-274, 1937.

Brooks, Sheilagh Thompson: Skeletal age at death: The reliability of cranial and pubic age indicators. *Am J Phys Anthropol, 13:* 567-597, 1955.

Brues, A. M.: Identification of skeletal remains. *J Crim Law, Criminol and Pol Sci, 48:* 551-563, 1958.

Bruno, G.: Über senile Strukturveränderungen der proximalen Humerus-epiphyse. *Fortschr Roentgenstr, 50:* 287-289, 1934.

Burns, K. R., and Maples, W. R.: Estimation of age from individual adult teeth. *J For Sci, 21:* 343-356, 1976.

Bussy, L.: Étienne Rollet (1862-1937). *Arch d'Opht, n.s. 1*(8): 681-690, 1937.

Charney, Michael: The Big Thomson flood disaster. *Am Acad For Sci Book of Abstracts* (Ann Meeting, San Diego, CA), No. 31, Feb., 1977.

Cherry, Donald G., and Angel, J. Lawrence: Personality reconstruction from unidentified remains. *FBI Law Enf Bull, 46*(8): 12-15, 1977.

Cleland, John: On certain distinctions of form hitherto unnoticed in the human pelvis, characteristic of sex, age, and race. In Cleland, John, Mackay, John Yule, and Young, Robert Bruce: *Memoirs and Memoranda in Anatomy,* Vol. I, pp. 95-103, Edinburgh, 1889.

Cobb, W. Montague: Skeleton. In Lansing, Albert I. (Ed.): *Cowdry's Problems of Ageing; Biological and Medical Aspects.* 3rd ed., pp. 791-856, Baltimore, Williams & Wilkins, 1952.

Cole, Fay-Cooper: George A. Dorsey. *Am Anthropol, 33:* 413-414, 1931.

Cook, S. F., and Heizer, R. F.: The quantitative investigation of aboriginal sites: Analyses of human bone. *Am J Phys Anthropol, 5:* 201-219, 1947.

Cornwall, I. W.: *Bones for the Archaeologist.* New York, Macmillan, 1956.

Culbert, W. L., and Law, F. M.: Identification by comparison with roentgenograms of nasal accessory sinuses and mastoid processes. *JAMA, 88:* 1634-1636, 1927.

Davies, D. A., and Parsons, F. G.: The age order of the appearance and union of the normal epiphyses as seen by X rays. *J Anat London, 62:* 58-71, 1927.

Derry, D. E.: See Pearson and Morant, 1934, pp. 270-271.

Dokládal, M.: A further contribution to the morphology of burned human bones. In Novotný, Vladímir (Ed.): *Proc Anthrop Congr, Prague and Humpolec* (1969). pp. 561-568, Prague, Academia, 1971.

Dorsey, George A.: A sexual study of the size of the articular surfaces of the long bones in aboriginal American skeletons. *Boston Med Surg J, 137*(4): 80-82, 1897.

Dorsey, George A.: The skeleton in medicolegal anatomy. *Chicago Med Recorder, 16:* 172-179, 1899.

Dupertuis, C. Wesley, and Hadden, John A., Jr.: On the reconstruction of stature from long bones. *Am J Phys Anthropol, 9:* 15-53, 1951.

Dutra, Frank R.: Identification of person and determination of cause of death from skeletal remains. *Arch Pathol, 38:* 339-349, 1944.

Dwight, Thomas: *The Identification of the Human Skeleton. A Medico-Legal Study.* [Prize essay, Massachusetts Medical Society.] Boston, 1878.

Dwight, Thomas: The sternum as an index of sex and age. *J Anat Physiol London, 15:* 327-330, 1881.

Dwight, Thomas: The sternum as an index of sex, height and age. *J Anat Physiol London, 24:* 527-535, 1890a.

Dwight, Thomas: The closure of the cranial sutures as a sign of age. *Boston Med Surg J, 122*(17): 389-392, 1890b.

Dwight, Thomas: Methods of estimating the height from parts of the skeleton. *Med Rec N Y, 46:* 293-296, 1894a. (Also reprinted as a 14-page pamphlet, New York.)

Dwight, Thomas: The range and significance of variations in the human skeleton. [Shattuck Lecture.] *Boston Med Surg J, 13* 1(4): 73- 76, 97-101, 1894b.

Dwight, Thomas: The size of the articular surfaces of the long bones as characteristics of sex; an anthropological study. *Am J Anat, 4:* 19-32, 1905.

Easton, Alan M., and Smith, Kenneth G. V.: The entomology of the cadaver. *Med Sci Law, 10:* 208-215, 1970.

Enlow, Donald H.: *Principles of Bone Remodeling.* (American Lecture Series in Anatomy No. 531.) Springfield, Thomas, 1963.

Evans, W. E.: The examination of hairs and fibers. In Gradwohl, R.B.H. (Ed.): *Legal Medicine,* pp. 479-499. St. Louis, Mosby, 1954.

Fawcett, Edward: The sexing of the human sacrum. *J Anat London, 72:* 633, 1938.

Fazekas, I. Gy., and Kósa, F.: Neuere Beiträge und vergleichende Unter-suchungen von Feten zur Bestimmung der Korperlänge auf Grund der Diaphysenmasse der Extremitätenknochen. *Deutsch Z Ges Gerichtl Med, 58:* 142-160, 1966.

von Fehling, H.: Die Form des Beckens biem Fötus und Neugeborenen und ihre Beziehung zu der beim Erwachsenen. *Arch f Gynaek Berlin, 10:* 80 pp., 1876.

Finnegan, Michael: Walnut Creek massacre: Identification and analysis. *Am J Phys Anthropol, 45:* 737-742, 1976.

Finnegan, Michael, and Schulter, Frances P.: Forensic discrimination between American Negro and white. *Am J Phys Anthropol, 42:* 300, 1975. (Abstract.)

Flecker, H.: Time of appearance and fusion of ossification centers as observed by roentgenographic methods. *Am J Roentgen, 47:* 97-159, 1942.

Foote, J. S.: A contribution to the comparative histology of the femur. *Smithsonian Contr Knowledge, 35*(3): x + 242 pp. and 35 pl., 1916.

Francis, Carl C., and Werle, Peter P. (with the assistance of Alten Behm): The appearance of centers of ossification from birth to five years. *Am J Phys Anthropol, 24:* 273-299, 1939.

Frédéric, J.: Untersuchungen über die normale Obliteration der Schädelnähte. *Z Morph Anthropol, 9:* 373-456, 1906.

Fujii, Akira: On the relation of long bone lengths of limbs to stature. *Juntendo Daigaku Taiiku Gakubu Kiyo* [*Jutendo Univ Bull Phys Ed*], *3:* 49-61, 1958. (In Japanese with English summary.)

Fully, Georges: Une nouvelle méthode de détermination de la taille. *Ann Méd Lég, 35:* 266-273, 1956.

Fully, Georges, and Pineau, H.: Détermination de la stature au moyen du squelette. *Ann Méd Lég, 40:* 145-154, 1960.

Garn, S. M.: The examination of head hair under the polarizing microscope. *Ann NY Acad Sci, 53:* 649-652, 1951.

Garn, S. M., and Lewis, A. B.: Relationship between the sequence of eruption of the mandibular molar and premolar teeth. *J Dent Res, 36:* 992-995, 1957.

Garn, S. M., Koski, K., and Lewis, A. B.: Problems in determining the tooth eruption sequence in fossil and modern man. *Am J Phys Anthropol, 15:* 313-331, 1957.

Garn, S. M., Lewis, A. B., Koski, K., and Polacheck, D. L.: The sex difference in tooth calcification. *J Dent Res, 37:* 561-567, 1958.

Gejvall, Nils-Gustaf: Cremations. In Brothwell, D., and Higgs, E. H. (Eds.): *Science in Archaeology,* pp. 379-390. New York, Praeger, 1963.

Gilbert, B. Miles: *Mammalian Osteo-Archaeology: North America.* Columbia, Missouri Archaeological Society, 1973.

Gilbert, B. Miles, and Bass, William M.: Seasonal dating of burials from the presence of fly pupae. *Am Antiq, 32:*534-535, 1967.

Gilbert, B. Miles, and McKern, Thomas W.: A method for aging the female *os pubis. Am J Phys Anthropol, 38:* 31-38, 1973.

Giles, Eugene: Sex determination by discriminant function analysis of the mandible. *Am J Phys Anthropol, 22:* 129-135, 1964.

Giles, Eugene: Sexing crania by discriminant function analysis: Effects of age and number of variables. *Proc VIII Intern Congr Anthropol Ethnol Sci, Tokyo, 1:* 59-61, 1970a.

Giles, Eugene: Discriminant function sexing of the human skeleton. In Stewart, T. D. (Ed.): *Personal Identification in Mass Disasters,* pp. 99-109. Washington, National Museum of Natural History, 1970b.

Giles, Eugene, and Elliot, Orville: Race identification from cranial measurements. *J For Sci, 7:* 147-157, 1962.

Giles, Eugene, and Elliot, Orville: Sex determination by discriminant function analysis of crania. *Am J Phys Anthropol, 21:* 53-68, 1963.

Glaister, John, and Brash, J. C.: *Medico-Legal Aspects of the Ruxton Case.* Edinburgh, E. & S. Livingstone, 1937.

Gleiser, Izaac, and Hunt, Edward E., Jr.: The permanent mandibular first molar: Its calcification, eruption and decay. *Am J Phys Anthropol 13:* 253-283, 1955.

Graves William Washington: Observations on age changes in the scapula. *Am J Phys Anthropol, 5:* 21-33, 1922. (Reprinted in Stewart and Trotter, Eds., 1954, pp. 245-263.)

Greulich, W. W., and Pyle, S. I.: *Radiographic Atlas of Skeletal Development of the Hand and Wrist.* Stanford, Stanford University Press, 1950. (2nd ed., 1959.)

Guinn, Vincent P.: Forensic neutron activation analysis. In Stewart, T. D. (Ed.): *Personal Identification in Mass Disasters,* pp. 25-35. Washington, National Museum of Natural History, 1970.

Gurdjian, E. S., Webster, J. E., and Lissner, H. R.: The mechanism of skull fracture. *Radiol, 54:* 313-339, 1950.

Gustafson, G.: Age determination on teeth. *J Am Dent Assn, 41:* 45-54, 1950.

Gustafson, G.: *Forensic Odontology.* New York, American Elsevier, 1966.

Hanna, R. E., and Washburn, S. L.: The determination of the sex of skeletons, as illustrated by a study of the Eskimo pelvis. *Human Biol, 25:* 21-27, 1953.

Hansen, G.: Die Altersbestimmung am proximalen Humerus- und Femurende im Rahmen der Identifizierung menschlicher Skelettreste. *Wiss Z Humboldt-Universität Berlin,* Math.-naturwiss. Reihe, *3:* 1-73, 1953-54.

Heglar, Roger: Paleoserology techniques applied to skeletal identification. *J For Sci, 17:* 358-363, 1972.

Helfman, P. M., and Bada, J. L.: Aspartic acid racemisation in dentine as a measure of ageing. *Nature, 262:* 279-281, 1976.

His, Wilhelm: Anatomische Forschungen ueber Johann Sebastian Bach's Gebeine und Antlitz' nebst Bemerkungen ueber dessen Bilder. *Abhandl d k sächs Gesellsch d Wissensch zu Leipz, 22* (whole ser. *37):* 379-420, 1895.

Hooton, Earnest A.: Medico-legal aspects of physical anthropology. *Clinics, 1:* 1612-1624, 1943.

Houghton, Philip: The relationship of the pre-auricular groove of the ilium to pregnancy. *Am J Phys Anthropol, 41:* 381-389, 1974.

Howells, W. W.: Factors of human physique. *Am J Phys Anthropol, 9:* 159-191, 1951.

Howells, W. W.: The cranial vault: Factors of size and shape. *Am J Phys Anthropol, 15:* 19-48, 1957.

Howells, W. W.: Détermination du sexe du bassin par fonction discriminante: Étude du matériel du Docteur Gaillard. *Bull Mém Soc Anthropol Paris,* xie sér., *7:* 95-105, 1964.

Howells, W. W.: Multivariate analysis for the identification of race from crania. In Stewart, T. D. (Ed.): *Personal Identification in Mass Disasters,* pp. 111-121. Washington, National Museum of Natural History, 1970.

Howells, W. W.: Cranial variation in man. A study by multivariate analysis of patterns of difference among recent human populations. *Papers Peabody Mus Archaeol Ethnol, Harvard Univ., 67:* xvi + 259 pp., 1973.

Hoyme, Lucile E.: The earliest use of indices for sexing pelves. *Am J Phys Anthrop, 15:* 537-546, 1957.

Hoyme, Lucile E.: *Human Skeletal Variation. Thesis,* Oxford University, Lady Margaret Hall, 1963.

Hrdlička, Aleš: *Physical Anthropology; its Scope and Aims; its History and Present Status in the United States.* Philadelphia, Wistar, 1919.

Hrdlička, Aleš: Anthropometry. Philadelphia, Wistar, 1920. (2nd ed. entitled *Practical Anthropometry,* 1939. See also Stewart, T. D., Ed., 1947.)

Hunt, Edward E., Jr., and Gleiser, Izaac: The estimation of age and sex of preadolescent children from bones and teeth. *Am J Phys Anthropol, 13:* 479-487, 1955.

Hurme, V. O.: Standards of variation of the eruption of the first six permanent teeth. *Yrb Phys Anthropol (1948), 4:* 181-200, 1949.

Hyrtl, Joseph: *Handbuch der topographischen Anatomie, etc.* 2 vol. Wien, 1865.

Ingalls, N. William: Observations on bone weights. *Am J Anat, 48:* 45-98, 1931.

Jacqueline, F., and Veraguth, P.: Étude radiologique de la tête fémoral du sujet agé. *Rev Rhum, 21:* 237-242, 1954.

Johnston, Francis E., and Snow, Charles E.: The reassessment of the age and sex of the Indian Knoll skeletal population: Demographic and methodological aspects. *Am J Phys Anthropol, 19:* 237-244, 1961.

Jones, F. Wood: Anatomical variation, and determination of age and sex of skeletons. In Smith, G. Elliot, and Jones, F. Wood: *Archaeological Survey of Nubia; Report for 1907-1908. Vol. II. Report on the Human Remains,* pp. 221-362. Cairo, National Printing Department, 1910.

Jurmain, Robert Douglas: *Distribution of Degenerative Joint Disease in Skeletal Populations.* Thesis, Harvard University, 1975.

Kerley, Ellis R.: The microscopic determination of age in human bone. *Am J Phys Anthropol, 23:* 149-163, 1965.

Kerley, Ellis R.: Age determination of bone fragments. *J For Sci, 14:* 59-67, 1969.

Kerley, Ellis R.: Estimation of skeletal age after about age 30. In Stewart, T. D. (Ed.): *Personal Identification in Mass Disasters,* pp. 57-70. Washington, National Museum of Natural History, 1970.

Kerley, Ellis R.: Special observations on skeletal identification. *J For Sci,* *17:* 349-357, 1972.

Kerley, Ellis R.: Forensic anthropology. In Wecht, Cyril H. (Ed.): *Legal Medicine Annual 1973,* pp. 161-198. New York, Appleton-Century-Crofts, 1973.

Kerley, Ellis R., and Rosen, S. I.: The identification of Polynesian head hair. *J For Sci, 18:* 351-355, 1973.

Kernan, Michael: Breathing life into dry bones. *Smithsonian,* 7(11): 116-123, 1977.

Knight, Bernard, and Lauder, Ian: Methods of dating skeletal remains. *Human Biol, 41:* 322-341, 1969.

Knox, R.: *The Anatomy of the Bones of the Human Body; a Series of Engravings, Copied from the Elegant Tables of Sue and Albinus by Edward Mitchell, Engraver; with Explanatory References by the Late John Barclay.* New Edition. Edinburgh, 1829.

Kollmann, J.: Die Weichteile des Gesichts und die Persistenz der Rassen. *Anat Anz, 15:* 165-177, 1898.

Kollmann, J. and Büchly, W.: Die Persistenz der Rassen und die Reconstruction der Physiognomie prähistorischer Schädel. *Arch Anthrop, 25:* 329-359, 1898.

Krause, W.: Ueber das weibliche Sternum. *Int Monatschr f Anat u Physiol Leipzig, 14:* 21-26, 1897.

Krogman, Wilton Marion: A guide to the identification of human skeletal material. *FBI Law Enf Bull, 8*(8): 3-31, 1939.

Krogman, Wilton Marion: Role of the physical anthropologist in the identification of human skeletal remains. *FBI Law Enf Bull, 12*(4): 17-40; *12*(5): 12-28, 1943.

Krogman, Wilton Marion: The reconstruction of the living head from the skull. *FBI Law Enf Bull, 15*(7): 11-18, 1946.

Krogman, Wilton Marion: The human skeleton in legal medicine: Medical aspects. In Levinson, S. D. (Ed.): *Symposium on Medicolegal Problems.* Ser. 2, pp. 1-90. Philadelphia, Lippincott, 1949.

Krogman, Wilton Marion: *The Human Skeleton in Forensic Medicine.* Springfield, Thomas, 1962.

Krogman, Wilton Marion: McGregor, John, and Frost, Bartlett: A problem in human skeletal remains. *FBI Law Enf Bull, 17*(6): 7-12, 1948.

Kronfeld, Rudolf: Development and calcification of the human deciduous and permanent dentition. *The Bur, 35:* 18-25, 1935. (Reprinted in Stewart and Trotter, Eds., 1954, pp. 3-10.)

Leclercq, Marcel: *Entomological Parasitology—the Relations between Entomology and the Medical Sciences.* New York, Pergamon, 1969.

Letterman, Gordon S.: The greater sciatic notch in American whites and Negroes. *Am J Phys Anthropol, 28:* 99-116, 1941.

Lewis, Arthur B., and Garn, Stanley M.: The relationship between tooth formation and other maturational factors. *Angle Orthodont, 30:* 70-77, 1960.

Lorke, D., Münzner, H., and Walter, E.: Zur Rekonstruktion der Körpergrösse eines Menschen aus den langen Gliedmassenknocken. *Deutsch Z Ges Gerichtl Med, 42:* 189-202, 1953.

von Luschka, Hubert: *Die Anatomie des Menschen,* etc. 3 vol. Tübingen, 1863-1869.

McGregor, J. H.: Restoring Neanderthal man. *Nat Hist, 26:* 288-293, 1926.

McKern, Thomas W.: The use of shortwave ultraviolet rays for the segregation of commingled skeletal remains. *Environmental Protection Res Div* (Quartermaster Res. & Dev. Center, U.S. Army, Natick, Mass.), Tech. Rep. EP-98, 1958.

McKern, Thomas W., and Stewart, T. D.: Skeletal age changes in young American males. Analysed from the standpoint of age identification. *Environmental Protection Res Div* (Quartermaster Res. & Dev. Center, U.S. Army, Natick, Mass.), Tech. Rep. EP-45, 1957.

Manouvrier, L.: La détermination de la taille d'après les grands os des membres. *Mém Soc Anthropol, Paris,* iie sér., *4:* 347-402, 1893.

Mant, A. Keith, and Furbank, R.: Adiopocere—a review. *J For Med, 4:* 18-35, 1957.

Maples, William R.: Identification based on pathology of the temporal bone. *Amer Acad For Sci Book of Abstracts* (Ann. Meeting, Washington, D.C.), p. 67, Feb., 1976.

Maresh, Marion M.: Linear growth of long bones of extremities from infancy through adolescence. *Am J Dis Child, 89:* 725-742, 1955.

Martin, Rudolf: *Lehrbuch der Anthropologie.* Rev. 2nd Ed. in 3 vol. ed. by Stefanie Oppenheim. Wien, 1928.

Masset, Cl.: Sur quelkues fâcheuses méthodes de détermination de l'âge des squelettes. *Bull Mém Soc Anthropol Paris,* xiiie sér., *3:* 329-336, 1976.

Matiegka, Jindřich: The testing of physical efficiency. *Am J Phys Anthropol,* 4: 223-230, 1921.

Matthews, W., and Billings, J. S.: The human bones of the Hemenway Collection in the United States Army Medical Museum in Washington. *Mem Nat Acad Sci, 6:* 139-286, 1891.

Merchant, Virginia Lucille: *A Cross-sectional Growth Study of the Protohistoric Arikara from Skeletal Material Associated with the Mobridge Site (39WW1), South Dakota.* Masters Thesis, American University, 1973.

Merchant, Virginia Lucille, and Ubelaker, Douglas H.: Skeletal growth of the protohistoric Arikara. *Am J Phys Anthropol, 46:* 61-72, 1977.

Meredith, Howard V.: Order and age of eruption for the deciduous dentition. *J Dent Res, 25:* 43-66, 1946. (Reprinted in Stewart and Trotter, Eds., 1954, pp. 11-34.)

Meredith, Howard V.: A chart on eruption of the deciduous teeth for the pediatrician's office. *J Pediatr, 38:* 482-483, 1951.

Montagu, M. F. A.: A study of man embracing error. *Technol Rev, 49:* 345-347, 356, 358, 360, 362, 1947.

Moorrees, C. F. A., Fanning, E. A., and Hunt, E. E., Jr.: Formation and resorption of three deciduous teeth in children. *Am J Phys Anthropol, 21:* 205-213, 1963.

Morse, Dan, Crusoe, Donald, and Smith, N. G.: Forensic archaeology. *J For Sci, 21:* 323-332, 1976.

Morse, Dan, Stoutamire, James, and Duncan, Jack: A unique course in anthropology. *Am J Phys Anthropol, 45:* 743-747, 1976.

Müller, Gertrude: Zur Bestimmung der Länge beschädigter Extremitätenknochen. *Anthrop Anz, 12:* 70-72, 1935.

Neep, Wesley A.: Procedures used by the U.S. Army to ensure proper identification of the Vietnam war dead and their acceptance by the next-of-kin. In Stewart, T. D. (Ed.): *Personal Identification in Mass Disasters,* pp. 5-9. Washington, National Museum of Natural History, 1970.

Nelson, Lee H.: Nail chronology as an aid to dating old buildings. *Hist News, 24*(11): 12 pp. (American Association for State and Local History Technical Leaflet No. 48), 1968.

Nemeskéri, János, Harsányi, Lászlo, and Acsádi, György: Methoden zur Diagnose des Lebensalters von Skelettfunden. *Anthropol Anz, 24:* 70-95, 1960.

Nuorteva, Pekka, Isokoski, Mauri, and Laiho, Kauno: Studies on the possibilities of using blowflies (Dipt.) as medicolegal indicators in Finland. 1. Report of four indoor cases from the city of Helsinki. *Ann Entomol Fennici, 33:* 217-225, 1967.

Olivier, Georges, and Pineau, Henri: Détermination de l'âge du foetus et de l'embryon. *Arch Anat (La Semaine des Hôpitaux), 6:* 21-28, 1958.

Olivier, Georges, and Pineau, Henri: Nouvelle détermination de la taille foetale d'après les longueurs diaphysaires des os longs. *Ann Méd Lég, 40:* 141-144, 1960.

Olsen, Stanley, J.: Mammal remains from archaeological sites. Part I. Southeastern and Southwestern United States. *Papers Peabody Mus Archaeol Ethnol, Harvard Univ, 56*(1): xii + 162 pp., 1964.

Orfila, M. J. B.: Leçons de Médecine Légale. 2 vol. Paris, 1821-23.

Orfila, M. J. B.: and Lesueur, O.: *Traité des Exhumations Juridiques, et Considérations sur les Changements Physiques que les Cadavres Eprouvent en se Pourrissant dans la Terre, dans l'Eau, dans les Fosses d'Aisance et dans le Fumier.* 2 vol., Paris, 1831.

Ortner, Donald J.: A recent occurrence of an African type of tooth mutilation in Florida. *Am J Phys Anthropol, 25:* 177-180, 1966.

Ortner, Donald J.: Description and classification of degenerative bone changes in the distal joint surfaces of the humerus. *Am J Phys Anthropol, 28:* 139-155, 1968.

Ortner, Donald J., Von Endt, David W., and Robinson, Mary S.: The effect of temperature on protein decay in bone; its significance in nitrogen dating of archaeological specimens. *Am Antiq, 37:* 514-520, 1972.

Paterson, R. S.: A radiological investigation of the epiphyses of the long bones. *J Anat London, 64:* 28-46, 1929.

Pearson, Karl: Mathematical contributions to the theory of evolution: On the reconstruction of the stature of prehistoric races. *Philos Trans Roy Soc London, 192A* (1898): 169-244, 1899.

Pearson, Karl: The skull of Robert the Bruce, King of Scotland 1274-1329. *Biometrika, 16:* 253-272, 1924.

Pearson, Karl: On the skull and portraits of George Buchanan. *Biometrika, 18:* 233-256, 1926.

Pearson, Karl: The skull and portraits of Henry Stewart, Lord Darnley, and their bearing on the tragedy of Mary, Queen of Scots. *Biometrika, 20B:* 1-104, 1928.

Pearson, Karl, and Bell, Julia: A study of the long bones of the English skeleton, I. The femur (Chapters 1 to 6). *Drapers' Co Res Mem (Biometric Ser. X), Dept. Applied Stat., Univ. London, Univ. College,* 1919.

Pearson, Karl, and Morant, G. M.: The Wilkinson head of Oliver Cromwell and its relationship to busts, masks, and painted portraits. *Biometrika, 26:* 269-378, 1934.

Phenice, T. W.: A newly developed visual method of sexing the os pubis. *Am J Phys Anthropol, 30:* 297-301, 1969.

Philipps, K. A.: The "nuts and bolts" of testifying as a forensic scientist. *J For Sci, 22:* 457-463, 1977.

Pommerol, F.: *Recherches sur la Synostose des Os du Crâne Considérée au Point de Vue Normal et Pathologique chez les Différentes Races Humaines.* Thèse, Paris, 1869.

Pons, José: The sexual diagnosis of isolated bones of the skeleton. *Human Biol, 27:* 12-21, 1955.

Pratt, H. S.: Harris Hawthorne Wilder. *Science, 67:* 479-481, 1928.

Prinsloo, I.: The identification of skeletal remains in Regina *versus* K and Another; the Howick Falls [Natal] murder case. *J For Med, 1:* 11-17, 1953.

Putschar, Walter G. J.: *Entwicklung, Wachstum und Pathologie der Beckenverbindungen des Menschen, mit besonderer Berücksichtigung von Schwangerschaft, Geburt und ihern Folgen.* Jena, Gustav Fischer, 1931.

Putschar, Walter G. J.: The structure of the human symphysis pubis with special consideration of parturition and its sequelae. *Amer J Phys Anthropol, 45:* 589-594, 1976.

Pyle, S. I., and Hoerr, N. L.: *Radiographic Atlas of Skeletal Development of the Knee.* Springfield, Thomas, 1955.

Ribbe, F. C.: *Étude sur l'Ordre d'Oblitération des Sutures du Crâne dans les Races Humaines.* Thèse, Paris, 1885.

Rollet, Étienne: *De la Mensuration des Os Longs des Membres dans ses*

Rapports avec l'Anthropologie, la Clinique et la Médecine Judiciaire. Lyon, 1889.

Rosen, S. I., and Kerley, Ellis R.: An epoxy method of embedding hair for histologic sectioning. *J For Sci, 16:* 236-240, 1971.

St. Hoyme: See Hoyme.

Schour, I., and Massler, M.: [*Chart entitled "Development of the Human Dentition."*] 2nd ed. Chicago, American Dental Association, 1944.

Schrantz, D.: Der Oberarmknochen und seine gerichtlichmedizinische Bedeutung aus dem Gesichtpunkte der Identität. *Deutsch Z Ges Gerichtl Med, 22:* 332-361, 1933.

Schrantz, D.: Age determination from the internal structure of the humerus. *Am J Phys Anthropol, 17:* 273-277, 1959.

Schultz, Adolph H.: The skeleton of the trunk and limbs of higher primates. *Human Biol, 2:* 303-438, 1930.

Schultz, Adolph H.: Proportions, variability and asymmetries of the long bones of the limbs and the clavicles in man and apes. *Human Biol, 9:* 281-328, 1937.

Schultz, Adolph H.: Age changes and variability in Gibbons; a morphological study on a population sample of a man-like ape. *Am J Phys Anthropol, 2:* 1-129, 1944.

Scott, D. B., Kaplan, Harry, and Wycoff, Ralph W. G.: Replica studies of changes in tooth surfaces with age. *J Dent Res, 28:* 31-47, 1949.

Sheldon, W. H.: *The Varieties of Human Physique; an Introduction to Constitutional Psychology.* New York, Harpers, 1940.

Simonin, C.: Identification des corps des soldats Américans inconnus. *Acta Med Leg Soc (Liège), 1:* 382-386, 1948.

Singer, R.: Estimation of age from cranial suture closure. *J For Med, 1:* 52-59, 1953.

Singleton, A. C.: The roentgenological identification of victims of the *Noronic* disaster. *Am J Roentgen, 66:* 375-384, 1951.

Smith, Sydney: Studies in identification. No. 3. *Police J London, 12:* 274-285, 1939a.

Smith, Sydney: Studies in identification. No. 4. *Police J London, 12:* 403-408, 1939b.

Smith, Sydney: Studies in identification and reconstruction. No. 13. *Police J London, 15:* 32-39, 1942.

Smith, Sydney: *Mostly Murder (with a Foreword by Earle Stanley Gardner.)* New York, McKay, 1960.

Snow, Charles E.: The identification of the unknown war dead. *Am J Phys Anthropol, 6:* 323-328, 1948a.

Snow, Charles E.: Indian Knoll skeletons of site Oh2, Ohio County, Kentucky *Univ Kentucky Repts Anthropol, 4:* 371-554, 1948b.

Snow, Clyde C., Gatliff, Betty P., and McWilliams, Kenneth R.: Reconstruction of facial features from the skull: An evaluation of its usefulness in forensic anthropology. *Am J Phys Anthropol, 33:* 221-227, 1970.

Steele, D. Gentry: *The Calcaneus and Talus: Discriminant Functions for Estimation of Sex Among American Whites and Negroes.* Thesis, University of Kansas, 1970a.

Steele, D. Gentry: Estimation of stature from fragments of long limb bones. In Stewart, T. D. (Ed.): *Personal Identification in Mass Disasters,* pp. 85-97. Washington, National Museum of Natural History, 1970b.

Steele, D. Gentry: The estimation of sex on the basis of the talus and calcaneus. *Am J Phys Anthropol, 45:* 581-588, 1976.

Stevenson, Paul H.: Age order of epiphyseal union in man. *Am J Phys Anthropol, 7:* 53-93, 1924.

Stevenson, Paul H.: On racial differences in stature long bone regression formulae for the Chinese (with an editorial note by Karl Pearson). *Biometrika, 21:* 303-318, 1929.

Stewart, Charles W.: *John Paul Jones. Commemoration at Annapolis, April 24, 1906.* Washington, Government Printing Office, 1907.

Stewart, T. D.: The tympanic plate and external auditory meatus in the Eskimo. *Am J Phys Anthropol, 17:* 481-496, 1933.

Stewart, T. D.: Skeletal remains with cultural associations from the Chicama, Moche, and Viru Valleys, Peru. *Proc US Nat Mus, 93:* 153-185, 1943.

Stewart, T. D.: Racial patterns in vertebral osteoarthritis. *Am J Phys Anthropol, 5:* 230-231, 1947. (Abstract.)

Stewart, T. D.: Medico-legal aspects of the skeleton. I. Sex, age, race, and stature. *Am J Phys Anthropol, 6:* 315-322, 1948.

Stewart, T. D.: What the bones tell. *FBI Law Enf Bull, 20*(2): 2-5, 19, 1951.

Stewart, T. D.: Resarch in human identification. (Editorial.) *Science, 118:* 3, 1953.

Stewart, T. D.: Evaluation of evidence from the skeleton. In Gradwohl, R. H. B. (Ed.): *Legal Medicine,* pp. 407-450, St. Louis, Mosby, 1954a.

Stewart, T. D.: Sex determination of the skeleton by guess and by measurement. *Am J Phys Anthropol, 12:* 385-392, 1954b.

Stewart, T. D.: Distortion of the pubic symphyseal surface in females and its effect on age determination. *Am J Phys Anthropol, 15:* 9-18, 1957.

Stewart, T. D.: The rate of development of vertebral osteoarthritis in American whites and its significance in skeletal age identification. *The Leech (Johannesburg), 28*(3-5): 144-151, 1958.

Stewart, T. D.: Bear paw remains closely resemble human bones. *FBI Law Enf Bull, 28*(11): 18-21, 1959.

Stewart, T. D.: Sternal ribs are aid in identifying animal remains. *FBI Law Enf Bull, 30*(7): 9-11, 1961.

Stewart, T. D.: Anterior femoral curvature; its utility for race identification. *Human Biol, 34:* 49-62, 1962a.

Stewart, T. D.: Comments on the reassessment of the Indian Knoll skeletons. *Am J Phys Anthropol, 20:* 143-148, 1962b.

Stewart, T. D.: The scapula of the first recognized Neanderthal skeleton. *Bonner Jahrb, 164:* 1-14, 1964.

Stewart, T. D.: Some problems in human palaeopathology. In Jarcho, Saul (Ed.): *Human Palaeopathology,* pp. 43-55. New Haven, Yale University Press, 1966.

Stewart, T. D.: Identification by skeletal structures. In Camps, Francis E. (Ed.): *Gradwohl's Legal Medicine,* 2nd ed., pp. 123-154. Bristol, Wright, 1968.

Stewart, T. D.: The effects of pathology on skeletal populations. *Am J Phys Anthropol, 30:* 443-450, 1969.

Stewart, T. D.: Identification of the scars of parturition in the skeletal remains of females. In Stewart, T. D. (Ed.): *Personal Identification in Mass Disasters,* pp. 127-135. Washington, National Museum of Natural History, 1970.

Stewart, T. D.: What the bones tell—today. *FBI Law Enf Bull, 41*(2): 16-20, 30-31, 1972.

Stewart, T. D.: Recent improvements in estimating stature, sex, age and race from skeletal remains. In Mant, A. Keith, (Ed.): *Modern Trends in Forensic Medicine—3,* pp. 193-211. London, Butterworths, 1973.

Stewart, T. D.: Evidence of handedness in the bony shoulder joint. *Am Acad For Sci Book of Abstracts* (Ann Meeting, Washington, D. C.), p. 68, Feb., 1976a.

Stewart, T. D.: Sacro-iliac osteophytosis. *Am J Phys Anthropol, 44:* 210, 1976b. (Abstract.)

Stewart, T. D.: An examination of selected post-cranial features recommended in the literature as good indicators of sex. *Am Acad For Sci Book of Abstracts* (Ann. Meeting, San Diego, CA), No. 125, Feb., 1977a.

Stewart, T. D.: History of physical anthropology. In Wallace, A. F. C., et al. (Eds.): *Perspectives on Anthropology 1976,* pp. 70-79. Washington, American Anthropological Association (Spec. Publ. No. 10), 1977b.

Stewart, T. D.: Forensic anthropology. In Goldschmidt, Walter (Ed.): *The Uses of Anthropology,* Washington, Amerocan Anthropological Association, In press.

Stewart, T. D. (Ed.): *Hrdlička's Practical Anthropometry.* 3rd ed. Philadelphia, Wistar, 1947. (4th ed., 1952.)

Stewart, T. D. (Ed.): *Personal Identification in Mass Disasters.* Washington, National Museum of Natural History, 1970.

Stewart, T. D., and Groome, John R.: The African custom of tooth mutilation in America. *Am J Phys Anthropol, 28:* 31-42, 1968.

Stewart, T. D., and Trotter, Mildred: Role of physical anthropology in the field of human identification. *Science, 122:* 883-884, 1955.

Stewart, T. D., and Trotter, Mildred (Eds.): *Basic Readings on the Identifi-*

cation of Human Skeletons: Estimation of Age. New York, Wenner-Gren Foundation, 1954.

Stewart, T. D., and Wedel, W. R.: The finding of two ossuaries on the site of the Indian village of Nacotchtanke (Anacostia). *J Washington Acad Sci, 27:* 213-219, 1937.

Suchey, Judy Myers: Problems in the aging of females using the pubic symphysis. *Am Acad For Sci* (Ann. Meeting, San Diego, CA), Paper No. 81, Feb., 1977. (Typescript copy.)

Sue, Jean Joseph: Sur les proportions du squelette de homme, examiné depuis l'âge le plus tendre, jusqu'à celui de vingtcinq, soixante ans & au delà. *Mém Math et Phys, Acad Sci Paris, 2:* 572-585, 1755.

Suk, V.: Fallacies of anthropological identification and reconstructions. A critique based on anatomical dissections. *Publ Fac Sci Univ Masaryk, Brno, 207:* 1-18, 1935.

Telkkä, Antti; Palkama, Arto, and Virtama, Pekka: Prediction of stature from radiographs of long bones in children. *J For Sci, 7:* 474-479, 1962.

Terry, Robert J.: Osteology and articulations. In Schaeffer; J. Parsons (Ed.): *Morris' Human Anatomy,* 10th ed., sections III and IV. Philadelphia, Blakiston, 1942.

Thieme, Frederick, and Otten, Charlotte M.: The unreliability of blood typing aged bone. *Am J Phys Anthropol, 15:* 387-397, 1957.

Thieme, Frederick, and Schull, W. J.: Sex determination from the skeleton. *Human Biol, 29:* 242-273, 1957.

Thomson, Arthur: The sexual differences of the foetal pelvis. *J Anat and Physiol London, 33:* 359-380, 1899.

Tibbetts, Gary Lynn: *Estimation of Stature from the Vertebral Column of American Negroes.* Masters Thesis, George Washington University, 1977.

Tidy, Charles Meymott: *Legal Medicine.* Vol. 1. New York, 1882.

Tildesley, M. L.: Sir Thomas Browne: His skull, portraits, and ancestry (with an introductory note by Sir Arthur Keith). *Biometrika, 15:* 1-76, 1923.

Todd, T. Wingate: Age changes in the pubic bone. *Am J Phys Anthropol, 3:* 285-334; *4:* 1-70, 333-424, 1920-21.

Todd, T. Wingate, and D'Errico, Joseph, Jr.: The clavicular epiphyses. *Am J Anat, 41:* 25-50, 1928. (Reprinted in Stewart and Trotter, Eds., 1954, pp. 161-166.)

Todd, T. Wingate, and Lyon, D. W., Jr.: Cranial suture closure; its progress and age relationship. *Am J Phys Anthropol, 7:* 325-384; *8:* 23-71, 149-168, 1924-25. (Parts I and II reprinted in Stewart and Trotter, Eds., 1954, pp. 265-347.)

Topinard, Paul: *Éléments d'Anthropologie Générale.* Paris, 1885a.

Topinard, Paul: De la restitution de la taille par les os longs. *Rev Anthropol,* 2e sér., 8: 134-140, 1885b.

Topinard, Paul: Procédé de mensuration des os longs, dans le but de reconstituer la taille. *Bull Mém Soc Anthropol Paris,* iiie sér., *8:* 73-83, 1885c.

Topinard, Paul, La formule de reconstitution de la taille d'après les os longs. *Rev Anthropol,* 3e sér., *3:* 469-471, 1888.

Trotter, Mildred: A preliminary study of estimation of weight of the skeleton. *Am J Phys Anthropol, 12:* 537-551, 1954.

Trotter, Mildred, and Duggins, Oliver H.: Hairs. In Emmel, V. M., and Cowdry, E.V. (Eds.): *Laboratory Techniques in Biology and Medicine.* 4th. ed., p.p. 195-6. Baltimore, Williams & Wilkins, 1964.

Trotter, Mildred: Estimation of stature from intact long limb bones. In Stewart, T. D. (Ed.): *Personal Identification in Mass Disasters,* pp. 71-83. Washington, National Museum of Natural History, 1970.

Trotter, Mildred, and Gleser, Goldine, C.: The effect of ageing on stature. *Am J Phys Anthropol, 9:* 311-324, 1951.

Trotter, Mildred, and Gleser, Goldine, C.: Estimation of stature from long bones of American whites and Negroes. *Am J Phys Anthropol, 10:* 463-514, 1952.

Trotter, Mildred, and Gleser, Goldine, C.: A re-evaluation of stature based on measurements taken during life and of long bones after death. *Am J Phys Anthropol, 16:* 79-123, 1958.

Trotter, Mildred and Gleser, Goldine C.: Corrigenda to "Estimation of stature from long limb bones of American whites and Negroes," American Journal Physical Anthropology (1952). *Am J Phys Anthropol, 47:* 355-356, 1977.

Trotter, Mildred, and Peterson, Roy R.: Ash weight of human skeletons in per cent of their dry, fat-free weight. *Anat Rec, 123:* 341-368, 1955 .

Ubelaker, Douglas H.: Reconstruction of demographic profiles from ossuary skeletal samples. A case study from the tidewater Potomac. *Smithsonian Contr Anthropol, 18:* 79 pp., 1974.

Ubelaker, Douglas H.: Problems in the microscopic determination of age at death. *Am Acad For Sci, Book of Abstracts* (Ann. Meeting, San Diego, CA), No. 128, Feb. 1977.

Ubelaker, Douglas H.: *Human Skeletal Remains: Excavation, Analysis, Interpretation.* Chicago, Aldine, 1978.

Ubelaker, Douglas H., and Willey, P.: Complexity in Arikara mortuary practice. *Plains Anthropol, 23:* 69-74, 1978.

Vallois, Henri V.: L'omoplate humaine; étude anatomique et anthropologique. *Bull Mém Soc Anthrop Paris,* viie sér., *9*(4-6): 129-168; *10:* 110-191; viiie sér., *3*(1-3): 3-153; ixe sér., *7*(1-3): 16-100, 1928-1946.

Vandervael, F.: Critères d'estimation de l'âge des squelettes entre 18 et 38 ans. *Bull du Comité Intern pour la Standardisation Anthropol Synthetique (Bologna),* Nos. 25-26: 67-82, 1952.

Vandervael, F.: L'identification anthropologique des mort inconnus de la guerre dans l'armée américaine. *Rev Méd Liége, 8:* 617-621, 1953.

Van Vark, Gerrit Nanning: *Some Statistical Procedures for the Investigation of Prehistoric Human Skeletal Material.* Thesis, Rijksuniversiteit de

Groningen, 1970.

Virchow, Hans: Einen Kopf, der zur Hälfe aus dem Schädel zur hälfe aus der Gesichtsmaske besteht. *Z Ethnol, 37:* 781-783, 1905.

Virchow, Hans: Die anthropologische Untersuchung der Nase. *Z Ehhnol, 44:* 289-337, 1912.

Virchow, Hans: Halb Schädel—halb Maske. *Z Ethnol, 46:* 180-186, 1914.

Wachholz, L.: Über die Altersbestimmung an Leichen auf Grund des Ossifikationsprozesses im obern Humerusende. *Friedreich's Bl Gerichtl Med Nürnb, 45:* 210-219, 1894.

Warren, Charles P.: Plants as decomposition vectors of skeletal human remains. *Indiana Academy of Sciences* (Paper read at 91st annual meeting, Butler University, October 31, 1975). (Typescript copy.)

Warren, John: Thomas Dwight, M.D., LL.D. *Anat Rec, 5:* 531-439 (portrait opposite p. 491), 1911.

Washburn, S. L.: Sex differences in the pubic bone. *Am J Phys Anthropol, 6:* 199-207, 1948.

Washburn, S. L.: Sex differences in the pubic bone of Bantu and Bushman. *Am J Phys Anthropol, 7:* 425-432, 1949.

Waterston, David: Bishop James Kennedy: An anthropological study of his remains. *Trans Roy Soc Edinburgh, 58* (1 and 2): 75-111, 1934.

Webb, William S., and Snow, Charles E.: The Adena people. *Univ Kentucky Rep Anthropol Archaeol, 6:* 1-369, 1945.

Welcker, H.: On the skull of Dante [translation of letters to J. Barnard Davis]. *Anthropol Rev, 5:* 56-71, 247-248, 1867.

Welcker, H. *Schiller's Schädel und Todenmaske, nebst Mittheilungen über Schädel und Todenmaske Kants.* Braunschweig, 1883.

Welcker, H.: Der Schädel Rafael's und die Rafaelporträts. *Arch Anthropol, 15:* 417-440, 1884.

Welcker, H.: Zur Kritik des Schillerschädels. *Arch Anthropol, 17:* 19-60, 1888.

Wells, Calvin: A study of cremation. *Antiquity, 34:* 29-37, 1960.

Wentworth, Bert, and Wilder, Harris Hawthorne: *Personal Identification, etc.* New and rev. ed. Chicago, 1932. (For 1st ed. see Wilder.)

Werner, Heinrich: *Die Dicke der menschlichen Gelenkknorpel.* Inaugural Dissertation, Berlin, 1897.

Wetherill, Charles M.: On adipocere, and its formation. *Trans Am Philos Soc Philadelphia, n.s. 11:* 1-25, 1860.

Wigmore, John H.: The Luetgert case. *Am Law Rev, 32:* 187-207, 1898.

Wilder, Harris Hawthorne: The physiognomy of the Indians of southern New England. *Am Anthropol, 14:* 415-436, 1912.

Wilder, Harris Hawthorne, and Wentworth, Bert: *Personal Identification: Methods for the Identification of Individuals, Living or Dead.* Boston, Gorham, 1918. (For 2nd ed. see Wentworth.)

AUTHOR INDEX

291

SUBJECT INDEX

A

Adipocere, formation of, 73; sign of fracture, 81; varying occurrence of, 73-4

Age, estimated from atrophic spots in scapula, 183-4, changes in joints, 108-10, 176-8, epiphyses, 147-57, cortical components of long bones, 184-9, developmental data, 126-7, femoral diaphyses, 129, 136, primary ossification centers, 138-40, pubic symphysis, 150-71, suture closure, 172-5, teeth, 141-9, 179-80

Age estimation, in general, 128; of fetuses, 129-31; planning research in, 13; reliability of, 137, 141, 171-3, 175, 178-9, 182-3, 186

Age profile chart, 186

American Academy of Forensic Sciences, certification in, 18; formation of, 17

American Indians (see also Arikara), distinguished from whites by discriminant functions, 237-8; shovel-shaped incisors in, 235

Angel, J. Lawrence, connection with Federal Bureau of Investigation, 30; method of examination, 41-2; observations on colonial skeletons, 37; role in seminar, 14

Animal bones (see also under animal name), as food debris, 45-6; identification to species, 45; mistaken for human fetuses, 47

Archeological situations, appearance of bones in, 74; source of case of left-handedness, 239

Archeological studies, of burned bones, 59-66, commingled bones, 39, insect remains, 70-1

Archeological technique, 30

Arikara, birth size of femoral diaphysis

in, 132-3; growth of femoral diaphysis in, 136

Arthritis, as indication of handedness, 242-4; use in estimating age, 107-10, 176-8

Asymmetries, 239-44, 270

Atlas, 139

Axis, primary ossification centers of, 139; use in estimating stature, 219-20

B

Baker, Paul, 14

Bear, bone microstructure in, 57; bones of paws of, 49-52

Beddoe, John, 193

Bias, 31-2

Birth size, 130-5

Blacks, contrasted with whites in body-weight estimation, 224, bone-weight estimation, 226, discriminant-function sexing, 89-90, 123, femoral morphology, 232-3, joint arthritis, 244, mean of sciatic-notch index, 118, range of ischium-pubis index, 114, skull dimensions, 236, skull morphology, 230-1, stature estimation, 203-8, 213-5, suture closure, 173

Blood grouping, 39-40

Bones (see also Animal and under name of bone), appearance of in archeological situations, 74; cleaning of, 33; cremation of, 59-67; evidence of dismemberment in, 33, 62; extraneous matter with, 33; fetal, 47; marks on, 33-5; nitrogen content of, 74-5; not related to crime, 36-8; odor in, 33, 69, 71; partial, 210-5; pathological changes in, 176-8, 249-50, 253; post-mortem loss of, 31; protection of, 36; reporting examination of, 40-2; restoration of, 35-6; roots in, 75; signs of cause of death in, 76-81, handed-